LUNSFORD/CONNORS

EasyWriter

A Pocket Guide

WITH A DIRECTORY OF
RESOURCES IN 15 DISCIPLINES

THE 20 MOST COMMON ERRORS

Research has found that aside from misspelling, the twenty errors listed below are the most common surface-level errors in the writing of U.S. college students. Checking your writing for them — and checking the listed sections of this book for help with them — will go a long way toward making you a more effective writer.

- Missing comma after an introductory element **19a**
- Vague pronoun reference **6c**
- Missing comma in a compound sentence **19b**
- Wrong word **13**
- Missing comma(s) with a nonrestrictive element **19c**
- Wrong or missing verb ending **2, 3**
- Wrong or missing preposition **17**
- Comma splice **7**
- Missing or misplaced possessive apostrophe **22a**
- Unnecessary shift in tense **12a**
- Unnecessary shift in pronoun **12b**
- Sentence fragment **8**
- Wrong tense or verb form **2, 12a, 16**
- Lack of agreement between subject and verb **3**
- Missing comma in a series **19d**
- Lack of agreement between pronoun and antecedent **6b**
- Unnecessary comma(s) with a restrictive element **19i**
- Fused sentence **7**
- Misplaced or dangling modifier **5a, 5c**
- Its/it's confusion **22b**

EASY WRITER

A Pocket Guide

ANDREA LUNSFORD
THE OHIO STATE UNIVERSITY

ROBERT CONNORS
UNIVERSITY OF NEW HAMPSHIRE

with a section for
multilingual writers by

FRANKLIN E. HOROWITZ
**TEACHERS COLLEGE
COLUMBIA UNIVERSITY**

ST. MARTIN'S PRESS
NEW YORK

Publisher: Marilyn Moller
Development editor: John Elliott
Managing editor: Erica T. Appel
Editorial assistant: Allison Rand
Marketing manager: Karen Melton
Art director: Lucy Krikorian
Text and cover design: Anna George
Composition: Jan Ewing, Ewing Systems, New York, NY

Library of Congress Catalog Card Number: 97-66124

Manufactured in the United States of America.

1 0 9 8 7
f   e d c b a

For information, write:
St. Martin's Press, Inc.
175 Fifth Avenue
New York, NY 10010

ISBN: 0-312-17085-8

HOW TO USE THIS BOOK

Whether you're a writing student, an engineer, or a psychologist, chances are that you're called on to write and do research often, maybe every day. Chances are also good that you often have questions you need answered about writing and research. *EasyWriter* aims to provide answers to such questions.

- Need to know how to document a source you found on the Web? Chapters 32–35 provide documentation guidelines for MLA, APA, Chicago, and CBE styles.

- Not sure whether to add a comma after an introductory word? Chapter 19 provides tips for using commas effectively.

- Wonder what tone and level of formality you should use in email? The FAQ on pp. 4–6 can help you decide.

- Want to be sure you haven't written any unintentional sentence fragments? Chapter 8 provides guidelines.

- Wonder where to start research for a biology project? Chapter 37 lists useful Web sites and journals in biology.

- Confused about when to use *lie* and when to use *lay?* Check the Glossary of Usage, pp. 242–52.

Ways into the book

- **Tables of Contents.** If you know what general topic you're looking for, the **Brief Contents** on the inside front cover will lead you to the chapter where you'll find that topic; if you're looking for a specific kind of information within a general topic (using commas in a series, rather than using commas in general, for example), the full **Contents** on the inside back cover can lead you to such specific information.

- **Index.** The index lists everything covered in the book. It's especially useful for finding specific words you need help with (*that* or *which*) but don't know the exact technical term for (*relative pronouns*).

- **FAQs about Online Writing.** If you have questions about online writing situations, you'll find answers on the FAQ pages in each section of this book. A directory to all these questions is on the back cover flap.

- **Yellow Pages for 15 Disciplines.** The yellow pages at the back of the book provide Web sites and journals in fifteen different subjects, listed alphabetically from art to sociology.

- **Most Common Errors.** On the front cover flap is a list of the twenty most common writing errors, with page references to places in the book where you can find help revising those errors.

- **Documentation Directories.** For information on documenting sources, see the directories for MLA (pp. 136, 141), APA (pp. 157, 161), Chicago (pp. 176, 182), and CBE (p. 190) styles.

- **Glossaries.** The **Glossary of Usage** gives help with troublesome words (*accept* and *except*, for example); the **Glossary of Terms** gives definitions of grammatical and online terms. Note that boldfaced terms throughout the book are all included in the Glossary of Terms.

We hope that *EasyWriter* will prove true to its name—a convenient source of information you can use quickly, efficiently, and easily.

WRITING

Q: What is most difficult for you in writing?

A: Starting a piece seems to be extremely difficult for me. . . . Perhaps the reason is that good writing is based on clear thinking, which is the hardest thing we have to do. It's as plain as that. It's hard to start to write because what you have to do is start to think.

– Roger Angell

A Writer's Choices

You sit down to dash off a quick **email** message to your best friend about a weekend reunion in Chicago. Later on, you put together a brief analysis of several cost-cutting possibilities for the manager of the wholesale produce company you're working for. And later still, just before calling it a day, you pull out the notes you took on your biology experiment and write up the lab report that is due tomorrow. In between, you probably do a lot of other writing as well—notes, lists, reminders, whatever.

These are the kinds of writing most of us do every day, more or less easily, yet each demands that we make various important choices. In your email message, you may choose to use a kind of shorthand, not even bothering to write complete sentences, since it's just a quick note to your best friend. For your boss, however, you will probably choose to be more formal—and "correct." And for your lab report, you will probably choose to follow the format demonstrated in your textbook. In each case, the choices you make are based on what is most *appropriate* for your purposes and audience. This chapter aims to help you think effectively about your writing choices.

1a Purposes

- If you are working on an assignment, be sure you understand what it asks you to do. Look for words like *persuade* or *recommend*, and make sure your response does what the assignment asks.
- What are your purposes for writing—to respond to a request? to learn about a subject? to make a recommendation? to express your feelings? Figuring out your purposes for writing is a key step to achieving them.

1b Audience

- Whom do you most want to reach? How well do you know them? Are they likely to be sympathetic—or unsympathetic—to your views?

- How are your readers different from you, and from one another? Think in terms of age, education, region, gender, ethnic and cultural heritage, politics, and other factors. What do you all have in common?
- What, if anything, do you want your audience to do as a result of what you write? How can you make clear what you want to happen?

1c Stance

- What is your relationship to your audience—student to instructor? superior to subordinate? colleague to colleague? citizen to members of a community? This relationship may well determine the level of formality of your writing.
- What is your own attitude toward your subject— positive? negative? curious? indifferent? Knowing your own stance can help you think about ways to get your readers to understand—and share—your views.

1d Genres and formats

- What kind of writing is most appropriate for your purpose and audience—a formal letter? a brochure? overhead transparencies? email? Make sure you know what formats are usually used in similar situations.
- What organizational features are appropriate for your purpose and audience? Do you need headings? a user-friendly organization that introduces and links ideas clearly so that readers can easily follow the text?

1e Evidence

- What kind of evidence will be most persuasive to your audience and most effective in the field you are working in—historical precedents? expert testimony? statistical data? experimental results? personal anecdotes? Knowing what kinds of evidence "count" most in a particular field or with particular audiences will help you make good and appropriate choices.

1f   Language and style

- What level of formality is most appropriate? extremely informal, as in email to a close acquaintance? moderately formal, as in a letter to someone you know only slightly? very formal, as in legal or institutional documents?

- What forms of address will be most appropriate for your audience? Do you know them well enough to use nicknames or slang? Is more formality called for? Should you use *he* or *she* or some gender-neutral way to refer to hypothetical readers?

- What kind of sentence style will be most appropriate? simple, straightforward sentences that convey information clearly and concisely? longer, descriptive sentences that create a picture in readers' minds or evoke emotional responses? lists of phrases to give directions? brief **sentence fragments** to get a point across quickly online in a **MOO** or **MUD**?

FAQ: WRITING ONLINE

Online writing takes many forms, including **EMAIL**, **LISTSERV** and **NEWSGROUP POSTINGS**, **HOMEPAGES**, **HYPERTEXTS**, **MOOS**, **MUDS**, and **IRCS**. In reading the following advice, check that it applies to the particular form you're using.

What online format conventions should you know?

- **Subject Lines.** In email and postings, pay special attention to the **SUBJECT LINE** in the address block: that is the place to state your purpose as clearly and succinctly as possible.

  > To: ulman.1@osu.edu
  > Subject: oops...

  This subject line may announce that you've made a mistake of some sort, but it gives no further clues to your purpose in writing. A much more helpful subject line would read:

  > Subject: Sorry to miss the meeting 10/3/97

- **Replies.** In email, you may sometimes use the "reply" function to send a message back to someone about a subject that is entirely different from the one stated in the original subject line. In such cases, you should change the subject line to reflect the change of

subject. Thus in a reply to a colleague who has written you under the subject of "trading work shifts," if you are changing the subject to ask something about vacation days in 1998, remember to change the subject line to read "Vacation days '98."

- **.Sig files.** Many writers conclude their online communications with a signature block (known as a **.SIG FILE**) that gives their name, title, address, phone and fax numbers, and so on. These signature files work not only to identify you but to establish your credentials and thus your authority. Keep your signature block as brief and straightforward as possible:

  Beverly Moss, Director   moss.1@osu.edu
  University Writing Center 614-292-5607
  Ohio State University   614-292-7816 (FAX)

- **Brevity.** In general, keep online messages and postings as concise as possible. Because readers need to scroll to read online text, shorter is often better. Consider limiting your lines to 60–70 characters in order to avoid one- or two-word lines that sometimes occur when one system **DOWNLOADS** to another.

- **Shouting.** Typing words in all capital letters can seem like SHOUTING and can be very annoying to readers. (Remember, too, that using all lowercase letters can make text hard to read and thus can also be annoying.)

- **Graphics.** Before sending any graphics, check to see that the recipients will be able to download them.

- **Type fonts.** For most academic and professional work, choose traditional fonts such as Courier, New Times Roman, or Arial in 11- or 12-point size. More exotic fonts such as Bellevue or Chicago are interesting but hard for many people to read.

- **MOOs and MUDs.** Learn from other participants what format conventions are in place.

What should you pay special attention to when you represent yourself online?

- **Introductions.** Include a brief introduction to any messages, especially if you are new to a group or aren't known to readers ("Hello from an interested participant in a recent workplace seminar at which you spoke. I am writing to . . ."). Doing so can help clarify the purpose of your message or posting and thus encourage prompt response.

- **Flaming.** Remember the golden rule: do unto others as you would have them do unto you. Sometimes writers say things online that they would never say in face-to-face communication. Be careful not to slip into

the kind of verbal harassment or other inconsiderate language known as FLAMING.

- **Proofreading.** Unless you are part of a speedy MOO or MUD conversation, proofread and spell-check your messages before you send them. The higher the stakes of the message, especially if it's likely to be printed out, the more care you should take to make sure it's as accurate as you can make it.

What should you remember about online audiences? How do they differ from "print" audiences?

- **Privacy.** Remember that the INTERNET is public and that online readers can take quick action in regard to your messages and postings, printing them out or forwarding them with the click of a MOUSE. If privacy is a prerequisite for a message you want to send, think twice before emailing or posting it.

- **Tone.** Though informal online exchanges can seem a lot like talking—indeed, a lot like face-to-face communication—remember that closeness to others doesn't happen instantly, online or off. Write according to how well you really know your audience, as well as according to the specific context. Your good friend may also be the company president; when you write to her about company business, you should ordinarily use an appropriately businesslike tone.

Online Resources

The Purdue Online Writing Lab provides handouts on writing-related issues as well as an extensive list of other useful resources on the Web:

    <http://www.owl@omni.cc.purdue.edu>

The University of Texas Undergraduate Writing Center offers resources on writing well in college, including handouts on specific issues such as revision, information on documentation and citation of sources, and links to other helpful sites.

    <http://uwc-server.fac.utexas.edu/resource/index.html>

The University of Missouri's Online Writery offers advice about writing via email as well as an open discussion list called The Writery Cafe.

    <http://www.missouri.edu/~writery>

Netiquette Home Page provides links to a Netiquette Quiz and an online version of Virginia Shea's *Netiquette*, with chapters on writing online, flaming, electronic style, and conventions guiding business and discussion-group netiquette.

    <http://www.albion.com/netiquette/index.html>

SENTENCE GRAMMAR

We learn a great deal about grammar from reading—and not grammar books but newspapers, novels, poetry, magazines, even the labels on cereal boxes.

— Lynn Z. Bloom,
Strategic Writing

Verbs

One Boston restaurant we know offers to bake, broil, pan-fry, deep-fry, poach, sauté, fricassee, blacken, or scallop any of the fish entrees on its menu. To someone ordering—or cooking—at this restaurant, the important distinctions lie entirely in the **verbs**. This chapter aims to help you use verbs appropriately.

2a Regular and irregular verb forms

A **regular verb** is one whose **past tense** and **past participle** are formed by adding *-ed* or *-d* to the **base form** of the verb.

BASE FORM	PAST TENSE	PAST PARTICIPLE
love	loved	loved
honor	honored	honored
obey	obeyed	obeyed

An **irregular verb** does not follow the *-ed* or *-d* pattern. If you are unsure about whether a verb form is regular or irregular, or what the correct form is, consult the following list or a dictionary. Dictionaries list any irregular forms under the entry for the base form.

Some common irregular verbs

BASE FORM	PAST TENSE	PAST PARTICIPLE
arise	arose	arisen
be	was/were	been
bear	bore	borne, born
beat	beat	beaten
become	became	become
begin	began	begun
bite	bit	bitten, bit
blow	blew	blown
break	broke	broken
bring	brought	brought
broadcast	broadcast	broadcast

BASE FORM	PAST TENSE	PAST PARTICIPLE
build	built	built
burn	burned, burnt	burned, burnt
burst	burst	burst
buy	bought	bought
catch	caught	caught
choose	chose	chosen
come	came	come
cost	cost	cost
cut	cut	cut
dig	dug	dug
dive	dived, dove	dived
do	did	done
draw	drew	drawn
dream	dreamed, dreamt	dreamed, dreamt
drink	drank	drunk
drive	drove	driven
eat	ate	eaten
fall	fell	fallen
feel	felt	felt
fight	fought	fought
find	found	found
fly	flew	flown
forget	forgot	forgotten, forgot
freeze	froze	frozen
get	got	gotten, got
give	gave	given
go	went	gone
grow	grew	grown
hang (suspend)[1]	hung	hung
have	had	had
hear	heard	heard
hide	hid	hidden
hit	hit	hit
keep	kept	kept

---

[1] *Hang* meaning "execute by hanging" is regular: *hang, hanged, hanged.*

BASE FORM	PAST TENSE	PAST PARTICIPLE
know	knew	known
lay	laid	laid
lead	led	led
leave	left	left
lend	lent	lent
let	let	let
lie (recline)[2]	lay	lain
lose	lost	lost
make	made	made
mean	meant	meant
meet	met	met
pay	paid	paid
prove	proved	proved, proven
put	put	put
read	read	read
ride	rode	ridden
ring	rang	rung
rise	rose	risen
run	ran	run
say	said	said
see	saw	seen
send	sent	sent
set	set	set
shake	shook	shaken
shoot	shot	shot
show	showed	showed, shown
shrink	shrank	shrunk
sing	sang	sung
sink	sank	sunk
sit	sat	sat
sleep	slept	slept
speak	spoke	spoken
spend	spent	spent
spread	spread	spread
spring	sprang, sprung	sprung

---

[2] *Lie* meaning "tell a falsehood" is regular: *lie, lied, lied.*

BASE FORM	PAST TENSE	PAST PARTICIPLE
stand	stood	stood
steal	stole	stolen
strike	struck	struck, stricken
swim	swam	swum
swing	swung	swung
take	took	taken
teach	taught	taught
tear	tore	torn
tell	told	told
think	thought	thought
throw	threw	thrown
wake	woke, waked	waked, woken
wear	wore	worn
win	won	won
wind	wound	wound
write	wrote	written

2b Lie *and* lay, *sit* and *set*, *rise* and *raise*

These pairs of verbs cause confusion because both verbs in each pair have similar-sounding forms and somewhat related meanings. In each pair, one of the verbs is **transitive**, meaning that it takes a **direct object** (*I lay the package on the counter*). The other is **intransitive**, meaning that it does not take an object (*He lies on the floor unable to move*). The best way to avoid confusing these verbs is to memorize their forms and meanings.

BASE FORM	PAST TENSE	PAST PARTICIPLE	PRESENT PARTICIPLE	-S FORM
lie (recline)	lay	lain	lying	lies
lay (put)	laid	laid	laying	lays
sit (be seated)	sat	sat	sitting	sits
set (put)	set	set	setting	sets
rise (get up)	rose	risen	rising	rises
raise (lift)	raised	raised	raising	raises

▶ The doctor asked the patient to ~~lay~~ *lie* on his side.

▶ She s̶a̶t̶ the vase on the table.
    set
    ^

▶ He r̶a̶i̶s̶e̶d̶ up in the bed and glared at me.
    rose
    ^

2c   Verb tenses

Tenses show when the action expressed by a verb takes place. The three simple tenses are the present tense, the past tense, and the future tense.

PRESENT TENSE	she *asks, writes*
PAST TENSE	she *asked, wrote*
FUTURE TENSE	she *will ask, will write*

More complex aspects of time, such as ongoing or completed actions or conditions, are expressed through progressive, perfect, and perfect progressive forms of the simple tenses.

PRESENT PROGRESSIVE	she *is asking, writing*
PAST PROGRESSIVE	she *was asking, writing*
FUTURE PROGRESSIVE	she *will be asking, writing*
PRESENT PERFECT	she *has asked, written*
PAST PERFECT	she *had asked, written*
FUTURE PERFECT	she *will have asked, written*
PRESENT PERFECT PROGRESSIVE	she *has been asking, writing*
PAST PERFECT PROGRESSIVE	she *had been asking, writing*
FUTURE PERFECT PROGRESSIVE	she *will have been asking, writing*

The simple tenses locate an action only within the three basic time frames of present, past, and future. Progressive forms express continuing actions; perfect forms express completed actions; perfect progressive forms express actions that continue up to some point in the present, past, or future.

▦ **Using the present tense for special purposes.** When writing about action in literary works, use the present tense of the verb rather than the past tense.

▶ Ishmael slowly c̶a̶m̶e̶ to realize all that w̶a̶s̶ at stake in
                comes   *is*
                   ^   ^

the search for the white whale.

General truths or scientific facts should be in the present tense, even when the predicate of the sentence is in the past tense.

▶ Pasteur demonstrated that his boiling process ~~made~~ *makes* milk safe.

When you are quoting, summarizing, or paraphrasing a work, use the present tense.

▶ Keith Walters ~~wrote~~ *writes* that the "reputed consequences and promised blessings of literacy are legion."

Note, however, that if you are documenting an essay using APA (American Psychological Association) style and reporting the results of your experiments or another researcher's work, this style calls for using the past tense (*wrote, noted*) or the present perfect (*has written, has reported*).

▶ Comer (1995) ~~notes~~ *noted* that protesters who deprive themselves of food (for example, Gandhi and Dick Gregory) are seen not as dysfunctional but rather as "caring, sacrificing, even heroic" (p. 5).

2d Sequencing verb tenses accurately

Careful and accurate use of **tenses** is important to clear writing. Even the simplest narrative describes actions that take place at different times. When you use the appropriate tense for each action, readers can follow such time changes easily. Most problems with sequence of tenses involve the use of the **past tense** instead of the **past perfect tense**.

▶ By the time he offered her the loan, she *had* declared bankruptcy.

The original sentence suggests that the two events occurred at the same time; the revised sentence makes it clear that the bankruptcy occurred first.

2e Using the appropriate voice

Voice tells whether a **subject** is acting (*He questions us*) or being acted upon (*He is questioned*). When the subject is acting, the verb is in the **active voice**; when the subject is being acted upon, the verb is in the **passive voice**. Most contemporary writers use the active voice as much as possible because it livens up their prose. To shift a sentence from passive to active voice, make the performer of the action the subject of the sentence.

>   *Researchers told the*
> ▶ ~~The~~ test administrator ~~was told~~ to give students an
>   *they gave*
> electric shock each time a wrong answer. ~~was given.~~

The passive voice can work to good advantage in some situations, however, such as when you want to emphasize the recipient of an action rather than the performer of the action.

> ▶ DALLAS, NOV. 22—President John Fitzgerald Kennedy was shot and killed by an assassin today.
>   – TOM WICKER, *New York Times*

2f Using the subjunctive mood

The **mood** of a verb indicates the attitude of the writer toward what he or she is saying. The **indicative mood** is used for stating facts or opinions and for asking questions: *I did the right thing.* The **imperative mood** is used for giving commands and instructions: *Do the right thing.* The **subjunctive mood** (used primarily in **dependent clauses** beginning with *that* or *if*) expresses wishes, suggestions, requests and requirements, and conditions that do not exist: *If I had done the right thing, I would not be in trouble now.* The present subjunctive uses the **base form** of the verb with all subjects.

> ▶ It is important that children *be* psychologically ready for a new sibling.

The past subjunctive is the same as the **simple past tense** except for the verb *be*, which uses *were* for all subjects.

> ▶ He spent money as if he *had* infinite credit.

▶ If the store *were* **better located, it would attract more customers.**

Because the subjunctive creates a rather formal tone, many people today tend to substitute the indicative mood in informal conversation.

▶ If the store *was* **better located, it would attract more customers.**

For academic or professional writing, use the subjunctive in the following contexts:

CLAUSES EXPRESSING A WISH

▶ He wished that his mother ~~was~~ *were* still living nearby.

IF CLAUSES EXPRESSING A CONDITION THAT DOES NOT EXIST

▶ If the federal government ~~was~~ *were* to ban the sale of

   tobacco, tobacco companies and distributors would

   suffer a great loss.

One common error is using *would* in both clauses. Use the subjunctive in the *if* clause and *would* in the other clause.

▶ If I ~~would have~~ *had* played harder, I would have won.

THAT CLAUSES EXPRESSING A SUGGESTION, REQUEST, OR REQUIREMENT

▶ The job demands that employees ~~are~~ *be* in good physical

   condition.

3

Subject-Verb Agreement

In everyday terms, the word *agreement* refers to an accord of some sort: you reach an agreement with your boss about salary; friends agree to go to a movie; the members of a family agree to share household chores. This meaning covers grammatical **agreement** as well. In standard academic varieties of English, **verbs** must agree with their **subjects** in **number** (singular or plural) and in **person** (first, second, or third).

To make a verb in the **present tense** agree with a third-person singular subject, add -*s* or -*es* to the **base form**.

▶ A vegetarian diet *lowers* the risk of heart disease.

To make a verb in the present tense agree with any other subject, use the base form of the verb.

▶ I *miss* my family.

▶ They *live* in another state.

Have and *be* do not follow the -*s* or -*es* pattern with third-person singular subjects. *Have* changes to *has; be* has irregular forms in both the present tense and the **past tense**.

▶ War *is* hell.

▶ The soldier *was* brave beyond the call of duty.

Subject-verb agreement tends to present a problem only with certain kinds of subjects and sentences.

3a   Subjects and verbs separated by other words

Sometimes the **simple subject** is separated from the verb by other words. Make sure the verb agrees with the subject and not with another **noun** that falls in between.

▶ Many books on the best-seller list ~~has~~ *have* little literary value.

> The simple subject is *books,* not *list.*

Be especially careful when you use *as well as, along with, in addition to, together with,* and similar phrases. They do not make a singular subject plural.

▶ The president, along with many senators, ~~oppose~~ *opposes* the bill.

▶ A passenger, as well as the driver, ~~were~~ *was* injured in the accident.

Though this sentence has a grammatically singular subject, it suggests the idea of a plural subject and would be
clearer with a compound subject: *The driver and a passenger were injured in the accident.*

3b Compound subjects

Compound subjects joined by *and* are generally plural.

▶ A backpack, a canteen, and a rifle ~~was~~ *were* issued to each
recruit.

When subjects joined by *and* are considered a single unit
or refer to the same person or thing, they take a singular verb form.

▶ John Kennedy's closest friend and political ally *was*
his brother.

▶ Drinking and driving ~~remain~~ *remains* a major cause of
highway fatalities.

In this sentence, *drinking and driving* is considered a single activity, and a singular verb is used.

With subjects joined by *or* or *nor*, the verb agrees with
the part closest to the verb.

▶ Neither my roommate nor my neighbors *like* my loud
music.

▶ Either the witnesses or the defendant *is* lying.

If you find this sentence awkward, put the plural noun
closest to the verb: *Either the defendant or the witnesses* <u>are</u>
lying.

3c Collective nouns and fractions as subjects

Collective nouns—such as *family, team, audience, group,
jury, crowd, band, class,* and *committee*—and fractions can
take either singular or plural verb forms, depending on
whether they refer to the group as a single unit or to the

multiple members of the group. The meaning of a sentence as a whole is your guide.

▶ **After deliberating, the jury *reports* its verdict.**

The jury acts as a single unit.

▶ **The jury still *disagree* on a number of counts.**

The members of the jury act as multiple individuals.

▶ **Two-thirds of the park ~~have~~ burned.** *has*

Two-thirds refers to the single unit of the park that burned.

▶ **Two-thirds of the students ~~was~~ commuters.** *were*

Two-thirds here refers to the students who commuted as individuals.

Treat phrases starting with *the number of* as singular and with *a number of* as plural.

SINGULAR   The number of applications for the internship *was* unbelievable.

PLURAL   A number of applicants *were* put on the waiting list.

3d Indefinite-pronoun subjects

Indefinite pronouns are those that do not refer to specific persons or things. Most take singular verb forms.

SOME COMMON INDEFINITE PRONOUNS

another	each	much	one
any	either	neither	other
anybody	everybody	nobody	somebody
anyone	everyone	no one	someone
anything	everything	nothing	something

▶ **Of the two jobs, neither *holds* much appeal.**

▶ **Each of the plays ~~depict~~ a hero undone by a tragic flaw.** *depicts*

Both, few, many, others, and *several* are plural.

▶ Though many *apply,* few *are* chosen.

All, any, enough, more, most, none, and *some* can be singular or plural, depending on the noun they refer to.

▶ All of the cake *was* eaten.

▶ All of the candidates *promise* to improve the schools.

3e *Who, which,* and *that* as subjects

When the **relative pronouns** *who, which,* and *that* are used as subjects, the verb agrees with the **antecedent** of the pronoun (6b).

▶ Fear is an ingredient that *goes* into creating stereotypes.

▶ Guilt, jealousy, and fear are ingredients that *go* into creating stereotypes.

Problems often occur with the words *one of the.* In general, *one of the* takes a plural verb form, but *only one of the* takes a singular form.

▶ Carla is one of the employees who always ~~works~~ work late.

Some employees always work late. Carla is among them. Thus *who* refers to *employees,* and the verb is plural.

▶ Sam is the only one of the employees who always ~~work~~ works overtime.

Only one employee always works overtime, and that employee is Sam. Thus *one,* and not *employees,* is the antecedent of *who,* and the verb form must be singular.

3f Linking verbs and complements

A **linking verb** should agree with its subject, which usually precedes the verb, not with the **subject complement**, which follows it.

▶ The signings of these treaties ~~is~~ *are* the topic of my talk.

The subject is *signings*, not *topic*.

▶ Nero Wolfe's passion ~~were~~ *was* orchids.

The subject is *passion*, not *orchids*.

3g Subjects with plural forms but singular meanings

Some words that end in -s seem to be plural but are singular in meaning and thus take singular verb forms.

▶ Measles still ~~strike~~ *strikes* many Americans.

Some **nouns** of this kind (such as *statistics* and *politics*) may be either singular or plural, depending on context.

SINGULAR   Statistics *is* a course I really dread.

PLURAL   The statistics in that study *are* highly questionable.

3h Subjects that follow the verb

In English, verbs usually follow subjects. When this order is reversed, it is easy to become confused. Make the verb agree with the subject, not with a **noun** that happens to precede it.

▶ Beside the barn ~~stands~~ *stand* a silo and several tractors.

The subject is *silo and several tractors*, so the verb must be *stand*.

In sentences beginning with *there is* or *there are* (or *there was* or *were*), *there* serves only as an introductory word; the subject follows the verb.

▶ There *are* five basic positions in classical ballet.

The subject, *positions*, is plural, so the verb must also be plural.

3i   Titles and words referred to as words

Titles of works and words referred to as words always take singular verb forms, even if their own forms are plural.

▶ *One Writer's Beginnings* ~~describe~~ describes Eudora Welty's childhood.

▶ *Steroids* ~~are~~ is a little word that packs a big punch in the world of sports.

3j   *She go, he need*

▶ **She go to work seven days a week.**

▶ **He need to get with the program.**

These two sentences follow the rules of some African American varieties of English, in which third-person singular verbs do not end with -*s* or -*es* and carry special nuances of meaning. (In standard academic English, these verb forms are *she goes* and *he needs*.) You will often see verb forms such as those in the sentences above in literature, especially in dialogue, and you may well quote passages using these varieties of English in your own writing. In most academic and professional writing, however, add -*s* or -*es*.

4

Adjectives and Adverbs

Adjectives and adverbs often bring indispensable differences in meaning to the words they modify. In basketball, for example, there is an important difference between a *flagrant* foul and a *technical* foul, a layup and a *reverse* layup, and an *angry* coach and an *abusively angry* coach. In each instance, the modifiers are crucial to accurate communication.

Adjectives modify **nouns** and **pronouns**, answering the questions which? how many? and what kind? **Adverbs** modify **verbs**, adjectives, and other adverbs;

they answer the questions how? when? where? and to what extent? Many adverbs are formed by adding *-ly* to adjectives (*slight, slightly*), but many are formed in other ways (*outdoors*) or have forms of their own (*very*).

4a Adjectives vs. adverbs

When adjectives come after **linking verbs**, they usually serve as a **subject complement**, to describe the subject: *I am <u>patient</u>*. Note that in specific sentences, some verbs may or may not be linking verbs—*look, appear, sound, feel, smell, taste, grow,* and *prove,* for instance. When a word following one of these verbs modifies the subject, use an adjective; when it modifies the verb, use an adverb.

ADJECTIVE   Otis Thorpe looked *angry*.

ADVERB   He looked *angrily* at the referee.

Linking verbs suggest a state of being, not an action. In the preceding examples, *looked angry* suggests the state of being angry; *looked angrily* suggests an angry action.

   In everyday conversation, you will often hear (and perhaps use) adjectives in place of adverbs. When you write in standard academic English, however, use adverbs to modify verbs, adjectives, and other verbs.

▶ You can feel the song's meter if you listen ~~careful.~~ *carefully.*

▶ The audience was ~~real~~ *really* disappointed by the show.

   Good, well, bad, and badly. The modifiers *good, well, bad,* and *badly* cause problems for many writers because the distinctions between *good* and *well* and between *bad* and *badly* are often not observed in conversation. Problems also arise because *well* can function as either an adjective or an adverb.

▶ I look ~~well~~ *good* in blue.

▶ Now that the fever has broken, I feel ~~good~~ *well* again.

▶ He plays the trumpet ~~good.~~ *well.*

▶ I feel ~~badly~~ ^{bad} for the Toronto fans.

▶ Their team played ~~bad.~~ ^{badly.}

4b Comparatives and superlatives

Most adjectives and adverbs have three forms: **positive**, **comparative**, and **superlative**. You usually form the comparative and superlative of one- or two-syllable adjectives by adding *-er* and *-est* to the positive form: *short, shorter, shortest*. With longer adjectives and with most adverbs, use *more* and *most: scientific, more scientific, most scientific; elegantly, more elegantly, most elegantly*. Some short adjectives and adverbs have irregular comparative and superlative forms: *good, better, best; badly, worse, worst*.

■ **Comparatives vs. superlatives.** In conversation, you will often hear the superlative form used even when only two things are being compared. When you write standard academic English, however, use the comparative.

▶ Of the two paintings, the one by Klee is the ~~most~~ ^{more} interesting.

■ **Double comparatives and superlatives.** **Double comparatives** and **double superlatives** unnecessarily use both the *-er* or *-est* ending and *more* or *most*. Occasionally, these forms can act to build a special emphasis, as in the title of Spike Lee's movie *Mo' Better Blues*. In academic and professional writing, however, do not use *more* or *most* before adjectives or adverbs ending in *-er* or *-est*.

▶ Paris is the ~~most~~ loveliest city in the world.

■ **Absolute concepts.** Some adjectives and adverbs—such as *perfect*, *final*, and *unique*—are absolute concepts, so it is illogical to form comparatives or superlatives of these words.

▶ Anne has ~~the most~~ ^a unique sense of humor.

5

Modifier Placement and Reference

To be effective, **modifiers** should refer clearly to the words they modify and be positioned close to those words. Consider, for example, a sign seen recently:

DO NOT USE THE ELEVATORS IN CASE OF FIRE.

Should we really avoid the elevators altogether, in case there is ever a fire? Repositioning the modifier *in case of fire* eliminates such confusion—and makes clear that we are to avoid the elevators only if there is a fire: IN CASE OF FIRE, DO NOT USE THE ELEVATORS. This chapter reviews the conventions of accurate modifier placement.

5a Misplaced modifiers

Modifiers can cause confusion or ambiguity if they are not close enough to the words they modify or if they seem to modify more than one word in the sentence.

▶ She teaches a seminar ~~this term~~ on voodoo ^*this term*^ at Skyline College.

Surely the voodoo was not at the college.

▶ Once deregulated, a price decline ^*the industry is*^ ~~in the industry~~ is expected.

The writer intended to say that the industry, not the price decline, was being deregulated.

▶ *After he lost the 1962 race,* Nixon said he would get out of politics. ~~after he lost the 1962 race.~~

The unedited sentence implies that Nixon planned to lose the race.

Limiting modifiers. Be especially careful with the placement of limiting modifiers such as almost, even, just, merely, and only. In general, these modifiers should be placed right before or after the words they modify. Putting them in other positions may produce not just ambiguity but a completely different meaning.

AMBIGUOUS	The court *only* hears civil cases on Tuesdays.
CLEAR	The court hears *only* civil cases on Tuesdays.
CLEAR	The court hears civil cases on Tuesdays *only*.

Squinting modifiers. If a modifier could refer either to the word before it or to the word after it, it is called a **squinting modifier**. Put the modifier where it clearly relates to only a single word.

SQUINTING	Students who practice writing *often* will benefit.
REVISED	Students who *often practice* writing will benefit.
REVISED	Students who practice writing will *often benefit*.

5b Disruptive modifiers

Be careful that modifiers do not disrupt the flow of a sentence, making it hard for readers to follow the progress of the thought.

► *If they are cooked too long, vegetables will*
~~Vegetables will, if they are cooked too long,~~ lose most of their nutritional value.

Split infinitives. In general, do not place a modifier between the *to* and the verb of an **infinitive** (*to often complain*). Doing so makes it hard for readers to recognize that the two go together.

► Hitler expected the British to fairly quickly *surrender*. ~~surrender.~~

In some sentences, however, a modifier sounds awkward if it does not split the infinitive. In such cases, it may be best to reword the sentence to eliminate the infinitive altogether.

SPLIT	I hope *to* almost *equal* my last year's income.
REVISED	I hope that I will earn almost as much as I did last year.

5c Dangling modifiers

Dangling modifiers are words or phrases that modify nothing in particular in the rest of the sentence. They often *seem* to modify something that is implied but not actually present in the sentence. Dangling modifiers frequently appear at the beginnings or ends of sentences. To revise them, often you need to add a **subject** that the modifier clearly refers to; sometimes you have to revise the modifier itself.

▶ Reluctantly, the hound <u>was given away</u> to a neighbor.
         our family gave away

In the original sentence, was the dog reluctant, or was someone else who is not mentioned?

▶ <u>As</u> a young boy, his grandmother told stories of her years as a country schoolteacher.
  When he was

His grandmother was never a young boy.

▶ <del>Thumbing through the magazine,</del> my eyes automatically noticed the perfume ads.
                    M
      as I was thumbing through the magazine.

Eyes cannot thumb through a magazine.

6

Pronouns

As words that stand in for **nouns**, **pronouns** carry a lot of weight in everyday discourse. For example:

> Take the Interstate until you come to Exit 3 and then Route 313. Go past it, and take the next exit, which will be Broadway.

These directions provide a good example of why it's important for a pronoun to refer clearly to a specific noun or pronoun antecedent. The word *it* could mean either Exit 3 or Route 313—or are they the same thing? This chapter aims to help you use pronouns accurately.

6a Pronoun case

Most speakers of English know intuitively when to use *I*, when to use *me*, and when to use *my*. Our choices reflect differences in **case**, the form a pronoun takes to indicate its function in a sentence. Pronouns functioning as **subjects** or **subject complements** are in the **subjective case** (*I*); those functioning as **objects** are in the **objective case** (*me*); those functioning as possessives are in the **possessive case** (*my*).

SUBJECTIVE	OBJECTIVE	POSSESSIVE
I	me	my/mine
we	us	our/ours
you	you	your/yours
he/she/it	him/her/it	his/her/hers/its
they	them	their/theirs
who/whoever	whom/whomever	whose

Case problems tend to occur in the following situations.

▨ **In subject complements.** Many Americans routinely use the objective case for subject complements, especially in conversation: *Who's there? It's me.* If the subjective case for a subject complement sounds stilted or awkward (*It's I*), try rewriting the sentence using the pronoun as the subject (*I'm here*).

She was the
▶ ~~The~~ first person to see Monty after the awards. ~~was she.~~
  ^   ^

▨ **Before gerunds.** Pronouns before a **gerund** should be in the possessive case.

▶ I remember *his* singing.

▨ **With *who, whoever, whom,* and *whomever*.** A common problem with pronoun case is deciding whether to use *who* or *whom*. Use *who* and *whoever*, which are subjective-case pronouns, for subjects or subject complements. Use *whom* and *whomever*, which are objective-case pronouns, for objects.

Two particular situations lead to confusion with *who* and *whom*: when they begin a question and when they introduce a **dependent clause** (8d). You can determine whether to use *who* or *whom* at the beginning of a ques-

tion by answering the question using a **personal pronoun**. If the answer is in the subjective case, use *who;* if it is in the objective case, use *whom.*

▶ ~~Who~~ did you visit?
   Whom

    I visited *them. Them* is objective; thus *whom* is correct.

▶ ~~Whom~~ do you think wrote the story?
   Who

    I think *she* wrote the story. *She* is subjective; thus *who* is correct.

The case of a pronoun in a dependent clause is determined by its function in the clause, no matter how that clause functions in the sentence. If the pronoun acts as a subject or subject complement in the clause, use *who* or *whoever.* If the pronoun acts as an object in the clause, use *whom* or *whomever.*

▶ Anyone can hypnotize someone ~~whom~~ wants to be
                       who

  hypnotized.

    The verb of the clause is *wants,* and its subject is *who.*

▶ ~~Whoever~~ the party suspected of disloyalty was executed.
   Whomever

    Whomever is the object of *suspected* in the clause *whomever the party suspected of disloyalty.*

In compound structures. When a pronoun is part of a compound subject, complement, or object, put it in the same case you would use if the pronoun were alone.

▶ When Zelda and ~~him~~ were first married, they lived in
               he

  New York.

▶ The boss invited ~~she~~ and her family to dinner.
              her

▶ This morning saw yet another conflict between my
  sister and ~~I.~~
         me.

In elliptical constructions. Elliptical constructions are those in which some words are understood but left out. When an elliptical construction ends in a pronoun,

put the pronoun in the case it would be in if the construction were complete.

▶ **His sister has always been more athletic than** *he* **[is].**

In some elliptical constructions, the case of the pronoun depends on the meaning intended.

▶ **Willie likes Lily more than** *she* **[likes Lily].**

   She is the subject of the omitted verb *likes*.

▶ **Willie likes Lily more than [he likes]** *her.*

   Her is the object of the omitted verb *likes*.

■ **With we and us before a noun.** If you are unsure about whether to use *we* or *us* before a **noun**, use whichever pronoun would be correct if the noun were omitted.

                      We
▶ ~~Us~~ fans never give up hope.
   ^

   Fans is the subject, so the subjective *we* is used.

                               us
▶ **The Rangers depend on** ~~we~~ **fans.**
                            ^

   Fans is the object of a preposition, so the objective *us* is used.

6b Pronoun-antecedent agreement

The **antecedent** of a pronoun is the **noun** or other pronoun that the pronoun refers to. A pronoun and its antecedent are said to "agree" when they match up in **person**, **number**, and **gender**.

SINGULAR   The *choirmaster* raised *her* baton.

PLURAL   The *boys* picked up *their* music.

■ **Compound antecedents.** When a compound antecedent is joined by *or* or *nor*, the pronoun agrees with the nearest antecedent. If the parts of the antecedent are of different genders or persons, however, this kind of sentence can be awkward and may need to be revised.

AWKWARD	Neither Annie nor Barry got his work done.
REVISED	Annie didn't get her work done, and neither did Barry.

When a compound antecedent contains both singular and plural parts, the sentence may sound awkward unless the plural part comes last.

AWKWARD	Neither the radio stations nor the newspaper would reveal *its* sources.
REVISED	Neither the newspaper nor the radio stations would reveal *their* sources.

Indefinite-pronoun antecedents. Indefinite pronouns are those that do not refer to specific persons or things. Most indefinite pronouns are always singular; a few are always plural. Some can be singular or plural depending on the context.

▶ One of the ballerinas lost *her* balance.

▶ Many in the audience jumped to *their* feet.

SINGULAR	Some of the furniture was showing *its* age.
PLURAL	Some of the farmers abandoned *their* land.

Sexist pronouns. Pronouns often refer to antecedents that may be either male or female. Writers used to use a masculine pronoun, known as the generic *he*, to refer to such antecedents: *A child needs a way to express himself. Everyone paid his own way.* In recent decades, however, many people have pointed out that such wording ignores or even excludes females—and thus should be revised: *Children need ways to express themselves. Everyone paid his or her own way.*

6c Clear pronoun reference

If a pronoun does not refer clearly to a specific **antecedent**, readers will have trouble following the meaning.

■ **Ambiguous antecedents.** When a pronoun could refer to more than one antecedent, revise the sentence to make the reference clear.

▶ The meeting between Bowman and Sonny makes ~~him~~ ^{Bowman} compare his own unsatisfying domestic life with one that is emotionally secure.

Who is the antecedent of *him* and *his*: Bowman or Sonny? The revision makes the reference clear by replacing a pronoun (*him*) with a noun (*Bowman*).

▶ Kerry told Ellen, "I ~~she~~ should be ready soon."

Reporting Kerry's words directly, in quotation marks, eliminates the ambiguity.

■ **Vague use of *it*, *this*, *that*, and *which*.** The words *it*, *this*, *that*, and *which* are often used to refer to something mentioned earlier. Like other pronouns, each of these words must refer to a specific antecedent.

▶ When the senators realized the bill would be defeated, they tried to postpone the vote but failed. ~~It~~ ^{The entire effort} was a fiasco.

▶ Nancy just found out that she won the lottery, ^{an event} which explains her sudden resignation from her job.

■ **Indefinite use of *you*, *it*, and *they*.** In conversation, we frequently use *you*, *it*, and *they* in an indefinite sense, in such expressions as *you never know* and *in the paper, it said*. In academic and professional writing, however, use *you* only to mean "you, the reader," and *it* or *they* only to refer to a clear antecedent.

▶ In Texas, ~~you~~ ^{one} often ~~hear~~ ^{hears} about the political influence of big oil corporations.

▶ ~~On~~ ^T/the Weather Channel, ~~it~~ said that Hurricane Fran will hit Virginia Beach tomorrow morning.

▶ ~~In France, they~~ ^{Most restaurants in France} allow dogs. ~~in most restaurants.~~

■ **Implied antecedents.** Sometimes a possessive may clearly *imply* a noun antecedent, but it does not serve as a clear antecedent.

▶ In ~~Welty's~~ *her* story, ~~she~~ *Welty* characterizes Bowman as a man unaware of his own isolation.

7

Comma Splices and Fused Sentences

A **comma splice** occurs when two **independent clauses** are joined with only a comma. We often see comma splices in advertising, where they can give slogans a catchy rhythm.

> Life's short, play hard.
> — NIKE ADVERTISEMENT

Another common pattern is a **fused** , or **run-on, sentence** , which occurs when two independent clauses are joined with no punctuation or no connecting word between them. The Nike advertisement as a fused sentence would be "Life's short play hard."

You will seldom if ever profit from using comma splices or fused sentences in academic or professional writing. In fact, doing so will almost always be identified as an error. This chapter will guide you in recognizing and revising comma splices and fused sentences.

7a Separating the clauses into two sentences

The simplest way to revise comma splices or fused sentences is to separate them into two sentences.

COMMA
SPLICE

My mother spends long hours every spring tilling the soil and moving manure /. *T*his part of gardening is nauseating.

If the two clauses are very short, making them two sentences may sound abrupt and terse, and some other method of revision would probably be preferable.

7b Linking the clauses with a comma and a coordinating conjunction

If the two clauses are closely related and equally important, you can join them with a comma and a **coordinating
conjunction** (*and, but, or, nor, for, so,* or *yet*).

FUSED
SENTENCE
    but
I should pay my tuition, I need a new car.

7c Linking the clauses with a semicolon

If the ideas in the two clauses are closely related and
you want to give them equal emphasis, another alternative is to link them with a semicolon.

COMMA
SPLICE
This photograph is not at all realistic; it

even uses dreamlike images to convey its

message.

Comma splices often result when writers link clauses
with a **conjunctive adverb** like *however* or *therefore* or a
transitional phrase like *in fact*. In such sentences, the
two clauses must be separated by a semicolon or by a
comma and a **coordinating conjunction**. In addition,
conjunctive adverbs and transitional phrases are usually set off from the second clause by a comma (19a, e).

COMMA
SPLICE
Many Third World countries have very

high birthrates; therefore, most of their

citizens are young.

7d Recasting the two clauses as one independent clause

When two independent clauses are spliced or fused,
you can sometimes reduce them to a single independent
clause.

FUSED
SENTENCE
    most
Many people complain that a large part of

    and
their mail is advertisements the rest is bills.

7e   Recasting one independent clause as a dependent clause

When one independent clause is more important than the other, try converting one to a **dependent clause**.

COMMA SPLICE

Although
Zora Neale Hurston is regarded as one of America's major novelists, she died in obscurity.

The first clause stands in contrast to the second one: in contrast to Hurston's importance today (she is held in high esteem) are the circumstances of her death (obscurity). In the revision, the writer chose to emphasize the second clause and to make the first one into a dependent clause by adding the subordinating conjunction *although*.

FUSED SENTENCE

, which reacted against mass production,
The arts and crafts movement called for handmade objects. ~~it reacted against mass production.~~

Both clauses discuss related aspects of the arts and crafts movement. In the revision, the writer chose to emphasize the first clause, the one describing what the movement advocated, and to make the second clause, the one describing what it reacted against, into a dependent clause.

8

Sentence Fragments

In literature and advertisements, you will find sentence fragments in frequent use. For example:

Our Lifetime Guarantee may come as a shock.

Or a strut. Or a muffler. Because once you pay to replace them, Toyota's Lifetime Guarantee covers parts and labor on any dealer-installed muffler, shock, or strut for as long as you own your Toyota! So if anything should ever go wrong, your Toyota dealer will fix it. *Absolutely free.*   — TOYOTA ADVERTISEMENT

As complete sentences, the information in the three italicized fragments would be less clever and far less memorable.

Sentence fragments are groups of words that are punctuated as sentences but lack some element grammatically necessary to a sentence. Though you will often see and hear sentence fragments, you will seldom if ever want to use them in academic or professional writing, where some readers might regard them as errors. Here are some ways to revise them.

8a Phrase fragments

Phrases are groups of words that lack a **subject**, a **verb**, or both. When a **verbal phrase**, a **prepositional phrase**, **noun phrase**, or an **appositive phrase** is punctuated like a sentence, it becomes a fragment. To revise such a fragment, attach it to an **independent clause**, or make it a separate sentence.

▶ NBC is broadcasting the debates⁄ With discussions afterward.

> The second word group is a prepositional phrase, not a sentence. The editing combines the phrase with an independent clause.

▶ One of our nation's most cherished concepts, ~~may be in~~ ~~danger.~~ The ideal of a good education for every child⁄,

may be in danger.

> *The ideal of a good education for every child* is an appositive phrase renaming the noun *concepts*. The editing attaches the fragment to the sentence containing the noun to which the appositive refers.

▶ Vivian stayed out of school for three months after Linda was born. *She did so to* ~~To~~ recuperate and to take care of her.

> *To recuperate and to take care of her* includes only a verbal and a verbal phrase. The revision—adding a subject (*she*) and a verb (*did*)—turns the fragment into a separate sentence.

8b Compound-predicate fragments

A fragment occurs when one part of a **compound predicate** is punctuated as a separate sentence although it lacks a **subject**. Such a fragment usually begins with *and, but,* or *or.* You can revise it by attaching it to the **independent clause** that contains the rest of the predicate.

▶ They sold their house/ ~~And~~ moved into an apartment.

    and

8c Fragments beginning with transitions

Transitional words and phrases like *also, and, but, for example, or,* and *that is* sometimes lead to fragments. If you introduce an example, an explanation, or an additional point with such a transition, be certain you write a sentence, not a fragment.

▶ Joan Didion has written on many subjects/ **~~Such~~** as the Hoover Dam and migraine headaches.

    such

The second word group is a phrase, not a sentence. The editing combines it with an independent clause.

8d Clause fragments

A **dependent clause** cannot stand alone as a sentence because it depends on an **independent clause** to complete its meaning. A dependent clause usually begins with a subordinating word such as *after, because, before, if, since, though, unless, until, when, where, while, who, which,* and *that.* You can usually combine a dependent-clause fragment with a nearby independent clause.

▶ When I decided to work part-time/ I gave up some earning potential.

If you cannot smoothly attach the clause to a nearby independent clause, try turning the dependent clause

into a sentence by deleting the opening subordinating word.

▸ Injuries in automobile accidents occur in two ways.

    A

~~When~~ ~~an~~ occupant either is hurt by something inside

the car or is thrown from the car.

FAQ: GRAMMAR ONLINE

How important are grammatical conventions when you do email and other online writing?

The answer to this question depends on the kind of online writing you are doing (EMAIL? WEB PAGE? MOO? HYPERTEXT essay?) and on your rhetorical situation—the context of your writing, your purpose, your audience and their expectations, the genre you are using, and the level of formality appropriate to your message.

- **Email.** If in doubt, stick to standard academic English punctuation and spelling, even if your diction and syntax are more informal. Much email is appropriately informal: it's often conversational, almost like talk: "Long time, no see—gimme some news, will you?" But if you're emailing your boss in response to a request, you will want to be more formal and to observe grammatical conventions: "I am responding to your request for an update on sales in the Northern region."

- **Postings.** If you're posting to a LISTSERV or NEWSGROUP whose members are largely unknown to you, look for any available FAQs before you begin: the information there may provide ground rules for postings, including expectations about writing conventions. It's also a good idea to look at other postings for a few days to get a sense of style and audience before posting anything yourself. If you are too casual or don't pay attention to grammatical conventions, you may send a message that you don't intend—that you are satisfied with sloppy work, for instance.

  Remember that postings, like email, can easily be printed out and circulated OFFLINE. In print, the informal "just between us" language and conventions may send unintentional signals to an even wider audience.

- **MOOs and MUDs.** In the fast-paced real-time communication of a MOO or MUD, however, paying careful attention to all conventions is very difficult. As a result, lapses of conventions and typographical errors are more likely to be tolerated.

You often see sentence fragments in online writing. How appropriate are they?

Take your cues from how formal or informal the message or posting is, what your purpose is in writing, and what your readers' expectations are. For informal email—a note to a close friend, a casual comment to a colleague—fragments can be appropriate. But much email, such as official business correspondence, needs to be more formal—especially if it might be forwarded or printed out.

How do you deal with acronyms such as HTML or MOO that need to be made plural or made into verbs?

The digital revolution has spawned many acronyms that are used routinely by online writers. To make them into plurals or verb forms, just follow the grammar of English nouns and verbs, with a few variations.

- To make an acronym plural, add a lowercase s without an apostrophe: MOOs, CDs, CPUs.

- To make an acronym into a past-tense verb, add an apostrophe + *d:* FTP'd, HTML'd.

- To make an acronym into a present participle, just add *ing:* FTPing, CCing.

- To make an acronym into a past participle, add an apostrophe + *d:* CC'd, ID'd.

When you use acronyms in your online writing, keep your readers in mind: if they may not understand what an acronym stands for, or if you don't know them well enough to judge, it is better to write it out.

What do the various parts of URLs mean? Is there an underlying "grammar" that helps you read them?

For many writers, Uniform Resource Locators (URLs) offer increasingly necessary ways to access information. Just as word order is important to the grammar of English sentences, so too is the order of the parts of a URL. You can read a URL for its meaning just as you can read a sentence, so knowing the "grammar" of URLs can help you use this locator, especially if you are trying to identify an error or typo in an address. The example below labels the parts of a URL: PROTOCOL, DOMAIN NAME, DIRECTORY PATH, and FILE NAME.

PROTOCOL	DOMAIN NAME	DIRECTORY PATH	FILE NAME

http://www.smpcollege.com/smp_english.easy_writer

SLASHES END PROTOCOL   SLASH ENDS DOMAIN NAME

Of particular importance is the final designation of the domain name. In the United States, the following designations appear (note, however, that domain names differ in other countries):

   com=commercial site

   edu=education site

   org=nonprofit organization site

   gov=governmental site

The domain name may also identify a country of origin:

   ca=Canada

   ar=Argentina

   ch=Switzerland

Most important of all, remember that a URL must be typed *exactly* as it appears, without any extra spaces, or you will not be able to access the site.

Do Web sites use any special grammatical conventions?

On the **WEB**, visuals and formatting are extremely important to the grammar of the overall page, and as sound becomes more available to ordinary writers, it too contributes to the "grammar" of any Web page. Hypertext links are also important to a site's logical, visual, and aural grammar, for they act as headings to direct readers' attention to certain topics or details.

Most people building **WEB SITES** want to put their best foot forward, creating a site that is aesthetically appealing, easy to navigate—and correct. If you want to stretch grammatical or other conventions for special effect on a Web site, make sure that readers will perceive what you have done as both intentional and effective.

Online Resources

Grammar and Style Notes provides explanations of conventions of grammar, style, and usage, broken into a file for each letter of the alphabet (click on "c" for information on commas, for example):

   <http://www.english.upenn.edu/~jlynch/Grammar/>

Professor Kitty Locker's Site offers expert advice on how to create an effective Web page of your own:

   <http://www.cohums.ohio-state.edu/english/People
   /Locker.1/web.htm>

SENTENCE STYLE

When you start writing—and I
think it's true for a lot of beginning
writers—you're scared to death
that if you don't get that sentence
right that minute it's never going
to show up again. And it isn't. But
it doesn't matter—another one
will, and it'll probably be better.
                            — Toni Morrison,
                            The Sight of Memory

Consistency and Completeness

If you listen carefully to the conversations around you, you will hear inconsistent and incomplete structures all the time, particularly during a lively or heated discussion. For instance:

> "The Bulls are . . . They must be . . . Man, they are absolutely the very best team . . . not in the League even . . . in the world."
> "Wait till the Jazz take them. Because you know that the Mailman will be more lethal than . . . he will be up to Jordan . . . for sure . . . just wait!"

In the flow of informal conversation, such structures pose few problems for speakers or listeners. But in writing, these "sentences" can seem mixed up, incoherent, even nonsensical. This chapter provides guidelines for recognizing and editing mixed and incomplete structures.

9a Consistent grammatical patterns

Beginning a sentence with one grammatical pattern and then switching to another one confuses readers.

MIXED The fact that I get up at 5:00 A.M., a wake-up time that explains why I'm always tired in the evening.

The sentence starts out with a **subject** (*The fact*) followed by a **dependent clause** (*that I get up at 5:00 A.M.*). The sentence needs a **predicate** to complete the **independent clause** but instead it moves to another **phrase** followed by a dependent clause (*a wake-up time that explains why I'm always tired in the evening*). Thus the independent clause is never completed, and what results is a fragment, or incomplete sentence.

REVISED The fact that I get up at 5:00 A.M. explains why I'm always tired in the evening.

Deleting *a wake-up time that* changes the rest of the sentence into a predicate.

REVISED   I get up at 5:00 A.M., a wake-up time
that explains why I'm always tired in
the evening.

Deleting *The fact that* turns the beginning of the sentence
into an independent clause.

9b Matching subjects and predicates

Another kind of mixed structure, called faulty predication,
occurs when a **subject** and **predicate** do not fit together
grammatically or simply do not make sense together.

▶ A characteristic that I admire is ~~a person who is kind.~~ ^{*kindness.*}

A person is not a characteristic.

▶ The rules of the corporation ^{*require that*} ~~expect~~ employees ~~to~~ be

on time.

Rules cannot expect anything.

Many cases of faulty predication result from using
forms of *be* when another **verb** would be stronger, as in
the constructions *is when, is where,* and *reason . . . is
because*. These constructions are inappropriate in academic or professional writing.

▶ A stereotype is ^{*an unfair characterization of*} ~~when someone characterizes~~ a group.
~~unfairly.~~

▶ A confluence is ^{*a place*} where two rivers join to form one.

▶ ~~The reason~~ I like to play soccer ~~is~~ because it provides
aerobic exercise.

9c Consistent compound structures

Sometimes writers omit certain words in compound
structures (6a). If the omitted word does not fit grammatically with other parts of the compound, the omis-
sion can be inappropriate.

▶ His skills are weak, and his performance ^{*is*} only average.

The omitted verb *is* does not match the verb in the other part of the compound (*skills are . . . performance is*), and so the writer must include it.

9d Logically consistent comparisons

When you compare two or more things, the comparison must be logically consistent.

> *Japan*
> ▶ ~~The Japanese economy~~ is more dependent on imported
> ^
> oil than any other industrialized country.

The original sentence illogically compared an economy with a country.

10

Conciseness

You can see the importance of conciseness in directions, particularly those on medicines. Consider the following directions found on one common prescription drug:

> Take one tablet daily with food. Avoid all alcohol. If symptoms persist, see doctor.

These directions aim to state the message as clearly and concisely as possible to relay important information on a small label. Squeezing words onto a three-inch label is probably not your ordinary writing situation, but more often than not, you will want to write as concisely as you can.

10a Eliminating redundant words

Sometimes writers add words for emphasis, saying that something is large *in size* or red *in color* or that two ingredients should be combined *together*. The italicized words are redundant, or unnecessary for meaning, as are the deleted words below.

> *A*
> ▶ ~~Compulsory~~ ⟨attendance at assemblies is required.

▶ The auction featured ~~contemporary~~ "antiques" made recently.

▶ Many different forms of hazing occur, such as physical ~~abuse~~ and mental abuse.

10b Eliminating empty words

Words that contribute little or no real meaning to a sentence include vague nouns like *area, aspect, factor,* and *situation* as well as vague **modifiers** like *definitely, major, really,* and *very.* Try simply deleting such words or thinking of a more specific way to say what you mean.

▶ ~~The~~ _H_ousing ~~situation~~ can ~~have a really significant~~ *strongly influence* ~~impact on the social aspect of~~ a student's *social* life.

10c Replacing wordy phrases

Many common phrases can be reduced to a word or two with no loss in meaning.

WORDY	CONCISE
at all times	always
at the present time	now/today
at that point in time	then
due to the fact that	because
in order to	to
in spite of the fact that	although, even though
in the event that	if
for the purpose of	for

10d Simplifying sentence structure

Using the simplest grammatical structures possible can tighten and strengthen your sentences considerably.

▶ Kennedy, ~~who was~~ only the second Roman Catholic ~~to be~~ nominated for the presidency by a major party, had to handle the religion issue ~~in a delicate manner.~~ *delicately.*

■ **Using strong verbs.** *Be* verbs (*is, are, was, were, been*) often result in wordiness.

▶ A high-fat, high-cholesterol diet ~~is bad for~~ your heart.
                                        harms

■ **Avoiding expletives.** Constructions such as *there is, there are,* and *it is* often add excess words to a sentence. Sometimes these **expletive** constructions provide emphatic ways to introduce a topic; often, however, your writing will be better without them.

▶ ~~There are~~ *M*any people ~~who~~ fear success because they believe they do not deserve it.

▶ ~~It is necessary for~~ *P*residential candidates *need* to perform well on television.

■ **Using active voice.** Try to use the **active voice** whenever possible. Some writing situations call for the **passive voice**, but it is always wordier than the active—and often makes for dull or even difficult reading (2e).

▶ ~~In Gower's research, it was~~ *Gower* found that pythons often dwell in trees.

11

Parallelism

If you look and listen, you will see parallel grammatical structures in everyday use. Bumper stickers often use parallelism to make their messages memorable (*Children on board; parents on Valium*), as do song lyrics and jump-rope rhymes. In addition to creating pleasing rhythmic effects, parallelism helps to clarify meaning.

11a Items in a series or list

All items in a series should be in parallel form—all **nouns**, all **verbs**, all **prepositional phrases**, and so on. Such parallelism makes a series both graceful and easy to follow.

▶ In the eighteenth century, armed forces could fight *in open fields* and *on the high seas.* Today, they can clash *on the ground anywhere, on the sea, under the sea,* and *in the air.*

— DONALD M. SNOW AND EUGENE BROWN,
The Contours of Power

The parallel structure of the italicized phrases, and of the two sentences themselves, emphasizes the contrast between the eighteenth century and today.

▶ The quarter horse skipped, pranced, and ~~was sashaying~~ *sashayed* onto the track.

▶ The children ran down the hill, skipped over the lawn, *jumped* and into the swimming pool.

▶ The duties of the job include baby-sitting, house-cleaning, and ~~preparation of~~ *preparing* meals.

Items in a list and on a formal outline should be parallel.

▶ Kitchen rules: (1) Coffee to be made only by library staff. (2) Coffee service to be closed at 4:00 P.M. (3) Doughnuts to be kept in cabinet. (4) ~~No faculty members should handle coffee materials.~~ *Coffee* materials not to be handled by faculty.

11b Paired ideas

Parallel structures can help you pair two ideas effectively. The more nearly parallel the two structures are, the stronger the connection between the ideas will be.

▶ We die. That may be the meaning of life. But we *do* language. That may be the measure of our lives.

— TONI MORRISON

▶ Writers are often more interesting on the page than in ~~person.~~ *the flesh.*

In these examples, the parallel structures help to point out an important contrast between two ideas or acts.

With conjunctions. When you link ideas with *and, but, or, nor, for, so,* or *yet,* try to make the ideas parallel in structure. Always use the same structure after both parts of a **correlative conjunction**: *either . . . or, both . . . and, neither . . . nor, not . . . but, not only . . . but also, just as . . . so,* and *whether . . . or.*

▶ Consult a friend in your class or who is good at math.

   who is (inserted above "or who")

▶ The wise politician promises the possible and should accept the inevitable.

   accepts (replacing "should accept")

▶ I wanted not only to go away to school but also to New England.

   live in (inserted before "New England")

11c Words necessary for clarity

In addition to making parallel elements grammatically similar, be sure to include any words—**prepositions**, **articles**, **verb** forms, and so on—that are necessary for clarity.

▶ We'll move to a town near the ocean or Mexico.

   to (inserted before "Mexico")

To a town near Mexico or to Mexico? The editing clarifies the meaning.

12
Shifts

A shift in writing is an abrupt change of some sort that results in inconsistency. Sometimes writers shift deliberately, as Dave Barry does in saying he "would have to say that the greatest single achievement of the American medical establishment is nasal spray." His shift in tone from the serious (the American medical establishment) to the banal (nasal spray) is intended to make us laugh. Unintentional shifts, on the other hand, can be jolting and confusing to readers.

12a Shifts in tense

If the verbs in a passage refer to actions occurring at different times, they may require different tenses. Be careful, however, not to change tenses for no reason.

▶ A few countries produce almost all of the world's
  affects
  illegal drugs, but addiction ~~affected~~ many countries.
  ^

12b Shifts in voice

Do not shift without reason between the active voice (she *sold* it) and the passive voice (it *was sold*). Sometimes a shift in voice is justified, but often it may only confuse readers.

                                             me
▶ Two youths approached ~~me~~, and ~~I was~~ asked for my
                                           ^
  wallet.

The original sentence shifts from the active (*youths approached*) to the passive (*I was asked*), so it is unclear who asked for the wallet. Making both verbs active clears up the confusion.

12c Shifts in point of view

Unnecessary shifts between first person (*I, we*), second person (*you*), and third person (*he, she, it, one,* or *they*) or between singular and plural subjects can be very confusing to readers.

  You
▶ ~~One~~ can do well on this job if you budget your time.
  ^

Is the writer making a general statement or giving advice to someone? Eliminating the shift eliminates this confusion.

▶ Nurses receive much less pay than doctors, even
        nurses have
  though ~~a nurse has~~ the primary responsibility for
         ^
  daily patient care.

The writer had no reason to shift from plural (*nurses*) to singular (*a nurse*).

12d Shifts between direct and indirect discourse

When you quote someone's exact words, you are using **direct discourse**: *She said, "I'm an editor."* When you report what someone says without repeating the exact words, you are using **indirect discourse**: *She said she is an editor.* Shifting between direct and indirect discourse in the same sentence can cause problems, especially with questions.

             he
▶ Bob asked what ͜could he do to help̷.͜

The editing eliminates an awkward shift by reporting Bob's words. The sentence could also be edited to quote Bob directly: *Bob asked, "What can I do to help?"*

12e Shifts in diction

Watch out for shifts in your diction (choice of words) that could confuse readers and leave them wondering what your real attitude toward your topic is.

INCONSISTENT

Since taking office, Prime Minister Chrétien has been bombarded with really gross news, including tons of strikes, record unemployment, several scandals, and even bitching from colleagues in his own party.

REVISED

Since taking office, Prime Minister Chrétien has been bombarded with unrelenting bad news, including a wave of strikes, record unemployment, several scandals, and even sniping from colleagues in his own party.

The shift in diction from formal to highly informal gives an odd, disjointed sound to the passage. As revised, the passage is easier to read because the words are consistently formal.

FAQ: SENTENCE STYLE ONLINE

Does online writing need to be very concise?

Readers of online writing can't flip pages back and forth. Instead, they have to scroll down and back up, or print out and then read. Moreover, much online communication is meant to be instantaneous, composed of short exchanges and quick replies to queries. The speed of communication, small screens, even scarce **BANDWIDTH**—all encourage concise, directly stated messages. Unless your writing is meant to be **DOWNLOADED** and printed out, try to use screen space efficiently.

- **Homepages. HOMEPAGES** must use space to maximum effect, giving necessary information via images and words, and also including links to other pages and documents. Though these linked documents may be quite lengthy, the homepage leading you to them needs to be concise.

- **MOOs and MUDs.** Brevity is even more important in **MOOS** and **MUDS**, where many people interact simultaneously. MOOs and MUDs tend to invite very short exchanges, often just a sentence or two.

How much stylistic polishing does online writing call for?

As always, the answer depends on your rhetorical situation. If the outcome of a particular piece of online writing is very important to you (an award or promotion, say, or a contract, or a Web page you are responsible for designing), then the more polished your prose the better. Make sure it's correct, accurate, and persuasive.

Many **EMAIL** or **NEWSGROUP** postings, however, seek to convey particular pieces of information in the quickest and easiest way possible. Such messages need only be polished enough to be clear. And in MOOs and MUDs, writing contributions are so short and done so rapidly that polished prose is not expected.

Online Resources

The Online Elements of Style provides Strunk and White's classic advice on usage and style:

<http://www.columbia.edu/acis/bartleby/strunk>

Writer's Workbench Style Program offers information on stylistic issues such as average sentence length, sentence type, voice of verbs, and kinds of sentence openers. It includes links to other programs on diction, spelling, punctuation, and so on:

<http://www.emo.com/wwb/wwb_sty.html>

WORD CHOICE

A word is dead
When it is said,
Some say.
I say it just
Begins to live
That day.
         – Emily Dickinson

Appropriate, Precise Language

One restaurant's "down-home beef stew" may be similar to another's "boeuf bourguignon," but in each case the choice of language says something not only about how the beef is prepared but also about what kind of restaurant is serving it. This chapter will help you choose words that are clear and appropriate for your purpose, topic, and audience.

13a Language variety

English comes in many varieties, which differ in pronunciation, vocabulary, rhetoric, and grammar. Your regional variety, for example, may determine whether you order a hero, a poor boy, a hoagie, a submarine, a grinder, or a *cubano*. In addition to numerous varieties of English, which include ethnic and occupational as well as regional ones, many other languages are spoken in the United States.

One variety of English, often referred to as the "standard," is that taught in schools, represented in this and all other textbooks, used in the national media, and written and spoken by those wielding the most social and economic power. As the language used in business and most public institutions, standard academic English is a variety you will want to be completely familiar with. Standard academic English, however, is only one of many effective varieties of English and itself varies from the very formal style used in scholarly writing to the informal style characteristic of casual conversation.

13b Appropriate levels of formality

In an email or letter to a friend or close associate, informal language is often appropriate. For most academic and professional writing, however, more formal language is appropriate because you are addressing people you do not know well.

EMAIL TO SOMEONE YOU KNOW WELL

Mirna is great—hire her if you can!

LETTER OF RECOMMENDATION TO SOMEONE YOU DO NOT KNOW

I am pleased to recommend Mirna Mendez. She will bring good ideas and extraordinary energy to your organization.

■ **Slang and colloquial language.** Slang, extremely informal language, is often confined to a relatively small group and changes very quickly, though some slang gains wide use (*yuppie, bummer*). Colloquial language (*a lot, in a bind, snooze*) is less informal, more widely used, and longer lasting than most slang.

Writers who use slang and colloquial language can run the risk of not being understood or of not being taken seriously. If you are writing for a general audience about arms-control negotiations and you use the term *nukes*, some readers may not know what you mean, and others may be irritated by what they see as a frivolous reference to a deadly serious subject.

■ **Jargon.** Jargon is the special vocabulary of a trade or profession that enables members to speak and write concisely to one another. Jargon should usually be reserved for a specific technical audience.

JARGON

The VDTs in composition were down last week.

REVISED FOR A GENERAL AUDIENCE

The video display terminals in the composing room were not working last week.

■ **Stuffy language and euphemisms.** Stuffy or pompous language is unnecessarily formal for the purpose, audience, or topic. Hence it often gives writing an insincere or unintentionally humorous tone, making a writer's ideas seem insignificant, or even unbelievable.

STUFFY

Pursuant to the August 9 memorandum regarding petroleum supply exigencies, it is incumbent upon us to endeavor to make maximal utilization of telephonic communication in lieu of personal visitation.

REVISED

> As of August 9, petroleum shortages require us to use the telephone instead of personal visits whenever possible.

Euphemisms make unpleasant ideas seem less harsh. *Your position is being eliminated* seeks to soften the blow of being *fired* or *laid off;* the British call this employment situation being *declared redundant,* and Canadians refer to being *made surplus.* Use euphemisms with great care. Although they can appeal to an audience by showing that you are considerate of people's feelings, euphemisms can also sound phony or evasive.

13c Denotation and connotation

The words *maxim, epigram, proverb, saw, saying,* and *motto* all carry roughly the same denotation, or dictionary meaning. Because of their different connotations or associations, however, *proverb* would be the appropriate word to use in reference to a saying from the Bible, *saw* in reference to the kind of wisdom handed down anonymously, *epigram* in reference to a witty statement by someone like Dave Barry.

Note the differences in connotation among the following three statements:

▶ Students Against Racism erected a barrier on the campus oval, saying it symbolizes "the many barriers to those discriminated against by university policies."

▶ Left-wing agitators threw up an eyesore right on the oval to try to stampede the university into giving in to their demands.

▶ Supporters of human rights challenged the university's investment in racism by erecting a protest barrier on campus.

The first statement is the most neutral, merely stating facts (and quoting the assertion about university policy to represent it as someone's words rather than as "facts"); the second, by using words with negative connotations (*agitators, eyesore, stampede*), is strongly critical; the third, by using words with positive connotations (*supporters of human rights*) and presenting assertions as facts (*the university's investment in racism*), gives a favorable slant to the story.

13d General and specific diction

Effective writers balance general words (those that name groups or classes) with specific words (those that identify individual and particular things). Abstractions, which are types of general words, refer to things we cannot perceive through our five senses. Specific words are often concrete, naming things we can see, hear, touch, taste, or smell.

GENERAL	LESS GENERAL	SPECIFIC	MORE SPECIFIC
book	dictionary	unabridged dictionary	my 1998 edition of *Webster's Dictionary*

ABSTRACT	LESS ABSTRACT	CONCRETE	MORE CONCRETE
culture	visual art	painting	*Starry Night*

13e Figurative language

One good way to communicate is by using figurative language, or figures of speech. Such language paints pictures in readers' minds, allowing them to "see" a point and hence understand more readily and clearly.

Similes, metaphors, and analogies. Similes use *like, as, as if,* or *as though* to make explicit the comparison between two seemingly different things.

▶ **The Digital Revolution is whipping through our lives like a Bengali typhoon.**   – LOUIS ROSSETTO

Metaphors are implicit comparisons, omitting the *like, as, as if,* or *as though* of similes.

▶ **Unix is the Swiss Army Knife of the Net.**
     – THOMAS MANDEL

Analogies compare similar features of two dissimilar things; they explain something unfamiliar by relating it to something familiar.

▶ **One Hundred and Twenty-fifth Street was to Harlem what the Mississippi was to the South, a long traveling river always going somewhere, carrying something.**
     – MAYA ANGELOU, *The Heart of a Woman*

■ **Clichés and mixed metaphors.** A cliché is an overused figure of speech such as *busy as a bee*. By definition, we use clichés all the time, especially in speech, and many serve quite usefully as shorthand for familiar ideas. But if you use such paint-by-numbers language to excess in your writing, readers are likely to conclude that what you are saying is not very new or interesting—or true.

Mixed metaphors make comparisons that are inconsistent.

▶ The lectures were like brilliant comets streaking
                  dazzling
    through the night sky, ~~showering~~ listeners with
             ^

    flashes
    ~~a torrential rain~~ of insights.
    ^

The images of streaking light and heavy precipitation were inconsistent; in the revised sentence, all of the images relate to light.

14

The Language of Common Ground

The supervisor who refers to her staff as "team members" (rather than as "my staff" or as "subordinates") is choosing language intended to establish common ground with people who are important to her. This chapter will help you think about two ways that your own language can work to build common ground with others: considering carefully the sensitivities and preferences of others, and watching for words that carry stereotypes and betray assumptions not directly stated.

14a Stereotypes and other assumptions

Children like to play; U.S. citizens value freedom. These broad statements contain stereotypes, standardized or fixed ideas about a group. To some extent, we all think in terms of stereotypes, and sometimes they can be helpful in making generalizations. Stereotyping any individual on the basis of generalizations about a group, however, can sometimes lead to inaccurate and

even hurtful conclusions. Thus careful writers will want to make sure that language doesn't stereotype any group *or* individual.

Other kinds of unstated assumptions that enter into thinking and writing can destroy common ground by ignoring differences between others and ourselves. For example, a student in a religion seminar who uses *we* to refer to Christians and *they* to refer to members of other religions had better be sure that everyone in the class is Christian, or some of them may feel left out of this discussion.

Sometimes stereotypes even lead writers to call special attention to a personal characteristic or group affiliation when it is not necessary or relevant to the point, as in "a woman bus driver," "a Jewish doctor," "a lesbian politician," or "an elderly but still active golfer." Nevertheless, deciding whether to describe an individual as a member of a group is often difficult. The following sections suggest some ways that your language can build—rather than destroy—common ground.

14b Assumptions about gender

At one time, writers always referred to hypothetical doctors or engineers as *he* and to nurses and secretaries as *she* (and then labeled any woman who worked as a doctor a *woman doctor* or any man who worked as a nurse as a *male nurse*, as if to say, "they're exceptions"). Such sexist language—words and phrases that stereotype or ignore members of either sex or that unnecessarily call attention to gender—can usually be revised fairly easily. There are several alternatives to using masculine pronouns to refer to persons of unknown sex:

▶ ~~A lawyer~~ *Lawyers* must pass the bar exam before ~~he~~ *they* can begin to practice.

▶ A lawyer must pass the bar exam before he *or she* can begin to practice.

▶ A lawyer must pass the bar exam before ~~he can begin~~ *beginning* to practice.

Here are some other suggestions for revising common kinds of sexist language:

INSTEAD OF	TRY USING
anchorman, anchorwoman	anchor
chairman, chairwoman	chair, chairperson
congressman	member of Congress, representative
male nurse	nurse
man, mankind	humans, human beings, humanity, the human race, humankind
mothering	parenting
steward, stewardess	flight attendant
woman engineer	engineer

14c Assumptions about race and ethnicity

Generalizations about racial and ethnic groups can result in especially harmful stereotyping. Such assumptions underlie statements that suggest, for instance, that all Asian Americans excel in math and science, or that all Germans are efficient. In building common ground, writers must watch for any language that ignores differences not only among individual members of a race or ethnic group but also among subgroups. Writers must be aware, for instance, of the many nations to which Native Americans belong and of the diverse places from which Americans of Spanish-speaking ancestry have emigrated.

   Preferred terms. Referring to a group in terms that its members desire is sometimes not an easy task, for preferences change and even vary widely. The word *colored*, for example, was once widely used in the United States to refer to Americans of African ancestry. By the 1950s, the preferred term had become *Negro*; in the 1960s, *black* came to be preferred by most, though certainly not all, members of that community. Then, in the late 1980s, some leaders of the community urged that *black* be replaced by *African American*. The word *Oriental*, once used to refer to people of East Asian descent, is now often considered offensive. Many of those U.S. citizens once

referred to as *American Indians* now prefer *Native Americans*. Among Americans of Spanish-speaking descent, the preferred terms are many: *Chicano/Chicana, Hispanic, Latin American, Latino/Latina, Mexican American, Dominican,* and *Puerto Rican,* to name but a few.

Clearly, then, ethnic terminology changes often enough to challenge even the most careful writers. The best advice may be to consider your words carefully, to *listen* for the way members of groups refer to themselves (or *ask* their preferences), and to check any term you're unsure of in a current dictionary.

FAQ: WORD CHOICE ONLINE

How and when should digital jargon be used?

Like all jargon, the terms emerging in the digital age can be irritating and incomprehensible—or extremely helpful. If the jargon is concrete and specific, it can help clarify concepts, providing a useful shorthand for an otherwise lengthy explanation. Saying "Sorry, but for the time being I'm limited to asynchronous communication, primarily email" sends a pretty straightforward message, one that is faster to read than "Sorry, but for the time being I'm limited to the kinds of electronic communication that depend on sending and receiving messages at different times only, and primarily to email."

Frequently used terms (such as ASYNCHRONOUS COMMUNICATION and EMAIL) are the ones online writers should know. Other terms, like the jargon in this sentence— "Savvy wavelet compression is the fiber signpost of the virtual chillout room"—may be appropriate for techies talking to one another, but they are not very useful to those trying to communicate with a nontechnical or general audience. Before you use technical jargon, remember your readers: if they will not understand the terms, then take the time to say what you need to say in everyday language.

When is it appropriate to use digital acronyms like IMHO and F2F?

Along with the new jargon have come quite a few new acronyms, which also serve as a kind of shorthand. Such acronyms may be appropriate for some informal online communication, but you should avoid them in academic or other formal writing. Here are some acronyms we find particularly useful:

ASCII   American Standard Code for Information Interchange

BBS	bulletin board system
BTW	by the way
FAQ	frequently asked questions
FTP	file transfer protocol
FWIW	for what it's worth
HTML	hypertext markup language
HTTP	hypertext transfer protocol
IMHO	in my humble opinion
IRC	Internet relay chat
ISP	Internet service provider
MOO	multi-user domain, object-oriented
MUD	multi-user domain
URL	uniform resource locator
WAIS	Wide Area Information Server

Online Resources

Webster's Dictionary Online uses a HYPERTEXT interface that allows you to search for definitions of any word in the dictionary—and can help you if you're not sure how to spell the word you want:

<http://c.gp.cs.cmu.edu:5103/prog/webster?>

Roget's Thesaurus can help you find synonyms:

<gopher://odie.niaid.nih.gov:70/77/.thesaurus/index>

Jargon File Resources, version 4.0 (1996), provides an index to all WEB resources related to the Jargon File and its print companion, *The New Hacker's Dictionary* (1996). The following URL allows you to search all jargon files and includes discussions of such topics as "how jargon works," "hacker writing style," and so on:

<http://www.ccil.org/jargon/jargon.html>

Hotwired's URL allows you to order the print version of *Wired Style* and to amplify and update the printed book's advice on how to use the new language of the digital age. For its Outtakes (things that didn't make it into the printed book) and Updates, **see:**

<http://www.hotwired.com/hardwired/wiredstyle/>

FOR MULTILINGUAL WRITERS

The history of the American people, the story of the peoples native to this continent and of those who immigrated here from every corner of the world, is told in the rich accents of Cherokee, Spanish, German, Dutch, Yiddish, French, Menomenie, Japanese, Norwegian, Arabic, Aleut, Polish, Navajo, Thai, Portuguese, Caribbean creoles, and scores of other tongues.

— Harvey Daniels

Nouns and Articles

Everyday life is filled with **nouns**: orange *juice*, the morning *news*, a *bus* to *work*, *meetings*, *lunch*, *email*, *Diet Coke*, *errands*, *dinner* with *friends*, a *chapter* in a good *book*. No matter what your first language is, it includes nouns. This chapter will focus on some of the ways English nouns and **articles** (*the* news, *a* book) differ from those in some other languages.

15a Count and noncount nouns

Nouns in English can be either count nouns or noncount nouns. As the name suggests, **count nouns** refer to distinct individuals or things that can be directly counted: *a doctor, a book, a tree; doctors, books, trees*. **Noncount nouns** refer to masses or collections of things or to other ideas that cannot be directly counted: *milk, grass, courage*. They can be quantified only in a broad, vague way or with a preceding phrase: *one quart of milk, three grains of rice, a great deal of courage, little information*.

Count nouns usually have singular and plural forms: *tree, trees*. Noncount nouns usually have only a singular form: *grass*.

COUNT	NONCOUNT
people (plural of *person*)	humanity
tables, chairs, beds	furniture
letters	mail
pebbles	gravel
words	advice

Some nouns can be either count or noncount, depending on meaning.

COUNT	Before there were video games, children played with *marbles*.
NONCOUNT	The floor of the palace was made of *marble*.

When you learn a noun in English, you need to learn whether it is count, noncount, or both. Two dictionaries

that supply this information are the *Oxford Advanced Learner's Dictionary* and the *Longman Dictionary of American English.*

15b Articles

The **definite article** *the* and the **indefinite articles** *a* and *an* are challenging to multilingual speakers. Many languages have nothing directly comparable to them, and languages that do have articles differ from English in the details of their use.

Using *the*. Use the definite article *the* with nouns whose identity is known or is about to be made known to readers. The necessary information for identification can come from the noun phrase itself, from elsewhere in the text, from context, from general knowledge, or from a superlative.

▶ Let's meet at *the* fountain in front of Dwinelle Hall.

The phrase *in front of Dwinelle Hall* identifies the specific fountain.

▶ A fire that started in a restaurant spread to a toy store. *The s* Store was saved, although it suffered water damage.

The store has been identified in the previous sentence.

▶ Professor to student in her office: "Please shut *the* door when you leave."

The professor expects the student to understand that she is referring to the door of her office.

▶ *The pope* ~~Pope~~ is expected to visit Africa in October.

There is only one living pope, and so his identity is clear.

▶ Willie is now *the* best singer in the choir.

The superlative *best* identifies the noun *singer.*

Using *a* or *an*. The indefinite articles *a* and *an* are used only with singular count nouns. Use *a* before a consonant sound: *a car*. Use *an* before a vowel sound: *an uncle*. Pay attention to sounds rather than to spelling: *a house, an hour*.

A or *an* tells readers they do not have enough information to identify what the noun refers to. Compare these sentences:

> I need *a* new *parka* for the winter.

> I saw *a parka* that I liked at Macy's, but it was too heavy.

The parka in the first sentence is hypothetical rather than actual. Since it is indefinite to the writer, it clearly is indefinite to the reader, and so it is used with *a*, not *the*. The second sentence refers to a very specific actual parka, but since the writer cannot expect the reader to know which one it is, it is used with *a* rather than *the*.

If you want to speak of an indefinite quantity, rather than just one indefinite thing, use *some* with a noncount noun or a plural count noun.

> This stew needs *some* more *salt*.

> I saw *some plates* that I liked at Gump's.

Using no article. Noncount and plural count nouns can be used with no article to make generalizations.

> In this world nothing is certain but *death* and *taxes*.
> — BENJAMIN FRANKLIN

The absence of an article indicates that Franklin refers not to a particular death or specific taxes but to death and taxes in general.

Here English differs from many other languages—Greek or Spanish or German, for example—that use the definite article to make generalizations. In English, a sentence like *The snakes are dangerous* can refer only to particular, identifiable snakes, not to snakes in general.

16

Verbs and Verb Phrases

When there are things to do, **verbs** tell us what they are—from the street signs that say *stop* or *yield* to email commands such as *send* or *delete*. So verbs might be

called the heartbeat of prose, especially in English, where they are necessary parts of sentences. If you speak Russian or Arabic, you might wonder what is wrong with the sentence *Where Main Street?* But unlike sentences in those and many other languages, English sentences must have a verb: *Where is Main Street?* This chapter will focus on some of the other ways English verbs differ from verbs in other languages.

16a Verb phrases

Verb phrases can be built up out of a **main verb** and one or more **auxiliary verbs**, such as *My cat is drinking milk* or *My cat may have been drinking milk*. Verb phrases have strict rules of order. If you try to rearrange the words in either of these sentences, you will find that most alternatives are impossible. You cannot say *My cat drinking is milk* or *My cat have may been drinking milk*.

■ **Auxiliary and main verbs.** In *My cat may have been drinking milk*, the main verb *drinking* is preceded by three auxiliaries: *may, have*, and *been*. *May* is a **modal**, which must be followed by the **base form** (*have*). *Have* indicates that the **tense** is **perfect**, and it must be followed by a **past participle** (*been*). *Been* (or any other form of *be*), when it is followed by a **present participle** (such as *drinking*), indicates that the tense is **progressive**. A form of *be* can also represent **passive voice**, but then the following verb form must be a past participle, as in *My cat may have been bitten by a dog*.

Auxiliaries must be in the following order: modal + perfect *have* + progressive *be* + passive *be*.

      perf pass   main
▶ Sonya *has been invited* to stay with a family in Prague.

Only one modal is permitted in a verb phrase.

      will be able to speak
▶ She ~~will can speak~~ Czech much better soon.
         ^

Every time you use an auxiliary, you should be careful to put the next word in the appropriate form.

■ **Modal + base form.** Use the base form of the verb after the modals *can, could, will, would, shall, should, may, might*, and *must*: *Alice can read Latin*. In many other lan-

guages, modals like *can* or *must* are followed by the infinitive (*to* + base form). Do not substitute an infinitive for the base form.

▶ Alice can ~~to~~ read Latin.

■ **Perfect *have, has,* or *had* + past participle.** To form the perfect tenses, use *have, has,* or *had* with a past participle: *Everyone <u>has gone</u> home. They <u>have been</u> working all day.*

■ **Progressive *be* + present participle.** A progressive form of the verb is signaled by two elements, a form of the auxiliary *be* (*am, is, are, was, were, be,* or *been*) and the present participle (*-ing* form) of the main verb: *The children <u>are studying</u>.* Be sure to include both elements.

▶ The children ^{are} studying in school.

▶ The children are ^{studying} ~~study~~ in school.

Some verbs are rarely used in progressive forms. These are verbs that express unchanging conditions or mental states rather than deliberate actions: *believe, belong, cost, hate, know, like, love, mean, need, own, resemble, understand, weigh.*

■ **Passive *be* + past participle.** Use *am, is, are, was, were, being, be,* or *been* with a past participle to form the passive voice: *Tagalog <u>is spoken</u> in the Philippines.* Notice that the difference between progressive *be* and passive *be* is that with the progressive, the following word ends in the *-ing* of the present participle, but with the passive, the following word never ends in *-ing* and instead becomes the past participle.

Meredith *is* studying music.

Natasha *was* taught by a famous violinist.

16b Infinitives and gerunds

Knowing when to use **infinitives** or **gerunds** may be a challenge to multilingual writers. Here are some hints that will help you.

My adviser urged me *to apply* to several colleges.

Her *writing* a strong letter of recommendation made a big difference.

Why was an infinitive used in the first sentence and a gerund in the second? In general, infinitives represent intentions, desires, or expectations, and gerunds represent facts. The gerund in the second sentence calls attention to the fact that a letter was actually written; the infinitive in the first sentence conveys the idea that the act of applying was something desired, not an accomplished fact.

The association of fact with gerunds and of intention with infinitives can help you know in the majority of cases whether to use an infinitive or a gerund when another **verb** immediately precedes it.

Gerunds

Jerzy *enjoys going* to the theater.

We *resumed working* after our coffee break.

Kim *appreciated getting* candy from Sean.

Infinitives

Kumar *expected to get* a good job after graduation.

Last year, Fatima *decided to become* a math major.

The strikers have *agreed to go* back to work.

A few verbs can be followed by either an infinitive or a gerund. With some, such as *begin* or *continue*, the choice makes little difference in meaning. With others, however, the difference in meaning is striking.

Carlos was working as a medical technician, but he *stopped to study* English.

Carlos *stopped studying* English when he left the United States.

The infinitive indicates that Carlos intended to study English when he left his job. We are not told whether he actually did study English. The gerund indicates that Carlos actually did study English, but later stopped.

The distinction between fact and intention is not a rule but only a tendency, and it can be superseded by other rules. Use a gerund—never an infinitive—directly following a **preposition**.

> This fruit is all right for ~~to eat.~~
> *eating.*
>   ^

You can also get rid of the preposition and keep the infinitive.

> This fruit is all right ~~for~~ to eat.

A full list of verbs that can be followed by an infinitive and verbs that can be followed by a gerund can be found in the *Index to Modern English,* by Thomas Lee Crowell Jr. (McGraw-Hill, 1964).

16c Conditional sentences

English pays special attention to whether or not something is a fact, or to the degree of confidence a speaker or writer has in the truth or likelihood of an assertion. English distinguishes among many different types of conditional sentences, those that focus on questions of truth and that are introduced by *if* or its equivalent. Following are examples of several different conditional sentences. Each sentence makes different assumptions about the likelihood that what is stated in the **clause** beginning with *if* is true, and each then draws the corresponding conclusion in the main clause.

> If you *practice* (or *have practiced*) writing frequently, you *know* (or *have learned*) what your chief problems are.

This sentence assumes that what is stated in the *if* clause may very well be true; the alternatives in parentheses indicate that any tense that is appropriate in a simple sentence may be used in both the *if* clause and the main clause.

> If you *practice* writing for the rest of this term, you *will* (or *may*) *get* a firmer grasp of the process.

This sentence makes a prediction about the future and again assumes that what is stated may very well turn out to be true. Only the main clause uses the **future tense** (*will get*) or some other **modal** that can indicate future time (*may get*). In this case, the *if* clause must use the **present tense**, even though it, too, refers to the future.

> If you *practiced* (or *were to practice*) writing every single day, it *would* eventually *seem* much easier to you.

This sentence casts some doubt on the likelihood that what is stated will be put into effect. In the *if* clause, the verb is either past—actually, **past subjunctive** (2f)—or *were to* + the base form, though it refers to future time. The main clause has *would* + the base form of the main verb.

> If you *practiced* writing on Mars, you *would find* no one to show your work to.

This sentence contemplates an impossibility at present or in the foreseeable future. As with the preceding sentence, the past subjunctive is used in the *if* clause, although past time is not being referred to, and *would* + the base form is used in the main clause.

> If you *had practiced* writing in ancient Egypt, you *would have used* hieroglyphics.

This sentence shifts the impossibility back to the past; obviously you are not going to find yourself in ancient Egypt. But since past forms have already been used in the preceding two sentences, this one demands a form that is "more past": the **past perfect** in the *if* clause, and *would* + the **present perfect** form of the main verb in the main clause.

17

Prepositions and Prepositional Phrases

If you were traveling by rail and asked for directions, it would not be helpful to be told to "take the Chicago train." You would need to know whether to take the train *to* Chicago or the one *from* Chicago. Words such as *to* and *from*, which show the relations between other words, are **prepositions**. Not all languages use prepositions to show such relations, and English differs from other languages in the way prepositions are used. This chapter provides guidelines for using prepositions in English.

17a Using the right preposition

Even if you usually know where to use prepositions, you may have difficulty from time to time knowing

which preposition to use. Each of the most common prepositions, whether in English or in other languages, has a wide range of different applications, and this range never coincides exactly from one language to another. See, for example, how English speakers use *in* and *on*.

The peaches are *in* the refrigerator.

The peaches are *on* the table.

Is that a diamond ring *on* your finger?

Spanish uses one preposition (*en*) in all these sentences, a fact that might lead you astray in English.

▶ Is that a ruby ring ~~in~~ *on* your finger?

There is no easy solution to the challenge of using English prepositions idiomatically, but the following strategies can make it less formidable.

• Keep in mind typical examples of each preposition.

IN   The peaches are *in* the refrigerator.
      There are still some pickles *in* the jar.

Here the object of the preposition *in* is a container that encloses something.

ON   The peaches are *on* the table.
      The book is *on* the top shelf.

Here the object of the preposition *on* is a horizontal surface that supports something with which it is in direct contact.

• Learn other examples that show some similarities and some differences in meaning.

IN   You shouldn't drive *in* a snowstorm.

Like a container, the falling snow surrounds and seems to enclose the driver.

ON   Is that a diamond ring *on* your finger?

Like a horizontal surface, a finger can support a ring with which it is in contact.

• Use your imagination to create mental images that can help you remember figurative uses of prepositions.

IN   Michael is *in* love.

Imagine a warm bath in which Michael is immersed (or a raging torrent, if you prefer to visualize love that way).

ON   I've just read a good book *on* computer science.

Imagine a shelf labeled COMPUTER SCIENCE on which the book you have read is located.

- Try to learn prepositions not in isolation but as part of a system. For example, in identifying the location of a place or an event, the three prepositions *in, on,* and *at* can be used. *At* specifies the exact point in space or time.

AT   Meet me tomorrow *at* 9:30 A.M. *at* 160 Main Street.

Expanses of space or time within which a place is located or an event takes place might be seen as containers and so require *in*.

IN   My family arrived *in* the United States *in* January.

On must be used in two cases: with the names of streets (but not the exact address) and with days of the week or month.

ON   The airline's office is *on* Fifth Avenue.
        I'll be moving *on* September 30.

17b Using two-word verbs

Some words that look like prepositions do not always function as prepositions. Consider the following two sentences:

The balloon rose *off* the ground.

The plane took *off* without difficulty.

In the first sentence, *off* is a preposition that introduces the **prepositional phrase** *off the ground.* In the second sentence, *off* neither functions as a preposition nor introduces a prepositional phrase. Instead, it combines with *took* to form a two-word **verb** with its own meaning.

Such a verb is called a *phrasal verb,* and the word *off,* when used in this way, is called an adverbial particle. Many prepositions can function as particles to form phrasal verbs.

The verb + particle combination that makes up a phrasal verb is a tightly knit entity that usually cannot be separated.

> The plane *took off* without difficulty. [not *took* without difficulty *off*]

The exceptions are some of the many phrasal verbs that are **transitive**, meaning that they take a **direct object**. Some of these verbs have particles that may be separated from the verb by the object.

> I *picked up my baggage* at the terminal.

> I *picked my baggage up* at the terminal.

If a personal pronoun is used as the direct object, it *must* separate the verb from its particle.

> I *picked it up* at the terminal.

In some idiomatic two-word verbs, the second word is a preposition. With such verbs, the preposition can never be separated from the verb.

> We *ran into* our neighbor on the plane. [not *ran* our neighbor *into*]

Every comprehensive dictionary includes information about the various adverbial particles and prepositions that a verb can combine with, but only some dictionaries distinguish verb + particle from verb + preposition. The *Longman Dictionary of American English* is one that does.

18

Sentence Structure

Sound bites surround us, from Nike's "Just do it" to Avis's "We try harder." These short, simple sentences may be memorable, but they don't tell us very much. Ordinarily, we need more complex sentences to convey meaning. Sentences are not formed in the same way in every language. This chapter will focus on English sentences.

18a Expressing subjects and objects explicitly

With few exceptions, English demands that an explicit **subject** accompany an explicit **predicate** in every sentence. Though you might write *Went from Yokohama to Nagoya* in an email message or on a postcard to a friend, in most varieties of spoken and written English, the extra effort of explicitly stating who went is not simply an option but an obligation.

In fact, every **dependent clause** must have an explicit subject.

▶ They flew to London on the Concorde because ~~was~~ fast.
                                       it

English even requires a kind of "dummy" subject to fill the subject position in certain kinds of sentences. Consider the following sentences:

It is raining.

There is a strong wind.

Speakers of Spanish, for example, might be inclined to leave out dummy subjects. In English, however, *it* and *there* are indispensable.

▶ ~~Is~~ raining.
  It is

▶ ~~Is~~ a strong wind.
  There is

Transitive verbs typically require that **objects** also be explicitly stated, and in some cases even other items of information as well. For example, it is not enough to tell someone *Give!* even if it is clear what is to be given to whom. You must say *Give it to me* or *Give her the passport* or some other such sentence.

18b Keeping words in appropriate order

In English sentences, **subjects**, **verbs**, and **objects** must usually be arranged in a certain order. In the following sentence, each element is in an appropriate place.

▶ subject | verb | object | adverb
   Omar | reads | books | voraciously.

This sentence would also be acceptable if written as *Omar voraciously reads books* or *Voraciously Omar reads books,* but no other alternatives are possible. Only the **adverb** can be moved.

If you speak Turkish, Korean, Japanese, or another language in which the verb must come last, you may have to make a special effort never to write such a sentence as *Omar books voraciously reads,* which is not acceptable in English.

If you speak Russian or another language that permits a great deal of freedom in word order, you must never interchange the position of subject and object (*Books reads Omar voraciously*) is not acceptable English. Also, avoid separating the verb from its object (*Omar reads voraciously books*).

FAQ: MULTILINGUAL WRITERS ONLINE

What online resources are particularly helpful for multilingual writers?

The Virtual English Language Center provides an "idiom of the week," a "fable of the month," sound clips for pronunciation, online tests for comprehension and vocabulary, EMAIL, pen-pal programs, and more:

<http://www.comenius.com>

Dave's ESL Cafe offers games, activities, and—best of all—daily updates:

<http://www.eslcafe.com/>

English for Internet offers live CHATS, placement tests, and free English classes (which fill up quickly):

<http://www.study.com>

Grammar Safari allows you to learn grammar in context, with hundreds and sometimes thousands of examples of particular English words shown in the context of real-life communication:

<http://deil.lang.uiuc.edu/web.pages/grammarsafari.html>

schMOOzeU is a MOO devoted to practicing conversation:

<http://schmooze.hunter.cuny.edu:8888/>

WordWatch focuses on English vocabulary, with a new entry every day:

<http://www.wordsmith.org/awad/index.html>

PUNCTUATION/ MECHANICS

"You can show a lot with a look.
. . . It's punctuation."

– Clint Eastwood

Commas

It's hard to go through a day without encountering directions of some kind, and commas often play a crucial role in how you interpret instructions. See how important the comma is in the following directions for making hot cereal:

Add Cream of Wheat slowly, stirring constantly.

The comma here tells the cook to *add the cereal slowly*. If the comma came before the word *slowly,* however, the cook might add all of the cereal at once and *stir slowly*—perhaps ending up with lumpy cereal. This chapter aims to help you use commas correctly and effectively.

19a To set off introductory elements

In general, use a comma after any word, phrase, or clause that precedes the subject of the sentence.

▶ Eventually, I wondered whether I should move.

▶ In fact, only you can decide.

▶ In Fitzgerald's novel, the color green takes on great symbolic qualities.

▶ Sporting her "lucky" shoes, Jamie prepared for the race.

▶ To win the contest, Connor needed courage.

▶ Pens poised, we waited for the lecture to begin.

▶ Since my mind was not getting enough stimulation, I decided to read some good literature.

Some writers omit the comma if the introductory element is short and does not seem to require a pause after it.

▶ Suddenly she realized her mistake.

19b To separate clauses in compound sentences

A comma usually precedes a **coordinating conjunction** (*and, but, or, nor, for, so,* or *yet*) that joins two **independent clauses** in a **compound sentence**.

▶ The title may sound important, but *administrative clerk* is only a euphemism for *photocopier.*

With very short clauses, you can sometimes omit the comma if there is no chance the sentence will be misread without it.

▶ She saw her chance and she took it.

Use a semicolon rather than a comma when the clauses are long and complex or contain their own commas.

▶ There is no royal path to good writing; and such paths as exist do not lead through neat critical gardens, various as they are, but through the jungles of self, the world, and of craft.

— JESSAMYN WEST

19c To set off nonrestrictive elements

Nonrestrictive elements are **clauses**, **phrases**, and words that do not limit, or restrict, the meaning of the words they modify. Since such elements are not essential to the meaning of a sentence, they should be set off from the rest of the sentence with commas. **Restrictive elements**, on the other hand, *do* limit meaning; they should *not* be set off by commas.

RESTRICTIVE

Drivers *who have been convicted of drunken driving* should lose their licenses.

In the preceding sentence, the clause *who have been convicted of drunken driving* is essential to the meaning because it limits the word it modifies, *Drivers,* to only those drivers who have been convicted of drunken driving. Therefore it is *not* set off by commas.

NONRESTRICTIVE

> The two drivers involved in the accident, *who have been convicted of drunken driving,* should lose their licenses.

In this sentence, however, the clause *who have been convicted of drunken driving* is not essential to the meaning because it does not limit what it modifies, *The two drivers involved in the accident,* but merely provides additional information about these drivers. Therefore, it *is* set off with commas.

To decide whether an element is restrictive or nonrestrictive, mentally delete the element, and then see if the deletion changes the meaning of the rest of the sentence or makes it unclear. If the deletion does change the meaning, the element is probably restrictive, and you should not set it off with commas. If it does not change the meaning, the element is probably nonrestrictive and requires commas.

■ Adjective and adverb clauses. An adjective clause that begins with *that* is always restrictive; do not set it off with commas. An adjective clause beginning with *which* may be either restrictive or nonrestrictive; however, some writers prefer to use *which* only for nonrestrictive clauses, which they set off with commas. An adverb clause that follows a main clause usually does *not* require a comma to set it off unless the adverb clause expresses the idea of contrast.

NONRESTRICTIVE CLAUSES

▶ I borrowed books from the rental library of Shakespeare and Company, *which was the library and bookstore of Sylvia Beach at 12 rue de l'Odeon.*
>   — ERNEST HEMINGWAY, *A Moveable Feast*

The adjective clause describing Shakespeare and Company is not necessary to the meaning of the independent clause and therefore is set off with a comma.

▶ The park soon became a popular gathering place,
^
although some nearby residents complained about

the noise.

The adverb clause *although some nearby residents complained about the noise* expresses the idea of contrast; therefore it is set off with a comma.

RESTRICTIVE CLAUSES

▶ The claim *that men like seriously to battle one another to some sort of finish* is a myth.
— JOHN McMURTRY,
"Kill 'Em! Crush 'Em! Eat 'Em Raw!"

The adjective clause is necessary to the meaning of the sentence because it explains which claim is a myth; therefore it is not set off with commas.

▶ The man/who rescued her puppy/won her eternal gratitude.

The adjective clause *who rescued her puppy* is necessary to the meaning because it identifies the man, and so it takes no commas.

Phrases. Participial phrases may be restrictive or nonrestrictive. Prepositional phrases are usually restrictive but are not always essential to the meaning of a sentence and are thus set off with commas.

NONRESTRICTIVE PHRASES

▶ The bus drivers, rejecting the management offer, remained on strike.

Using commas around the phrase makes it nonrestrictive, telling us that all of the drivers remained on strike.

▶ The bodyguards, in dark suits and matching ties, looked quite intimidating.

The phrase *in dark suits and matching ties* does not limit the meaning of *bodyguards* but only gives additional information about them; therefore it is set off by commas.

RESTRICTIVE PHRASES

▶ The bus drivers/rejecting the management offer/ remained on strike.

Without the commas, the sentence says that only some bus drivers—the ones who rejected the offer—remained on strike, implying that other drivers returned to work.

▶ The men in dark suits and ties were the bodyguards.

The phrase *in dark suits and ties* limits the meaning of *men* and so is not set off by commas.

Appositives. An **appositive** is a **noun** or **noun phrase** that renames a nearby noun. When an appositive is not essential to identify what it renames, it is set off with commas.

NONRESTRICTIVE APPOSITIVES

▶ Beethoven's opera**,** *Fidelio***,** includes the famous
   "Prisoner's Chorus."

   Beethoven wrote only one opera, so its name is *not* essential to the meaning of the sentence and therefore is set off with commas.

RESTRICTIVE APPOSITIVES

▶ Mozart's opera/*The Marriage of Figaro*/was considered
   revolutionary.

   The opera's name, *The Marriage of Figaro,* is essential to the meaning of the sentence because Mozart wrote more than one opera. Therefore it is *not* set off with commas.

19d To separate items in a series

You may often see a series with no comma after the next-to-last item, particularly in newspaper writing. Omitting the comma can cause confusion, however, and you will never be wrong if you include it.

▶ He has plundered our seas, ravaged our coasts, burnt
   our towns, and destroyed the lives of our people.
                                    – DECLARATION OF INDEPENDENCE

▶ The long**,** twisting**,** muddy road led to a shack in the
   woods.

▶ Diners had a choice of broccoli, green beans, peas**,**
   and carrots.

   Without the comma after *peas,* you wouldn't know if there were three choices (the third being a *mixture* of peas and carrots) or four.

19e To set off parenthetical and transitional expressions

Parenthetical expressions add comments or information. Because they often interrupt the flow of a sentence, they are usually set off with commas.

▶ Some studies, incidentally, have shown that chocolate, of all things, helps to prevent tooth decay.

Transitionals are words such as *however* and *furthermore* and other words and phrases used to connect parts of sentences. They are usually set off with commas.

▶ Ceiling fans are, moreover, less expensive than air conditioners.

▶ Ozone is a byproduct of dry cleaning, for example.

19f To set off contrasting elements, interjections, direct address, and tag questions

▶ On official business it was she, *not my father,* one would usually hear on the phone or in stores.
– RICHARD RODRIGUEZ,
"Aria: A Memoir of a Bilingual Childhood"

▶ The story is narrated objectively at first, *subjectively toward the end.*

▶ *My God,* who wouldn't want a wife?
– JUDY BRADY, "I Want a Wife"

▶ Remember, *sir,* that you are under oath.

▶ The governor vetoed the tax bill, *didn't she?*

19g To set off parts of dates and addresses

■ **Dates.** Use a comma between the day of the week and the month, between the day of the month and the year, and between the year and the rest of the sentence, if any.

► The war began on Thursday, January 17, 1991, with
air strikes on Iraq.

Do not use commas with dates in inverted order or with
dates consisting of only the month and the year.

► She dated the letter *26 October 1996.*

► Thousands of Germans swarmed over the wall in
November 1989.

Addresses and place-names. Use a comma after
each part of an address or place-name, including the
state if there is no zip code. Do not precede a zip code
with a comma.

► Forward my mail to the Department of English, The
Ohio State University, Columbus, Ohio 43210.

► Portland, Oregon, is much larger than Portland,
Maine.

19h To set off quotations

Commas set off a quotation from words used to introduce the source of the quotation. A comma following a
quotation goes *inside* the closing quotation mark.

► A German proverb warns, "Go to law for a sheep, and
lose your cow."

► "All I know about grammar," said Joan Didion, "is its
infinite power."

Do not use a comma after a question mark or exclamation point.

► "Out, out damned spot!/" cries Lady Macbeth.

Do not use a comma to introduce a quotation with *that*
or when you do not quote the speaker's exact words.

► The writer of Ecclesiastes concludes/that "all is
vanity."

► Patrick Henry said/he wanted either liberty or death.

19i Unnecessary commas

Excessive use of commas can spoil an otherwise fine sentence.

▨ **Around restrictive elements.** Do not use commas to set off **restrictive elements**—elements that limit, or define, the meaning of the words they modify or refer to. Such elements are essential to meaning and therefore should not be set off with commas (19c).

▶ I don't let my children watch TV shows/ that are violent.

The *that* clause restricts the meaning of *TV shows,* so the comma should be omitted.

▶ The actress/ Rosemary Harris/ has returned to Broadway.

▨ **Between subjects and verbs, verbs and objects or complements, and prepositions and objects.** Do not use a comma between a **subject** and its **verb**, a verb and its **object** or **complement**, or a **preposition** and its object. This rule holds true even if the subject, object, or complement is a long **phrase** or **clause**.

▶ Watching movies late at night/ has become an important way for me to relax.

▶ Parents must decide/ how much TV their children may watch.

▶ The winner of/ the trophy for outstanding community service stepped forward.

▨ **In compound constructions.** In compound constructions (other than **compound sentences**), do not use a comma before or after a **coordinating conjunction** that joins the two parts (19b).

▶ A buildup of the U.S. military/ and deregulation of major industries were the Reagan administration's goals.

The *and* joins parts of a compound subject, which should not be separated by a comma.

▶ **Mark Twain trained as a printer/ and worked as a steamboat pilot.**

The *and* joins parts of a compound predicate, which should not be separated by a comma.

■ **In a series.** Do not use a comma before the first or after the last item in a series.

▶ **The auction included/ furniture, paintings, and china.**

▶ **The swimmer took slow, powerful/ strokes.**

20

Semicolons

If you've ever pored over the fine print at the bottom of an ad for a big sale, then you've seen plenty of semicolons in action. Here's an example from a Bloomingdale's ad.

> Store Hours—SUN., 12–6; MON. through FRI., 10–9:30; SAT., 10–8.

The semicolons separate the information for one day's hours from the next. Semicolons create a pause stronger than that of a comma but not as strong as the full pause of a period.

20a To link independent clauses

Though a comma and a **coordinating conjunction** often join **independent clauses** (19b), semicolons provide writers with subtler ways of signaling closely related clauses. The clause following a semicolon often restates an idea expressed in the first clause, and it sometimes expands on or presents a contrast to the first.

▶ **Immigration acts were passed; newcomers had to prove, besides moral correctness and financial solvency, their ability to read.**
                    — MARY GORDON, "More Than Just a Shrine"

Gordon uses a semicolon to join the two clauses, giving the sentence an abrupt rhythm that suits the topic: laws that imposed strict requirements.

▶ Fuel oil, natural gas, and electricity are popular
sources of energy for heating homes/; ^t^The least pol-
luting, however, is solar energy.

If two independent clauses joined by a coordinating
conjunction contain commas, you may use a semicolon
instead of a comma before the conjunction to make the
sentence easier to read.

▶ Every year, whether the Republican or the Democratic
party is in office, more and more power drains away
from the individual to feed vast reservoirs in far-off
places; and we have less and less say about the shape
of events which shape our future.
                                   – WILLIAM F. BUCKLEY JR.,
                                   "Why Don't We Complain?"

20b To link independent clauses joined by conjunctive adverbs or transitional phrases

A semicolon—not a comma—should link **independent clauses** joined by a **conjunctive adverb** like *however* or *therefore* or a transitional phrase like *as a result* or *for example*. Using a comma in this construction creates a **comma splice** error (see Chapter 7).

▶ The circus comes as close to being the world in microcosm as anything I know; in a way, it puts all the rest of show business in the shade.
                                   – E.B. WHITE, "The Ring of Time"

▶ Every kid should have access to a computer/; ^further-
more, access to the Internet should be free.

20c To separate items in a series containing other punctuation

Ordinarily, commas separate items in a series (19d). But when the items themselves contain commas or other punctuation, semicolons will make the sentence easier to read.

▶ Anthropology encompasses archaeology, the study of ancient civilizations through artifacts/; linguistics, the study of the structure and development of language/; and cultural anthropology, the study of language, customs, and behavior.

20d Misused semicolons

A comma, not a semicolon, should separate an **independent clause** from a **dependent clause** or phrase.

▶ The police found fingerprints/, which they used to identify the thief.

A colon, not a semicolon, should introduce a series or list.

▶ The tour includes visits to the following art museums/: the Prado, in Madrid; the Louvre, in Paris; and the Rijksmuseum, in Amsterdam.

21

End Punctuation

Periods, question marks, and exclamation points often appear in advertising to create special effects:

> The experts say America Online is a well-designed, easy-to-use service.
> So what are you waiting for?
> Get your hands on America Online today!

End punctuation tells us how to read each sentence—as a matter-of-fact statement, an ironic query, or an emphatic order. This chapter will guide you in using appropriate end punctuation in your own writing.

21a Periods

Use a period to close sentences that make statements, give mild commands, or make polite requests.

▶ **All books are either dreams or swords.**
— AMY LOWELL

▶ **Never use a foreign phrase, a scientific word or a jargon word if you can think of an everyday English equivalent.**
— GEORGE ORWELL,
"Politics and the English Language"

▶ **Would you please close the door.**

A period also closes indirect questions , which report rather than ask questions.

▶ **I asked how old the child was.**

In American English, periods are also used with most abbreviations.

Mr.	Jr.	Ph.D.
Ms.	B.C.	R.N.
P.M./p.m.	B.C.E.	Sen.

Some abbreviations do not require periods. Among them are the postal abbreviations of state names, such as *FL* and *TN*, and most groups of initials (*GE, CIA, DOS, AIDS, YMCA, UNICEF*). If you are not sure whether a particular abbreviation should include periods, check a dictionary. (See Chapter 26 for more about abbreviations.)

Do not use an additional period when a sentence ends with an abbreviation that has its own period.

▶ **The social worker referred me to Evelyn Pintz, M.D./**

21b Question marks

Use question marks to close sentences that ask direct questions.

▶ **Who will be left to celebrate a victory made of blood and fire?**
— THICH NHAT HANH, "Our Green Garden"

▶ **How is the human mind like a computer, and how is it different?**
— BERGER AND THOMPSON, *The Developing Person Through Childhood and Adolescence*

Question marks do not close *indirect* **questions**, which report rather than ask questions.

▶ **She asked whether I opposed his nomination.**

21c Exclamation points

Exclamation points show surprise or strong emotion. Use them very sparingly because they can distract your readers or suggest that you are exaggerating.

▶ **In those few moments of geologic time will be the story of all that has happened since we became a nation. And what a story it will be!**
        – JAMES RETTIE, "But a Watch in the Night"

▶ **This university is so large, so varied, that attempting to tell someone everything about it would take three years!.**

22

Apostrophes

The little apostrophe can sometimes make a big difference in meaning. A friend of ours found that out when he agreed to look after a neighbor's apartment while she was out of town. "I'll leave instructions on the kitchen counter," the neighbor said as she gave him her key. Here are the instructions he found: "The cat's food is on the counter. Once a day on the patio. Thanks. I'll see you on Friday."

Because the note said *cat's,* our friend expected one cat—and when he saw one, he put it and the food outside on the patio. When the neighbor returned, she found one healthy cat—and a second, very weak one that had hidden under the bed. The difference between *cat's* and *cats'* in this instance almost cost his neighbor a cat.

22a To signal possessive case

The **possessive case** denotes ownership or possession of one thing by another. Add an apostrophe and *-s* to form the possessive of most singular **nouns**, including

those that end in -*s*, and of **indefinite pronouns** (3d).
The possessive forms of **personal pronouns** do not take
apostrophes: *yours, his, hers, its, ours, theirs.*

▶ The *bus's* fumes overpowered her.

▶ Katherine *Hepburn's* first movies are considered
classics.

▶ *Anyone's* guess is as good as mine.

Plural nouns. To form the possessive case of plural
nouns not ending in -*s*, add an apostrophe and -*s*. For
plural nouns ending in -*s*, add only the apostrophe.

▶ Robert Bly helped to popularize the *men's* movement.

▶ The *clowns'* costumes were bright green and orange.

Compound nouns. To form the possessive case of
compound nouns, make the last word in the group
possessive.

▶ Both her *daughters-in-law's* birthdays fall in July.

Two or more nouns. To signal individual possession
by two or more owners, make each noun possessive.
To signal joint possession, make only the last noun possessive.

▶ Great differences exist between *John Wayne's and
Henry Fonda's* films.

Wayne and Fonda appeared in different films.

▶ *MacNeil and Lehrer's* television program focused on
current issues.

MacNeil and Lehrer participated in the same program.

22b To signal contractions and omissions

Contractions are two-word combinations formed by
leaving out certain letters, which are indicated by an
apostrophe.

it is, it has/it's   I would/I'd   will not/won't

Contractions are common in conversation and informal
writing. Academic and professional work, however,
often calls for greater formality.

Apostrophes also signal omissions in some common phrases.

rock and roll   class of 1999
rock 'n' roll   class of '99

■ **Distinguishing *it's* and *its*.** Remember the difference between the possessive pronoun *its* and the contraction *it's*. *Its* is the possessive form of *it*. *It's* is a contraction for *it is* or *it has*.

▶ This disease is unusual; *its* symptoms vary from person to person.

▶ *It's* a difficult disease to diagnose.

22c To form some plurals

Use an apostrophe and -*s* to form the plural of numbers, letters, symbols, and words referred to as words.

▶ The gymnasts need marks of *8*'s and *9*'s to qualify for the finals.

▶ The computer prints *e*'s whenever there is an error in the program.

▶ I marked special passages with a series of three ***'s.

▶ The five *Shakespeare*'s in the essay were spelled five different ways.

As in the above examples, italicize numbers, letters, and words referred to as words, but do not italicize the plural ending.

You can write the plural of years with or without the apostrophe (1990's or 1990s). Whichever style you follow, be consistent.

23

Quotation Marks

"Hilarious!" "A great family movie!" "Two thumbs up!" Claims of this kind leap out from most movie ads, always set off by quotation marks. In fact, the quotation marks are a key component of such statements, indicating that the praise comes from people other than the

movie promoter. In other words, it is praise that we should believe. This chapter provides tips for using quotation marks for many purposes.

23a To signal direct quotation

▶ Bush called for a "kinder, gentler" country.

▶ She smiled and said, "Son, this is one incident that I will never forget."

Use quotation marks to enclose the words of each speaker within running dialogue. Mark each shift in speaker with a new paragraph.

> "But I can see you're bound to come," said the father. "Only we ain't going to catch us no fish, because there ain't no water left to catch 'em in."
> "The river!"
> "All but dry."
> – EUDORA WELTY, "Ladies in Spring"

Single quotation marks. Single quotation marks enclose a quotation within a quotation. Open and close the quoted passage with double quotation marks, and change any quotation marks that appear *within* the quotation to single quotation marks.

▶ Baldwin says, "The title 'The Uses of the Blues' does not refer to music; I don't know anything about music."

Long quotations. If you wish to quote a long passage, set the quotation off by starting it on a new line and indenting it from the left margin. This format, known as block quotation, does not require quotation marks. In the style recommended by the Modern Language Association (MLA), block quotation is used for prose quotations of four typed lines or more, and the block is indented one inch, or ten spaces (see 32d). In American Psychological Association (APA) style, block quotation is used for any quotation of forty words or more, and the block is indented five spaces (see 33d). The following example illustrates MLA style:

> In *Winged Words: American Indian Writers Speak,* Leslie Marmon Silko describes her early education, saying:
>> I learned to love reading, and love books, and the printed page, and therefore was

motivated to learn to write. The best thing . . . you can have in life is to have someone tell you a story . . . but in lieu of that . . . I learned at an early age to find comfort in a book, that a book would talk to me when no one else would. (145)

Quoting poetry. In MLA style, include brief quotations of poetry (fewer than four lines) within your text. Separate the lines of the poem with slashes, each preceded and followed by a space.

In one of his best-known poems, Robert Frost remarks, "Two roads diverged in a yellow wood, and I— / I took the one less traveled by / And that has made all the difference."

To quote more than three lines of poetry, indent each line one inch or ten spaces from the left margin, and do not use quotation marks. When you quote poetry, take care to follow the indentation, spacing, capitalization, punctuation, and other features of the original passage.

The duke in Robert Browning's poem "My Last Duchess" is clearly a jealous, vain person, whose arrogance is illustrated through this statement:

> She thanked men,—good! but thanked
> Somehow—I know not how—as if she ranked
> My gift of a nine-hundred-years-old name
> With anybody's gift.

23b To enclose titles of short works and definitions

Use quotation marks to enclose the titles of short poems, short stories, articles, essays, songs, sections of books, and episodes of television and radio programs. Quotation marks are also used around definitions.

▶ **"Dover Beach" moves from calmness to sadness.** [poem]

▶ **Alice Walker's "Everyday Use" is about more than just quilts.** [short story]

▶ **In social science, the term** *sample size* **means "the number of individuals being studied in a research project."**
— BERGER AND THOMPSON, *The Developing Person Through Childhood and Adolescence*

23c With other punctuation

Periods and commas go *inside* closing quotation marks.

▶ **"Don't compromise yourself," said Janis Joplin. "You are all you've got."**

Colons, semicolons, and footnote numbers go *outside* closing quotation marks.

▶ **I felt only one emotion after finishing "Eveline": pity.**

▶ **Everything is dark, and "a visionary light settles in her eyes"; this vision, this light, is her salvation.**

▶ **Tragedy is defined by Aristotle as "an imitation of an action that is serious and of a certain magnitude."[1]**

Question marks, exclamation points, and dashes go *inside* if they are part of the quoted material, *outside* if they are not.

▶ **Gently shake the injured person while asking, "Are you all right?"**

▶ **What is the theme of "The Birth-Mark"?**

For information on using quotation marks with footnotes and in bibliographical references, see Chapters 32–35.

23d Misused quotation marks

Do not use quotation marks for indirect quotations—those that do not use someone's exact words.

▶ **Mother smiled and said that ⸕she would never forget the incident.⸕**

Do not use quotation marks just to add emphasis to particular words or phrases.

▶ **Much time was spent speculating about their ⸕relationship.⸕**

Do not use quotation marks around slang or colloquial language; they create the impression that you are apologizing for using those words. If you have a good reason

to use slang or a colloquial term, use it without quotation marks.

▶ After our twenty-mile hike, we were completely exhausted and ready to ⫽turn in.⫽

24

Other Punctuation

Parentheses, brackets, dashes, colons, slashes, and ellipses are all around us. Pick up the television listings, for instance, and you will find all these punctuation marks in abundance.

> **P.O.V.:** "A Litany for Survival—The Life and Work of Audre Lorde." 10 P.M. (13) An hour-long documentary about the poet, who died of cancer in 1992 at 58. [Time approximate after pledge drive]

This chapter will guide you in using these marks to signal relationships among sentence parts, to create particular rhythms, and to help readers follow your thoughts.

24a Parentheses

Use parentheses to enclose material that is of minor or secondary importance in a sentence— material that supplements, clarifies, comments on, or illustrates what precedes or follows it.

▶ Inventors and men of genius have almost always been regarded as fools at the beginning (and very often at the end) of their careers.
> — FYODOR DOSTOYEVSKY

▶ During my research, I found problems with the flat-rate income tax (a single-rate tax with no deductions).

Parentheses are also used to enclose textual citations and numbers or letters in a list.

▶ Freud and his followers have had a most significant impact on the ways abnormal functioning is understood and treated (Joseph, 1991).
> — RONALD J. COMER, *Abnormal Psychology*

▶ **Five distinct styles can be distinguished: (1) Old
New England, (2) Deep South, (3) Middle American,
(4) Wild West, and (5) Far West or Californian.**
— ALISON LURIE, *The Language of Clothes*

■ **With other punctuation.** A period may be placed
either inside or outside a closing parenthesis, depending on whether the parenthetical text is part of a larger
sentence. A comma is always placed *outside* a closing
parenthesis (and never before an opening one).

▶ **Gene Tunney's single defeat in an eleven-year career
was to a flamboyant and dangerous fighter named
Harry Greb ("The Human Windmill"), who seems to
have been, judging from boxing literature, the dirtiest
fighter in history.**
— JOYCE CAROL OATES, "On Boxing"

24b Brackets

Use brackets to enclose parenthetical elements in material that is itself within parentheses. Also use brackets to
enclose explanatory words or comments that you are
inserting into a quotation. If your keyboard does not
include keys for brackets, draw them in by hand.

▶ **Eventually the investigation had to examine the major
agencies (including the previously sacrosanct National
Security Agency [NSA]) that were conducting covert
operations.**

▶ **As Curtis argues, "[Johnson] saw [the war] as a game
or wrestling match in which he would make Ho Chi
Minh cry 'uncle.'"**

The bracketed words replace the words *he* and *it* in the
original quotation.

In the quotation in the following sentence, the artist
Gauguin's name is misspelled. The bracketed word *sic*,
which means "so," tells readers that the person being
quoted—not the writer who has picked up the quotation—made the mistake.

▶ **One admirer wrote, "She was the most striking woman
I'd ever seen—a sort of wonderful combination of Mia
Farrow and one of Gaugin's [*sic*] Polynesian nymphs."**

24c Dashes

Use pairs of dashes to insert a comment or to highlight material in a sentence.

▶ The pleasures of reading itself—who doesn't remember?—were like those of Christmas cake, a sweet devouring.   – EUDORA WELTY, "A Sweet Devouring"

▶ Mr. Angell is addicted to dashes and parentheses—small pauses or digressions in a narrative like those moments when the umpire dusts off home plate or a pitcher rubs up a new ball—that serve to slow an already deliberate movement almost to a standstill.
    – JOEL CONARROE, *New York Times Book Review*

A single dash can be used to emphasize material at the end of a sentence, to mark a sudden change in tone, to indicate hesitation in speech, or to introduce a summary or explanation.

▶ In the twentieth century it has become almost impossible to moralize about epidemics—except those which are transmitted sexually.
    – SUSAN SONTAG, *AIDS and Its Metaphors*

▶ New York is a catastrophe—but a magnificent catastrophe.   – LE CORBUSIER

▶ As the officer approached his car, the driver stammered, "What—what have I done?"

▶ In walking, the average adult person employs a motor mechanism that weighs about eighty pounds—sixty pounds of muscle and twenty pounds of bone.
    – EDWIN WAY TEALE

On most typewriters and with some word-processing software, a dash is made with two hyphens (--) with no spaces before, between, or after. In some software, the solid dash can be typed—as it is in this book—by selecting it from the symbols menu.

Dashes give more emphasis than parentheses to the material they enclose or set off. Use them sparingly, not only because they are somewhat informal but also because they can create a jerky, disconnected effect that can make it hard for readers to follow your thought.

24d Colons

Use a colon to introduce an explanation, an example, an appositive, a series, a list, or a quotation.

▶ The men may also wear the getup known as Sun Belt Cool: a pale beige suit, open-collared shirt (often in a darker shade than the suit), cream-colored loafers and aviator sunglasses.
— ALISON LURIE, *The Language of Clothes*

▶ At the baby's one-month birthday party, Ah Po gave him the Four Valuable Things: ink, inkslab, paper, and brush.   — MAXINE HONG KINGSTON, *China Men*

▶ We began a series of workshops on nonviolence, and we repeatedly asked ourselves: "Are you able to accept blows without retaliation?"
— MARTIN LUTHER KING JR.,
"Letter from Birmingham Jail"

Colons are also used after salutations in formal letters; with numbers indicating hours, minutes, and seconds; with ratios; with biblical chapters and verses; with titles and subtitles; and in bibliographic entries.

▶ Dear Dr. Ashdown:

▶ 4:59 P.M.

▶ a time of 2:15:06

▶ a ratio of 5:1

▶ I Corinthians 3:3–5

▶ *The Joy of Insight: Passions of a Physicist*

▶ New York: St. Martin's, 1998

Misused colons. Do not put a colon between a **verb** and its **object** or **complement** (unless the object is a quotation), between a **preposition** and its **object**, or after such expressions as *such as, especially,* and *including.*

▶ Some natural fibers are: cotton, wool, silk, and linen.

▶ In poetry, additional power may come from devices such as: simile, metaphor, and alliteration.

24e Slashes

Use slashes to mark line divisions between two or three lines of poetry quoted within text. When using a slash to separate lines of poetry, precede and follow it with a space (see 23a).

▶ In Shakespeare's Sonnet 29, the persona states, "For thy sweet love rememb'red such wealth brings / That then I scorn to change my state with kings."

Use a slash to separate alternatives.

▶ Psychologists continue to study the male/female ratio for some personality disorders.

24f Ellipses

Ellipses, or ellipsis points, are three equally spaced dots. You usually use ellipses to indicate that you have omitted something from a quoted passage. Ellipses have been used in the following example to indicate two omissions—one in the middle of the first sentence and one at the end of that sentence.

ORIGINAL TEXT

> Much male fear of feminism is the fear that, in becoming whole human beings, women will cease to mother men, to provide the breast, the lullaby, the continuous attention associated by the infant with the mother. Much male fear of feminism is infantilism—the longing to remain the mother's son, to possess a woman who exists purely for him.   – ADRIENNE RICH

WITH ELLIPSES

> As Adrienne Rich argues, "Much male fear of feminism is the fear that . . . women will cease to mother men. . . . Much male fear of feminism is infantilism—the longing to remain the mother's son, to possess a woman who exists purely for him."

When you omit the last part of a quoted sentence, add a period before the ellipses—for a total of four dots. Be sure a complete sentence comes before and after the four points. If your shortened quotation ends with a

source citation (such as a page number, a name, or a title), follow these steps:

1. Use three ellipsis points but no period after the quotation.
2. Add the closing quotation mark, closed up to the third ellipsis point.
3. Add the source of documentation in parentheses.
4. Use a period to indicate the end of the sentence.

▶ Hawthorne writes, "My friend, whom I shall call Oberon—it was a name of fancy and friendship between him and me . . ." (575).

You can also use ellipses to indicate a pause or a hesitation in speech.

▶ Then the voice, husky and familiar, came to wash over us—"The winnah, and still heavyweight champeen of the world . . . Joe Louis."
— MAYA ANGELOU, *I Know Why the Caged Bird Sings*

25

Capitalization

Capital letters are a key signal in everyday life. Look around any store to see their importance: you can shop for Levi's or any blue jeans, for Coca-Cola or any cola, for Kleenex or any tissues. In each of these instances, the capital letter indicates a particular brand. This chapter will help you use capitals appropriately.

25a The first word of a sentence

The first word of a sentence is always capitalized. If you are quoting a full sentence, capitalize the first word of the quotation unless you are introducing the quotation with *that*.

▶ I overheard Alex say, "Graduation will be traumatic."

▶ She said that "graduation will be traumatic."

Capitalization of an independent clause following a colon is optional.

▶ Gould cites the work of Darwin: The [*or* the] theory of natural selection incorporates the principle of evolutionary ties among all animals.

Capitalize a sentence within parentheses unless the parenthetical sentence is inserted into another sentence.

▶ Combining the best in Japanese engineering with the attitude of Evel Knievel (on a good day), the new MK9 is one bad hog. (It's also an ergonomically correct one.)
— WIRED, July 1996

▶ Men are supposed to be warriors (he who flinches is a "coward") and studs (have you ever said "what a stud!" to mean "what a great guy"?).
— SONIA MAASIK AND JACK SOLOMON, *Signs of Life in the USA*

When citing poetry, follow the capitalization of the original poem. Though most poets capitalize the first word of each line, some do not.

▶ Morning sun heats up the young beech tree leaves and almost lights them into fireflies
— JUNE JORDAN, "Aftermath"

25b Proper nouns and proper adjectives

Capitalize **proper nouns** (those naming specific persons, places, and things) and most **adjectives** formed from proper nouns. All other nouns are **common nouns** and are not capitalized unless they are used as part of a proper noun: *a street*, but *Elm Street*.

Capitalized nouns and adjectives include personal names; months, days of the week, and holidays (but not seasons of the year or parts of the academic year); geographical names; structures and monuments; ships, trains, aircraft, and spacecraft; organizations, businesses, and government institutions; academic institutions and courses; historical events and eras; religions and their deities, followers, and sacred writings; nationalities; languages; and trade names.

PROPER	COMMON
Alfred Hitchcock, Hitchcockian	a director
January	winter
Friday	fall semester
Labor Day	a holiday
Pacific Ocean	an ocean
Africa, African	a continent
Brazil, Brazilian	a nation
Golden Gate Bridge	a bridge
Challenger	a space shuttle
Library of Congress	a federal agency
General Motors Corporation	a blue-chip company
University of California	a state university
Chemistry 102	a chemistry course
Shays's Rebellion	a rebellion
the Renaissance	the fifteenth century
God	a god
the Koran	a prayer book
Catholicism, Catholics	a religion
Kurds, Kurdish	a nationality
Dutch	a language
Xerox copies	photocopies

25c Titles before a proper name

Capitalize personal titles when used before a name. When used alone or following a name, most titles are not capitalized. One common exception is the word *president*, which many writers capitalize when it refers to the President of the United States.

Professor Lisa Ede	my history professor
Dr. Garth Essig	Garth Essig, the doctor

25d Titles of works

Capitalize most words in titles of books, articles, speeches, stories, essays, plays, poems, documents, films, paintings, and musical compositions. Do not capi-

talize **articles** (*a, an, the*), short **prepositions**, **conjunctions**, and the *to* in an **infinitive** unless they are the first or last words in a title or subtitle.

Walt Whitman: A Life	Declaration of Independence
"As Time Goes By"	*Sense and Sensibility*

25e Compass directions

Capitalize compass directions only if the word designates a specific geographical region.

▶ John Muir headed west, motivated by the desire to explore.

▶ The South is becoming increasingly Republican.

25f Family relationships

Capitalize family relationships only if the word is used as part of a name or as a substitute for the name.

▶ When she was a child, my mother shared a room with her aunt.

▶ I could always tell when Mother was annoyed with Aunt Rose.

26

Abbreviations and Numbers

Any time you open up a telephone book, you see an abundance of abbreviations and numbers, as in the following listing from the Berkeley directory:

Oaks Theater   1875 Solano Av   Brk

Abbreviations and numbers allow writers to present detailed information in a small amount of space. This chapter explains the conventions for using abbreviations and numbers in academic and professional writing.

26a Abbreviations

Certain titles, including those indicating academic degrees, are normally abbreviated when used before or after a person's name.

Mr. Jason Bowen   Henry Louis Gates Jr.

Dr. Edward Davies   Karen Lancry, M.D.

Other titles, including religious and government titles, can be abbreviated before a full name but should be written out before a last name alone.

Rev. Fleming Rutledge   Reverend Rutledge

Prof. Jaime Mejia   Professor Mejia

Sen. Trent Lott   Senator Lott

Business, government, and science terms. If you are sure your readers will understand them, use common abbreviations such as CBS, DNA, and CIA. If an abbreviation may be unfamiliar, however, spell out the term the first time you use it, and give the abbreviation in parentheses. After that, use the abbreviation by itself. Use abbreviations such as *Co., Inc., Corp.,* and *&* only if they are part of a company's official name.

▶ The Comprehensive Test Ban (CTB) Treaty was first proposed in the 1950s. For those nations signing it, the CTB would bring to a halt all nuclear weapons testing.

▶ Sears, Roebuck & Co. was the only large ~~corp.~~ *corporation* in town.

With numbers. The following abbreviations are acceptable with specific years and times.

399 B.C. ("before Christ")

A.D. 49 (*anno Domini,* Latin for "in the year of our Lord")

210 B.C.E. ("before the common era")

184 C.E. ("common era")

11:15 A.M. (*or* a.m.)

9:00 P.M. (*or* p.m.)

Symbols such as % and $ are acceptable with figures ($11) but not with words (*eleven dollars*). Units of measurement can be abbreviated in charts and graphs (*4 in.*) but not in the body of a paper (*four inches*).

In notes and source citations. Some abbreviations are used in notes and in source citations but are not appropriate in the body of a paper.

cf.	compare (*confer*)
e.g.	for example (*exempli gratia*)
et al.	and others (*et alia*)
etc.	and so forth (*et cetera*)
i.e.	that is (*id est*)
N.B.	note well (*nota bene*)

In addition, except in notes and source citations, do not abbreviate such terms as *chapter, page,* and *volume* or the names of months, states, cities, or countries. Two exceptions are *Washington, D.C.,* and *U.S.,* which is acceptable as an adjective but not as a noun: *U.S. borders* but *in the United States.*

26b Numbers

If you can write out a number in one or two words, do so. Use figures for longer numbers.

▶ Her screams were ignored by ~~38~~ thirty-eight people.

▶ A baseball is held together by ~~two hundred sixteen~~ 216 red stitches.

If one of several numbers *of the same kind* in the same sentence requires a figure, use figures for all the numbers.

▶ An audio system can range in cost from ~~one hundred dollars~~ $100 to $2,599.

When a sentence begins with a number, either spell out the number or rewrite the sentence.

▶ ~~119~~ One hundred nineteen years of CIA labor cost taxpayers sixteen million dollars.

Most readers find it easier to read figures than three-word numbers; thus the best solution may be to rewrite this sentence: *Taxpayers spent sixteen million dollars for 119 years of CIA labor.*

In general, use figures for the following:

ADDRESSES	23 Main Street, 175 Fifth Avenue
DATES	September 17, 1951; 4 B.C.E.; the 1860s
DECIMALS AND FRACTIONS	65.34, 8½
PERCENTAGES	77 percent (*or* 77%)
EXACT AMOUNTS OF MONEY	$7,348; $1.46 trillion; $2.50; 35 (*or* thirty-five) cents
SCORES AND STATISTICS	an 8–3 Red Sox victory, a mean score of 600, an average age of 22
TIME OF DAY	6:00 A.M.

27

Italics

The slanted type known as italics is more than just a pretty typeface. Indeed, italics give words special meaning or emphasis. In the sentence "Many people read *People* on the subway every day," the italics tell us that *People* is a publication. You may have a word processor that produces italic type; if not, underline words that you would otherwise italicize.

27a For titles

In general, use italics for titles of long or complete works; use quotation marks for shorter works (23b).

BOOKS	*Beloved*
CHOREOGRAPHIC WORKS	Agnes de Mille's *Rodeo*
FILMS AND VIDEOS	*Shine*
LONG MUSICAL WORKS	*Brandenburg Concertos*
LONG POEMS	*The Bhagavadgita*
MAGAZINES AND JOURNALS	*Newsweek, New England Journal of Medicine*
NEWSPAPERS	the Cleveland *Plain Dealer*
PAINTINGS AND SCULPTURE	Georgia O'Keeffe's *Black Iris*

PAMPHLETS	Thomas Paine's *Common Sense*
PLAYS	*Rent*
RADIO SERIES	*All Things Considered*
RECORDINGS	the Fugees' *The Score*
SOFTWARE	*Quicken*
TELEVISION SERIES	*The Simpsons*

Do not italicize sacred books, such as the Bible and the Koran; public documents, such as the Constitution and the Magna Carta; or the titles of your own papers.

27b For words, letters, and numbers used as terms

▶ One characteristic of some New York speech is the absence of postvocalic *r*, for example, pronouncing *four* as "fouh."

27c For non-English words

Italicize words from other languages unless they have become part of English—the French "bourgeois," for example. If a word is in an English dictionary, it does not need italics. Always italicize Latin genus and species names.

▶ At last one of the phantom sleighs gliding along the street would come to a stop, and with gawky haste Mr. Burness in his fox-furred *shapka* would make for our door. — VLADIMIR NABOKOV, *Speak, Memory*

▶ The caterpillars of *Hapalia*, when attacked by the wasp *Apanteles machaeralis*, drop suddenly from their leaves and suspend themselves in air by a silken thread.
— STEPHEN JAY GOULD, "Nonmoral Nature"

27d For aircraft, spacecraft, ships, and trains

Spirit of St. Louis   Amtrak's *Silver Star*
Discovery   USS *Iowa*

27e For emphasis

Italics can help to create emphasis in writing, but use them sparingly for this purpose. It is usually better to create emphasis with sentence structure and word choice.

▶ **Great literature and a class of literate readers are nothing new in India. What is new is the emergence of a gifted generation of Indian writers *working in English.*** — SALMAN RUSHDIE

28

Hyphens

Hyphens show up every time you make a left-hand turn, wear a T-shirt, get one-on-one tutoring, listen to hip-hop, or eat Tex-Mex food. Sometimes the dictionary will tell you whether to hyphenate a word. Other times, you will have to apply some general rules, which you will find in this chapter.

28a In compound nouns and verbs

Some **compound nouns** and verbs are one word, some are separate words, and some require hyphens. Consult a dictionary to be sure.

ONE WORD	rowboat, homepage, download
SEPARATE WORDS	high school, parking meter, shut up
WITH HYPHENS	city-state, sister-in-law, cross-fertilize

28b In compound adjectives

Hyphenate most **compound adjectives** before a noun. Do not hyphenate compound adjectives that follow a noun.

a *worn-out* coat	The coat was *worn out.*
a *well-liked* boss	Our boss is *well liked.*
a *six-foot* plank	The plank measures *six feet.*

Never hyphenate an *-ly* **adverb** and an adjective.

▶ They used a widely/distributed mailing list.

Use suspended hyphens in a series of compound adjectives.

▶ Each student did the work him- or herself.

28c In fractions and numbers

Hyphenate spelled-out fractions and numbers from twenty-one to ninety-nine.

two-sevenths   thirty-seven

28d With prefixes and suffixes

Most words containing a **prefix** or **suffix** are written without hyphens: *antiwar, gorillalike.* Here are some exceptions.

BEFORE CAPITALIZED WORDS	anti-Clinton, non-Catholic
WITH FIGURES	pre-1960, post-1945
WITH *ALL-, EX-,* AND *SELF-*	all-state, ex-partner, self-possessed
WITH *-ELECT*	mayor-elect
FOR CLARITY	re-cover, anti-inflation, troll-like

Re-cover means "cover again"; the hyphen distinguishes it from *recover,* meaning "get well." In *anti-inflation* and *troll-like,* the hyphens separate double and triple letters that make the words hard to read.

28e For word division

If you need to divide a word at the end of a line, do so only between syllables. All dictionaries show syllable breaks, so the best advice for dividing words correctly is simply to look them up. In addition, you should follow certain other conventions.

• Never divide one-syllable words or abbreviations, contractions, or figures.

- Do not divide a word unless you can leave at least two letters on each line.
- Divide compound words only between their parts. Divide words with **prefixes** or **suffixes** only after the prefix or before the suffix.

FAQ: PUNCTUATION AND MECHANICS ONLINE

How do you show italics online?

For programs that don't allow you to use italics, you can substitute other devices.

- To add emphasis to a word or phrase, use asterisks:

   The company homepage simply *must* be updated!

- To indicate a title, use the underline mark before and after the title:

   Thanks for the copy of _EasyWriter_, which arrived today.

Are there special rules for using capital letters online?

In general, follow the same conventions online that you would in print, capitalizing the first word of each sentence and proper nouns and adjectives. Some writers treat EMAIL almost like talk, writing hurriedly and not using any capital letters. This practice can be hard on your readers, however, and can result in text that looks unprofessional if it is printed out. Since email *is* often printed out, you should ordinarily follow the print conventions of capitalization. Here are some other tips for using capital letters.

- **Electronic addresses.** Follow the capitalization *exactly* in address lines: systems that are case sensitive may not recognize <Lunsford.8@Osu.edu> if the actual address is <lunsford.8@osu.edu>.

- **Shouting.** Capitalizing whole words or phrases for emphasis comes across to readers as SHOUTING. So instead of upper case, use asterisks to add emphasis: "Sorry for the abrupt response, but I am *very* busy."

- **InterCaps.** Some contemporary companies use capitals in the middle of their own or their products' names, often turning two words into one. Leave the capitals in, following the style you see in company advertising or on the product itself—*HotJava, WordPerfect, EasyWriter.*

What do the new online punctuation marks indicate?

/ The **forward slash** separates parts of URLS and WEB SITE addresses.

. The **dot** separates parts of email addresses and Web site addresses.

@ The **"at" sign** is part of every email address, indicating that you are "at" an electronic address.

<> **Angle brackets** can be used in printed texts to frame email addresses and Web site locations, making it possible to use them within sentences and with other punctuation.

_ The **underscore** is used in many URLs and Web site addresses, and around titles in online text.

~ The **tilde** appears in many URLs and Web site addresses as an indicator of the user or owner of the DIRECTORY PATH.

These marks are crucial for finding what you want. Even the familiar hyphen (-) can cause havoc if omitted—or if a dash (—) is substituted for it. So treat these punctuation marks with care—they are not optional!

• **Emoticons.** Some online writers combine punctuation marks and other keyboard characters to create (when viewed sideways) "facial expressions" that signal tone or attitude: a smile **:-)** signals a friendly hello or nod, whereas a frown **:-(** or a wink **;-)** or a laugh **:-D** signal other emotions. These little online punctuation marks, called EMOTICONS (or *smileys*), are today used primarily for fun, or to tease and puzzle readers. You should use them as you would other marks: only if they are appropriate to your topic and purpose, and only if they will be understood and accepted by your audience. As a general rule, leave emoticons out of most academic and professional writing.

How do you break a URL if it won't all fit on one line of printed text?

First, remember to signal the beginning and end of the URL with angle brackets (<>). Then, if you have to break it into two lines:

• Break it *after* the beginning PROTOCOL: <http://

• Break it *before* a punctuation mark: <http://www .smpcollege.com/online-4styles~help>

How do you know when to use hyphens with new compound words that are not yet in any dictionaries?

Many new compounds, especially those pertaining to technology, appear as one word, without hyphenation.

Helpful advice comes from *Wired Style:* "When in doubt, close it up." Hence *videogame, desktop, workstation, download, toolbar.*

How do you deal with money, weights and measurements, and phone numbers on the Internet?

Because the INTERNET reaches readers around the globe, you may need to use non-U.S. units. When using monetary figures online, use the currency of the nation you are writing about or to. For weights and measures, remember that the system of inches and pounds is largely limited to the United States; use metric measurements (meters, grams) when they are appropriate for the nation you are discussing. Begin phone numbers with a plus sign (+) followed by the international access code; then add the area, province, or city code in parentheses; and then add the local number, with spaces between:

+1 (212) 846 3119

+81 (5) 9232 6722

How do you mark paragraphs online if your program doesn't allow you to indent?

Long chunks of text are often difficult for readers to process, expecially when no diversity of font, use of italics, or boldfacing is possible. If you can't indent your online paragraphs, break your text into block paragraphs, leaving an extra space between each one. You can also help readers by stating the most important information at the beginning of each paragraph and by using numbered or bulleted lists to call attention to special items.

Online Resources

Grammar, Punctuation, and Capitalization: A Handbook for Technical Writers and Editors by Mary McCaskil has some chapters available online. The chapter on punctuation can be found at:

<http://sti.larc.nasa.gov/html/Chapt3/Chapt3-TOC.html>

A helpful program on punctuation can be found at:

<http://www.emo.com/wwb/wwb_sty.html>

RESEARCH

Research is formalized curiosity.
It is poking and prying with a
purpose.

- Zora Neale Hurston

Conducting Research

Your employer asks you to recommend a new email system. You need to plan a week's stay in Tokyo. Your twins want a clown for their fifth birthday party. An instructor assigns a term paper about an artist. Each of these situations calls for research, for examining various kinds of sources. And each calls for you to assess the data you collect, to synthesize your findings, and to come up with your own, original recommendation or conclusion. Many tasks that call for research, such as a term paper or a business report, require that your work culminate in a written document.

29a The research process

For academic research assignments, once you have chosen or been assigned a topic, you need to move as efficiently as possible to articulate a research question you want to answer about the topic and a hypothesis about the answer. Then, after some preliminary research, you can refine your hypothesis into a working thesis. Here's an example of the move from a general topic to a working thesis:

TOPIC	the art of Frida Kahlo
RESEARCH QUESTION	What were the influences on Kahlo's work?
HYPOTHESIS	The events of her own life were the central influences on Kahlo's work.
WORKING THESIS	Kahlo's unique style resulted not only from her life events but also from her familiarity with European and Mexican art.

29b Primary and secondary sources

Sources can be categorized as primary sources, or first-hand knowledge, and secondary sources—information

116

available from the research of others. Most research projects depend on both primary and secondary sources.

Primary sources are basic sources of raw information, including notes you take in the field; experiments, surveys, or interviews you conduct; objects or artwork you examine; literary works you read; performances you attend; and diaries, letters, eyewitness accounts, news reports, and historical documents. Secondary sources are accounts produced by other investigators, such as researchers' reports or analyses and critical writing, including reviews and biographies. Often what constitutes a primary or secondary source depends on your purpose. A critic's evaluation of a painting, for instance, is a secondary source for an essay on that painting, but it serves as a primary source for a study of that critic's writing.

29c Reference works

Libraries provide two necessary kinds of reference information: general background materials, which will provide an overview of your topic; and specialized materials, which may help direct your research and develop your working thesis.

GENERAL ENCYCLOPEDIAS

Collier's Encyclopedia, New Encyclopaedia Britannica

SPECIALIZED ENCYCLOPEDIAS

Encyclopedia of Asian History, Cambridge History of Africa, Harvard Guide to American History, Oxford Companion to English Literature

BIOGRAPHICAL RESOURCES

Dictionary of American Biography, Dictionary of National Biography, African American Biographies, Notable American Women, Chicano Scholars and Writers

ALMANACS, YEARBOOKS, NEWS DIGESTS, ATLASES

Facts on File, Statistical Abstracts of the United States, Atlas of World Cultures, National Geographic Atlas of the World

BOOK INDEXES, CD-ROM INDEXES

Books in Print, Cumulative Book Index, Paperbound Books in Print, CD-ROMs in Print

GENERAL PERIODICAL INDEXES/DATABASES

Book Review Digest, InfoTrac, New York Times Index, Readers' Guide to Periodical Literature, LEXIS-NEXIS, Dialog, Dow Jones News/Retrieval

SPECIALIZED PERIODICAL INDEXES AND ABSTRACTS

Arts and Humanities Citation Index, Biological Abstracts, PsycLIT

29d Computer databases

You may also search an electronic index or database to find specific articles that may prove to be good references for your research. You conduct a search in an electronic database by entering **keywords** (often referred to as **descriptors**), and you get back a list of every source that contains those keywords in its title, its text, or an abstract of the text. (Some sophisticated databases allow you to enter a direct question.)

Obviously, then, doing efficient database searches requires that you choose keywords carefully and observe the search logic for a particular database. Let's assume that you are preparing an academic report on urban life as represented in James Joyce's fiction and that you have located the electronic database called *MLA Bibliography of Books and Articles,* a major database for works of and about literature. Using *and* between keywords usually indicates that you want to find sources that deal with both keywords (for example, Joyce *and* Ireland, which yields 118 entries). Using *or,* however, instructs the software to call up every source in which either one keyword or the other shows up (Joyce *and* Dublin or Belfast). You can instruct the software to exclude articles that contain a specific term if you type in *not* before the term (Joyce *and* Ireland *not* Dublin, which yields 71 entries). In an electronic database search, the *or, and,* and *not* are known as **Boolean terms**.

Suppose you are working with the MLA database mentioned previously, and you enter the keywords *Kahlo, Frida,* and *American literature* as well as the Boolean term *and;* you would find that three articles contain both keywords. Here is the information on one of those three articles as it would appear on your screen

or on a printout at the time this book went to press. (Notice that the MLA format provides information using descriptor words in parentheses—*sau,* for example, is the MLA descriptor for subject-author.)

```
1 MLA
      AUTHOR: Salber, Linde; Stuhlmann,
              Gunther
      TITLE:  Artists--the Third Sex: A Few
              Thoughts on the Psychology of
              the Creative Age
      SOURCE: Anais: An International Journal
              1993 vii p59-68
      SUBJECTS COVERED:
      --(slt) American literature (tim)
      1900-1999 (sau) Nin, Anais (sau)
      Kahlo, Frida (sau) Andreas-Salome,
      Lou (sau) psychological approach
      --(slt) German literature (tim)
      1800-1899
```

29e The Internet

The **Internet** is a great global patchwork quilt of linked computer networks that can help you as a researcher by (1) letting you communicate with individuals and groups all over the world and (2) opening doors to other vast information resources. All you need is an account on a host computer and an Internet address.

Online discussion. The Internet allows you to find and communicate with groups of people who share your research interest—be it intercom systems, Tokyo, or Frida Kahlo. Such interest groups can be found through **listservs**, also called discussion groups or mailing lists. The Internet also gives you access to **Usenet**, a global collection of interest groups that share news—hence their other name, **newsgroups**. Instead of mail from these groups automatically coming to your electronic mailbox, as it does from listservs, you must electronically visit Usenet groups to get their news. Similarly, you can connect to an Internet bulletin board system, or **BBS**, where you can look over messages and files listed on menus. Or you can visit real-time

"virtual" conversation spaces in **MOOs**, **MUDs**, and **IRCs**. Above all, you can use **email** to keep up conversations with all kinds of groups and individuals.

▪ **Data gathering.** Many systems on the Internet allow you to access sources.

WORLD WIDE WEB

The **World Wide Web** is a network of linked sites, presented in "pages" that can feature sound, graphics, and video. Each site has its own uniform resource locator (URL), or address. You can leap from one **Web site** to another and to other kinds of Internet resources with the click of a **mouse**. To read a document on the Web that includes elements other than text, you must have a Web **browser** software tool, such as Mosaic, Netscape, or Explorer. To do research, you may use a Web **search engine** such as Yahoo! or Galaxy to help you do keyword searches.

GOPHER

Gopher is a browsing software system that can retrieve data for you from universities, companies, and other organizations. If your host computer has a gopher, you can select the information you want from the gopher's menu of information sources.

Using gopher often involves following a path from one menu to another before you get to a specific document. At times, you may lose track of how you actually located the material of interest to you. To simplify matters, you can use something called a **bookmark** to identify an important gopher location that you want to revisit. Over time, you may create a **bookmark list**, a sort of custom menu, that makes it easy for you to get to particular gopher sites.

ANONYMOUS FTP

Anonymous **FTP** (file transfer protocol) is a method for calling up and copying (at no cost) a huge and ever-expanding number of public files from host computers all over the Internet. The files, which may not be available via gopher or the World Wide Web, can be short documents or complete magazines (with pictures), audio clips, video clips, and even software that you can **download** to your computer.

ARCHIE

When you use anonymous FTP, you may know what kind of data you are looking for, but you probably do not know the exact name of the file that contains the data nor the Internet address at which that file resides. The solution is to tell another searching system called Archie what you are looking for. **Archie** allows you to search FTP sites for access to artwork, books, journals, photographs, sound tracks, and much more. Finally, Archie tells you how to locate the file so that you can download it.

WAIS

WAIS (wide area information servers, pronounced *ways*) provides a kind of index to specific files accessed through gopher, allowing you to search promising sources by using keywords and search logic. WAIS will list all the documents whose text contains the keywords you have specified, and it will give you the option of having the complete documents appear on your computer screen. The secret to using WAIS is figuring out which sources to search by keywords.

TELNET

Telnet allows you to make a telephone connection with another computer so that you can access on your computer the resources that are available to the other one.

29f The library catalog

A library catalog lists all the library's books. The traditional format for the library catalog is the card catalog. Today some libraries have a microfiche catalog, and many have transferred or are in the process of transferring their records to a computerized catalog. You can use public computer terminals to search for material or log on and access a library catalog from personal computers at remote locations. Most computerized catalogs provide clear instructions on how and when to type in information. As with a card catalog, you can search for holdings by author, title, or subject. With a computerized catalog, you can easily experiment with different subject headings. The computer screen displays entries

similar to those in a card catalog but may also indicate whether a book has been checked out and, if so, when it is due to be returned.

If the stacks are open to library users, take time to browse through the books near the one you have targeted. Very often you will find the other books in the area surrounding your book a more important treasure-trove than any bibliography or index.

29g Field research

Interviews. Some information is best obtained by asking direct questions of other people. If you can talk with an expert—in person, on the telephone, or via the Internet—you might get information you could not have obtained through any other kind of research. Here are some suggestions for planning an interview.

- Determine your exact purpose, and be sure it relates to your research question and your hypothesis.
- Set up the interview well in advance. Specify how long it will take, and if you wish to tape-record the session, ask permission to do so.
- Prepare a written list of factual and open-ended questions. Leave plenty of space for notes after each question. If the interview proceeds in a direction that seems fruitful, do not feel that you have to ask all of your prepared questions.
- Record the subject, date, time, and place of the interview.
- Thank those you interview, either in person or in a follow-up letter.

Observation. Trained observers report that making a faithful record of an observation requires intense concentration and mental agility. Here are some tips.

- Determine the purpose of the observation, and be sure it relates to your research and hypothesis.
- Develop an appropriate system for recording data. Consider using a "split" notebook or page: on one side, record your observations directly; on the other, record your thoughts or interpretations.

- Be aware that the way you record data will affect the final report, if only in respect to what you include in the notes and what you leave out.
- Record the date, time, and place of the observation.

■ **Opinion surveys.** Surveys usually depend on questionnaires. On any questionnaire, the questions should be clear and easy to understand and designed so that you can analyze the answers easily. Questions that ask respondents to say "yes" or "no" or to rank items on a scale are particularly easy to tabulate. Here are some additional suggestions for designing a questionnaire.

- Write out your purpose, and determine the kinds of questions you need to ask.
- Figure out how to reach respondents.
- Draft questions that call for short, specific answers.
- Test the questions on several people, and revise or drop any that are ambiguous or too hard or that take too much time to answer.
- For a questionnaire that is to be mailed, draft a cover letter. Provide an addressed, stamped return envelope, and be sure to state a deadline.
- On the final version of the questionnaire, leave adequate space for answers.
- Proofread the questionnaire.

30

Evaluating Sources

The quality of your research-based writing depends on the quality of your sources. Therefore, careful evaluation is in order for *all* sources, including those you gather in libraries or print sources, in online searches, or in the field.

30a Print sources

Use these guidelines to assess the usefulness of a print source.

- *Relevance.* Is the source closely related to your research question?

- *Author's and publisher's credentials and stance.* Is the author an expert on the topic? What is the author's stance on the issue(s) involved, and how does this influence the information in the source? Does the author support or challenge your own views? If you are evaluating a book published by a corporation, government agency, or interest group, what is the publisher's position on the topic? If you are evaluating an article, what kind of periodical published it? popular? academic? alternative?

- *Date of publication.* Recent sources are often more useful than older ones, particularly in the sciences. However, in some fields, the most authoritative works may be the older ones.

- *Level of specialization.* General sources can be helpful as you begin your research, but you may then need the authority or currentness of more specialized sources. On the other hand, extremely specialized works may be too hard to understand.

- *Audience.* Was the source written for the general public? specialists? advocates or opponents?

- *Cross-referencing.* Is the source cited in other works?

- *Length.* Is the source long enough to provide adequate detail?

- *Availability.* Do you have access to the source?

30b Electronic sources

Unlike most library-based research tools, much material on the **Internet** in general and the **World Wide Web** in particular is still the work of enthusiastic amateurs. Commercial advertisements, one-sided statements, and even false information are all jumbled together with good, reliable data. In this frontier electronic environment, you must be the judge of how accurate and useful materials are. Rely on the same kind of critical thinking you use to assess the usefulness of a print source; in addition, keep these questions in mind.

- Who has posted this document or **Web site** —an individual? an interest group? a company? a government agency? What can you determine about the poster's credibility?

- Who can be held accountable for the information in the document or site? How well and thoroughly does the document or site credit its own sources?
- How current is the document or site? Be especially cautious of undated materials.
- How effectively is the document or site designed? How user-friendly is it? If it is a Web site, are the links helpful? What effects do design, visuals, and sound have on the message?
- What is missing or omitted from the document or site? How do such exclusions affect how you can or cannot use the information?
- What perspective(s) are represented? If only one perspective is represented, how can you balance or expand this viewpoint?

30c Field research

If you have conducted experiments, surveys, interviews, observations, or other field research, make sure to review the results with a critical eye.

- Recheck all data and all conclusions to make sure they are accurate and warranted.
- Identify the exact time, place, and participants in all field research.
- Make clear what part you played in the research and how your role could have influenced the findings.
- If your research involved other people, get their permission to use their words. Ask whether you may use their names or whether the names should be kept confidential.

30d Critical reading and synthesis of data

After you have identified a potential source and decided to read it, you still need to determine if it merits a place in your research essay. Keeping these questions in mind can save you time as you dig into sources.

- How does the source material address your research question? How does it provide support for your working thesis?

- Does the source offer counterarguments to your working thesis? If so, what responses can you make?
- What is the author's stance or perspective? Is he or she an advocate of something? a strong opponent? an amused onlooker? a specialist? Are there any clues to what forces may have shaped the author's perspective?
- How does this stance affect the author's presentation?
- In what ways do you share—or not share—the author's stance?
- What is the author's tone—cautious? angry? flippant? serious?
- What is the author's main point? How much and what kind of evidence does the author use to support that point? How persuasive do you find the evidence?
- Do any of your other sources disagree with this source? If so, how are you going to handle this disagreement?
- What patterns or trends do the author's argument and evidence fall into? Can you synthesize this author's argument and evidence with arguments and evidence from other sources? What conclusions can you draw from those patterns or trends?

31

Using Sources

Every time you pick up *Consumer Reports* to check out its evaluation of an appliance or log on to the **Internet** to talk to owners of a software program you are interested in, you are calling on sources for help. All research builds on the careful and sometimes inspired use of sources—that research done by others. This chapter offers advice on making the most of all the sources you use.

31a Keeping clear records

As you locate and consider research sources—books, articles, Internet or **Web sites**, and so on—you should

create a working bibliography, a list of the sources that seem most likely to address your research question. Here are some guidelines for doing so.

- Use index cards (one for each source), a notebook, or a computer file. Record information so that you can arrange the entries alphabetically when you prepare the bibliography or list of works cited.

- For each *book*, record the following: call number or other location information; author(s) and/or editor(s); title and subtitle, if any; publisher's name and location; year of publication; other information you may find—translator, volume number, edition, and so on. If the book is made up of selections by a variety of authors, record the author(s) and title of the piece you are using and its inclusive page numbers.

- For each *periodical article*, list author(s); editor(s); article title and subtitle; periodical name, volume number, and date; and inclusive page numbers.

- For sources you find listed in *reference books*, note the name of the reference work and its location in case you need to check it again.

- For an *online source*, list the author (if available); title, document, file, or **Web site**; date of the material; name of the database or other **online** source; date you accessed the source; and the full electronic address or **URL** so that you can return to the source.

- For *other electronic sources*, try to obtain a printout of the source information instead of copying it by hand.

31b Taking notes

Though note-taking methods vary from one researcher to another, for each note you take you should (1) get down enough information to help you recall the major points of the source; (2) put the information in the form in which you are most likely to incorporate it into your research essay; and (3) label the note with shortened forms of the author's name and the title, the exact page number(s) the note comes from, a subject heading or theme, and the type of note it is—quotation, paraphrase, summary, your own comment.

■ **Quotations.** Quote—use an author's exact words—when the wording expresses a point so well that you cannot change it without weakening it; when the author is a respected authority whose opinion supports your own ideas; or when an author disagrees profoundly with others in the field. Here are guidelines for quoting.

- Copy the quotation carefully, with punctuation, capitalization, and spelling exactly as in the original.
- Enclose the quotation in quotation marks. (23a)
- Use brackets if you introduce words of your own into the quotation or make changes in it. Use ellipses if you omit material. (24b, f)
- If you later incorporate the quotation into your research essay, copy it from the note precisely, including brackets and ellipses.
- Record the author's name, shortened title, and page number(s) on which the quotation appears.
- Make sure you have a corresponding working bibliography entry. (31a)
- Label the note with a subject heading or theme.

■ **Paraphrases.** When you paraphrase, you put an author's major and minor points into *your own words and sentence structures.* If you wish to cite some of the author's words within the paraphrase, enclose them in quotation marks. Here are guidelines for paraphrasing.

- Include all main points and any important details in the same order in which the author presents them.
- State the meaning in your own words and sentence structures. If you want to include any language from the original, enclose it in quotation marks.
- Save for another note your own comments, elaborations, or reactions.
- Record the author's name, shortened title, and page number(s) on which the original material appeared.
- Make sure you have a corresponding working bibliography entry.
- Label the note with a subject heading, and identify it as a paraphrase to avoid confusion with a summary.
- Recheck the paraphrase against the original to be sure that the words and sentence structures are your own and that they express the author's meaning.

■ **Summaries.** A summary is a significantly shortened version of a passage or even a whole chapter or work that captures main ideas *in your own words*. Unlike a paraphrase, a summary uses just enough information to record the points you wish to emphasize. Here are some guidelines for summarizing accurately.

- Include just enough information to recount the main points you want to cite. A summary is usually far shorter than the original.

- Use your own words. If you include any language from the original, enclose it in quotation marks.

- Record the author, shortened title, and page number(s) on which the original material appeared.

- Make sure you have a corresponding working bibliography entry for the material.

- Label the note with a subject heading, and identify it as a summary to avoid confusion with a paraphrase.

- Recheck against the original any material you plan to use to be sure you have captured the author's meaning and that your words are entirely your own.

31c Incorporating source materials into your writing

Many fields have specific rules for incorporating source materials into a piece of writing. Here are some general guidelines.

■ **Direct quotations.** Because your essay is primarily your own work, limit your use of quotations to those necessary to your thesis or memorable for your readers. Use direct quotations for the following purposes:

- To incorporate a statement expressed so effectively by the author that it cannot be paraphrased without altering the meaning

- To allow the words of an authority on your topic to contribute to your credibility as a researcher

- To allow an author to state a position in his or her own words

- To create a particular effect

INTEGRATING QUOTATIONS INTO YOUR TEXT

Short quotations should run in with your text, enclosed by quotation marks. Longer quotations should be set off from the text. (See 23a and Chapters 32 and 33 for guidelines on when to set off quotations.) Integrate all quotations into your text so that they flow smoothly and clearly into the surrounding sentences. Use a signal phrase or **verb**, such as those underlined in these examples:

> A good seating arrangement can prevent problems; however, *withitness*, <u>as defined by Woolfolk</u>, works even better:
>
>> Withitness is the ability to communicate to students that you are aware of what is happening in the classroom, that you "don't miss anything." With-it teachers seem to have "eyes in the back of their heads." They avoid becoming too absorbed with a few students, since this allows the rest of the class to wander. (359)
>
> As Eudora Welty <u>notes</u>, "learning stamps you with its moments. Childhood's learning," she <u>continues</u>, "is made up of moments. It isn't steady. It's a pulse" (9).

When you write about literary and artistic works created in the past, generally follow Modern Language Association (MLA) style and use **present-tense verbs**, as in the second example above. (See Chapter 32.) However, if you are using the style recommendations of the American Psychological Association (APA), use signal phrases in the **past tense** or the **present-perfect form**. (See Chapter 33.)

> In *Abnormal Psychology*, Comer (1995) <u>emphasized</u> that Shakespeare's Othello blamed behavior on the moon: "She comes more near the earth than she was wont / And makes men mad."

BRACKETS AND ELLIPSES

In direct quotations, enclose in brackets any words you change or add, and indicate any deletions with ellipsis points.

> A farmer, Jane Lee, spoke to the Nuclear Regulatory Commission about the occurrences. "There is something wrong in the [Three Mile Island] area. It is happening within nature itself," she said, referring to human miscarriages, stillbirths, and birth defects in farm animals ("Legacy" 33).

Economist John Kenneth Galbraith has pointed out that "large corporations cannot afford to compete with one another. . . . In a truly competitive market someone loses. . . . American big business has finally learned that everybody has to protect everybody else's investment" (Key 17).

■ **Paraphrases and summaries.** Introduce paraphrases and summaries clearly, usually with a signal phrase that includes the author of the source, as the underlined words in this example indicate.

Professor Deborah Tannen offers her book *That's Not What I Meant!* to "women and men everywhere who are trying their best to talk to each other" (19). <u>Tannen goes on to illustrate</u> how communication between women and men breaks down <u>and then to suggest</u> that an awareness of "genderlects" can improve relationships (297).

31d Recognizing plagiarism and acknowledging sources

Plagiarism, the use of another's words without crediting that person, breaks trust with the research conversation you are a part of and with readers as well. As a mark of dishonesty, it can destroy the credibility of both research and researcher and can have serious consequences.

The safest way to avoid plagiarism is to acknowledge your use of all your sources, with the following *three exceptions*, which do not need to be credited:

- *Common knowledge*—a specific source of information most readers would be likely to know (that Bill Clinton was reelected president in 1996, for example)
- *Facts available in a variety of sources* (for instance, that water boils at 100 degrees Celsius or that the bombing of Pearl Harbor occurred on December 7, 1941)
- *Your own findings from field research* (interviews, observations, experiments, or surveys you have conducted, which should be announced as such)

For *all other source material,* give credit as fully as possible, using quotation marks around any quoted material, citing the source according to the documentation style required (see Chapters 32–35), and, if necessary, listing it in a bibliography or list of works cited. Acknowledge and give full credit to all the following:

- Facts not widely known; arguable assertions
- Judgments, opinions, and claims of others
- Statistics, charts, tables, and graphs from any source
- Help from friends, instructors, or others
- Material found on the Internet or World Wide Web, with the name of the author and the URL

FAQ: RESEARCH ONLINE

How do you gain access to the Internet?

In addition to a computer, you'll need two basic tools: a MODEM and a BROWSER, such as Netscape Navigator, Lynx, Mosaic, or Microsoft Explorer. Then you'll need an INTERNET service provider (ISP)—a school computing center, telephone or cable company, or other communal or government service—to connect your computer to the Internet and provide you with a USERNAME and password. For establishing your own Internet connection, check out the *Internet Starter Kit* by Adam Engst, a text that has versions for both Mac and Windows. It is available online at:

<http://www.mcp.com/hayden/iskm/iskw2/index.html> for Windows

<http://www.mcp.com/hayden/iskm/iskm3/index.html> for Mac

Where can you get more information and detailed help on navigating the Internet and the WWW?

Check out Andrew Harnack and Eugene Kleppinger's *Online! A Reference Guide to Using Internet Sources*. An online version is also available:

<http://www.smpcollege.com/online-4styles~help>

Another helpful online source can be found at:

<http://www.yahoo.com/Computers/World_Wide_Web/Beginner s Guides/>

How do you do online research efficiently?

Narrow your topic, and then come up with a list of specific KEYWORDS as soon as possible. Rather than searching for instances of a broad term like *cancer*, for example—which would call up thousands of possibilities—begin with the most specific topic you can, such as "metastatic colon cancer in teenagers."

How do you begin searching the Web?

Start by choosing the most appropriate and efficient SEARCH ENGINES for your topic; you can find a catalog of all search engines listed by category at <www.search.com>.

- **Subject Directory Search Engines**. The following sources index **WORLD WIDE WEB** contents by subject and are especially helpful if you know your general subject but haven't narrowed it to a specific subtopic.

  Yahoo! offers links to various fields (art, education, sports, and so on):

  <http://www.yahoo.com>

  The *Internet Services List* offers links in alphabetical order, from agriculture to the Web:

  <http://www.spectracom/islist>

  WWW Virtual Library provides links to Library of Congress topics:

  <http://www.w3.~org/pub/DataSources/bySubject/Overview.html>

  The Library of Congress WorldWideWeb HomePage provides links to information on all Internet sources:

  <http://lcweb.loc.gov>

- **Text Index Search Engines.** The following tools help you look for specific keywords and give links to documents containing those words. These engines are particularly helpful when you have already carefully limited your topic.

  Alta Vista is huge, indexing millions of **WEB PAGES** and **NEWSGROUP** messages; it allows you to search for a single term or for terms in combinations:

  <http://altavista.digital.com>

  Other popular and user-friendly engines include:

  Infoseek Guide <http://guide.infoseek.com>

  Lycos <http://www.lycos.com>

  Net Search <http://home.netscape.com/home/internet-search/html>

  Web Crawler <http://webcrawler.com>

How do you evaluate online sources?

Because almost anything—regardless of quality—may be published on the Internet and the Web, online research calls for very careful evaluation of sources. The questions that follow will help you assess online sources.

- **Authorship.** Who is the author of this site? What are the author's credentials? Who or what does the author represent? Check for a **HYPERLINK** to information about the author and for information at the bot-

tom of a Web page. Also try entering the author's name in a search engine to see what links it provides; if the author has a **HOMEPAGE**, you'll find it this way. On Usenet, you can try using DejaNews to search for other messages written by the author.

- **Sponsor.** Who sponsors the site? Read the Web address for clues. If a comparative review of new VCRs, for example, gives an address of <maritav @mitsubishi.com>, the review *may* favor Mitsubishi products. The final suffix in a **DOMAIN NAME** also tells something about the kind of group sponsoring the site:

  .com (commercial)
  .org (nonprofit organizations)
  .edu (educational institutions, usually universities)
  .gov (government agencies)
  .mil (military groups)
  .net (networks)

  Note also that geographical domains indicate country of origin: .ca (Canada), IE (Republic of Ireland), etc.

- **Links to Other Sources.** Does the site provide references and links to other sources? If possible, check out those sources.

- **Verifiability and Currency.** Can the information in the site be verified? How accurate and complete is the information? How current is it? Many sites include links to the sources of their information; check these out whenever possible. Remember, too, that the date when a source is posted is *not* necessarily the date when it was composed. Sites with no date are generally less reliable than those that are updated regularly.

Online Resources

For advice on doing online research, consult *Great Web Searching: Tricks of the Trade*, by Peggy Zorn, Mary Emanoil, Luc Marshall, and Mary Panek:

> <http://www.onlineinc.com/onlinemag/MayOL /zorn5.html>

Mary D. Been provides an *Annotated List of Guides for Evaluating Online Sources*:

> <http://www.marlboro.edu/~nickc/research/evallist .html>

Professor Kitty Locker's *Doing Research on the Web*, which is linked to her homepage, provides useful step-by-step guidance to online research:

> <http://www.cohums.ohio-state.edu/english/People /Locker.1/research.htm>

DOCUMENTATION

Adam was the only man who,
when he said a good thing, knew
that nobody had said it before
him.

– Mark Twain

MLA Style

This chapter discusses the basic format for Modern Language Association (MLA) style and provides examples of MLA documentation requirements for various kinds of sources. MLA style is widely used in literature and languages as well as in other fields. For further reference, consult the *MLA Handbook for Writers of Research Papers*, fourth edition, 1995.

32a In-text citations

MLA style requires parenthetical citations in the text of an essay to document quotations, paraphrases, summaries, and other material requiring documentation (31d). Keep your parenthetical citations short, and include all the information your readers need to locate the full citation in the list of works cited at the end of the text.

Place a parenthetical citation as near the relevant material as possible without disrupting the flow of the sentence. Pay attention in the following examples to *where* punctuation is placed in relation to the parentheses.

Directory to MLA style for in-text citations

1. AUTHOR NAMED IN A SIGNAL PHRASE. Ordinarily, you can use the author's name in a signal phrase—to introduce the material—and cite the page number(s) in parentheses.

> Herrera indicates that Kahlo believed in a "vitalistic form of pantheism" (328).

2. AUTHOR NAMED IN PARENTHESES. When you do not mention the author in a signal phrase, include the author's last name before the page number(s) in the parentheses, with no punctuation in between.

> In places, Beauvoir "sees Marxists as believing in subjectivity as much as existentialists do" (Whitmarsh 63).

3. TWO OR THREE AUTHORS. Use all the authors' last names.

> Gortner, Hebrun, and Nicolson maintain that "opinion leaders" influence other people in an organization because they are respected, not because they hold high positions (175).

4. FOUR OR MORE AUTHORS. Use the first author's name and *et al.* ("and others"), or name all the authors.

> Similarly, as Belenky, Clinchy, Goldberger, and Tarule assert, examining the lives of women expands our understanding of human development (7).

5. ORGANIZATION AS AUTHOR. Give the full name of a corporate author if it is brief or a shortened form if it is long.

> In fact, one of the leading foundations in the field of higher education supports the recent proposals for community-run public schools (Carnegie Corporation 45).

6. UNKNOWN AUTHOR. Use the full title of the work if it is brief or a shortened form if it is long.

> "Hype," by one analysis, is "an artificially engendered atmosphere of hysteria" ("Today's Marketplace" 51).

7. AUTHOR OF TWO OR MORE WORKS. If your list of works cited has more than one work by the same author, include the title in question or a shortened version of it.

> Gardner presents readers with their own silliness through his description of a

"pointless, ridiculous monster, crouched in
the shadows, stinking of dead men, murdered
children, and martyred cows" (<u>Grendel</u> 2).

8. AUTHORS WITH THE SAME LAST NAME. If your list of works
cited has works by authors with the same last name,
always include the authors' first *and* last names in the
signal phrases or in the parenthetical citations.

Children will learn to write if they are
allowed to choose their own subjects, James
Britton asserts, citing the Schools Council
study of the 1960s (37-42).

9. MULTIVOLUME WORK. Note the volume number first and
then the page number(s), with a colon and one space
between them.

Modernist writers prized experimentation
and gradually even sought to blur the line
between poetry and prose, according to
Forster (3: 150).

If you name only one volume of the work in your list of
works cited, you need include only the page number in
the parentheses.

10. LITERARY WORK. Because literary works are often
available in many different editions, first cite the page
number(s) from the edition you used followed by a
semicolon, and then give other identifying information
that will lead readers to the passage in any edition.
Indicate the act and/or scene in a play (*37; sc. 1*). For a
novel, indicate the part or chapter (*175; ch. 4*).

Resisting gossip, Wharton's character Lily
says, "What is truth? Where a woman is con-
cerned, it's the story that's easiest to
believe" (215; bk. 2, ch. 4).

For poems, instead of page numbers cite the part (if
there is one) and line(s), separated by periods. If you are
citing only line numbers, use the word *line(s)* in the first
reference (*lines 33–34*).

On dying, Whitman speculates "All goes
onward and outward, nothing collapses, /
And to die is different from what anyone
supposed, and luckier" (6.129-30).

For verse plays, give only the act, scene, and line numbers, separated by periods.

> As <u>Macbeth</u> begins, the witches greet Banquo
> as "Lesser than Macbeth, and greater"
> (1.3.65).

11. WORK IN AN ANTHOLOGY. For an essay, short story, or other piece of prose reprinted in an anthology, use the name of the author of the work, not the editor of the anthology, but use the page number(s) from the anthology.

> Narratives of captivity play a major role
> in early writing by women in the United
> States, as demonstrated by Silko (219).

12. BIBLE. Identify quotations by chapter and verse (*John 3:16*). Spell out the names of books mentioned in your text. In a parenthetical citation, use an abbreviation for books with names of five or more letters (*Gen.* for *Genesis*). If you use the King James Version, you do not need to include a works-cited entry.

13. INDIRECT SOURCE. Use the abbreviation *qtd. in* to indicate that you are quoting from someone else's report of a conversation, interview, letter, or the like.

> As Arthur Miller says, "When somebody is
> destroyed everybody finally contributes to
> it, but in Willy's case, the end product
> would be virtually the same" (qtd. in
> Martin and Meyer 375).

14. TWO OR MORE SOURCES IN THE SAME CITATION. Separate the information with semicolons.

> Some economists recommend that <u>employment</u> be
> redefined to include unpaid domestic labor
> (Clark 148; Nevins 39).

15. ENTIRE WORK OR ONE-PAGE ARTICLE. Include the reference in the text without any page numbers or parentheses.

> Thomas Hardy's tragic vision is given full
> vent in his <u>Jude the Obscure</u>.

16. WORK WITHOUT PAGE NUMBERS. If a work has no page numbers or is only one page long, you may omit the

page number. If a work uses paragraph numbers instead, use the abbreviation *par(s).*

> Whitman considered African American speech "a source of a native grand opera" in the words of Ellison (par. 13).

17. NONPRINT OR ELECTRONIC SOURCE. Give enough information in a signal phrase or parenthetical citation for readers to locate the source in the list of works cited. Usually give the author or title under which you list the source.

> Kahlo is seated with a Judas doll, identified in the film <u>Portrait of an Artist: Frida Kahlo</u> as a papier-mâché doll stuffed with firecrackers to be exploded on the day before Easter.

32b Explanatory and bibliographic notes

MLA style allows explanatory notes for information or commentary that does not readily fit into your text but is needed for clarification or further explanation. In addition, MLA style permits bibliographic notes for information about a source. Use superscript numbers in the text to refer readers to the notes, which may appear as endnotes (typed under the heading *Notes* on a separate page after the text but before the list of works cited) or as footnotes at the bottom of the page.

1. SUPERSCRIPT NUMBER IN TEXT

> Stewart emphasizes the existence of social contacts in Hawthorne's life so that the audience will accept a different Hawthorne, one more attuned to modern times than the figure in Woodberry.[3]

2. NOTE

> [3]Woodberry does, however, show that Hawthorne <u>was</u> often an unsociable individual. He emphasizes the seclusion of Hawthorne's mother, who separated herself from her family after the death of her husband, often even taking meals alone (28). Woodberry seems to imply that Mrs. Hawthorne's isolation rubbed off onto her son.

32c List of works cited

A list of works cited is an alphabetical list of the sources you have referred to in your essay. (If your instructor asks you to list everything you have read as background, call the list *Works Consulted*.) Here are some guidelines for preparing entries for such a list.

Directory to MLA style for a list of works cited

Books

The basic information for a book includes three elements, each followed by a period: the author's name, last name first; the title and subtitle, underlined or italicized; and the city of publication, a shortened form of the publisher's name, and the date.

1. ONE AUTHOR

> Herrera, Hayden. <u>Frida: A Biography of Frida Kahlo</u>. New York: Harper, 1983.

2. TWO OR THREE AUTHORS

> Appleby, Joyce, Lynn Hunt, and Margaret Jacob. <u>Telling the Truth about History</u>. New York: Norton, 1994.

3. **FOUR OR MORE AUTHORS.** Either give the first author listed on the title page, followed by a comma and *et al.* ("and others"), or list all the names.

> Belenky, Mary Field, Blythe Clinchy, Jill
>   Goldberger, and Nancy Tarule. <u>Women's
>   Ways of Knowing</u>. New York: Basic, 1986.

4. **ORGANIZATION AS AUTHOR**

> American Chemical Society. <u>Handbook for
>   Authors of Papers in the American
>   Chemical Society Publications</u>. Washing-
>   ton: American Chemical Soc., 1978.

5. **UNKNOWN AUTHOR**

> <u>The New York Times Atlas of the World</u>. New
>   York: New York Times Books, 1980.

6. **TWO OR MORE BOOKS BY THE SAME AUTHOR**

> Lorde, Audre. <u>A Burst of Light</u>. Ithaca:
>   Firebrand, 1988.
> ---. <u>Sister Outsider</u>. Trumansburg: Crossing,
>   1984.

7. **EDITOR**

> Wall, Cheryl A., ed. <u>Changing Our Own
>   Words: Essays on Criticism, Theory, and
>   Writing by Black Women</u>. New Brunswick:
>   Rutgers UP, 1989.

8. **AUTHOR AND EDITOR**

> James, Henry. <u>Portrait of a Lady</u>. Ed. Leon
>   Edel. Boston: Houghton, 1963.

9. **SELECTION IN AN ANTHOLOGY**

> Gordon, Mary. "The Parable of the Cave."
>   <u>The Writer on Her Work</u>. Ed. Janet
>   Sternburg. New York: Norton, 1980.
>   27-32.

10. **TWO OR MORE ITEMS FROM AN ANTHOLOGY**

> Baker, Houston A., Jr. "There Is No More
>   Beautiful Way." Donalson 856-63.
> Donalson, Melvin, ed. <u>Cornerstones: An
>   Anthology of African American Litera-
>   ture</u>. New York: St. Martin's, 1996.

11. TRANSLATION

Zamora, Martha. <u>Frida Kahlo: The Brush of Anguish</u>. Trans. Marilyn Sode Smith. San Francisco: Chronicle, 1990.

12. EDITION OTHER THAN THE FIRST

Kelly, Alfred H., Winfred A. Harbison, and Herman Belz. <u>The American Constitution: Its Origins and Development</u>. 6th ed. New York: Norton, 1983.

13. ONE VOLUME OF A MULTIVOLUME WORK

Foner, Philip S., and Ronald L. Lewis, eds. <u>The Black Worker</u>. Vol. 3. Philadelphia: Lippincott, 1980. 8 vols.

14. TWO OR MORE VOLUMES OF A MULTIVOLUME WORK

Foner, Philip S., and Ronald L. Lewis, eds. <u>The Black Worker.</u> 8 vols. Philadelphia: Lippincott, 1980.

15. PREFACE, FOREWORD, INTRODUCTION, OR AFTERWORD

Schlesinger, Arthur M., Jr. Introduction. <u>Pioneer Women: Voices from the Kansas Frontier</u>. By Joanna L. Stratton. New York: Simon, 1981. 11-15.

16. ARTICLE IN A REFERENCE WORK

Johnson, Peder J. "Concept Learning." <u>Encyclopedia of Education</u>. 1971.

"Traquair, Sir John Stewart." <u>Encyclopaedia Britannica</u>. 11th ed. 1911.

17. BOOK THAT IS PART OF A SERIES

Moss, Beverly J., ed. <u>Literacy across Communities</u>. Written Language Series 2. Cresskill: Hampton, 1994.

18. REPUBLICATION

Scott, Walter. <u>Kenilworth</u>. 1821. New York: Dodd, 1956.

19. GOVERNMENT DOCUMENT

> United States. Cong. House. <u>Report of the
>   Joint Subcommittee on Reconstruction</u>.
>   39th Cong., 1st sess. H. Rept. 30.
>   1865. New York: Arno, 1969.
> U.S. Bureau of the Census. <u>Historical
>   Statistics of the United States,
>   Colonial Times to 1870</u>. Washington:
>   GPO, 1975.

20. PAMPHLET

> <u>Why Is Central America a Conflict Area?</u>
>   Opposing Viewpoints Pamphlets. St.
>   Paul: Greenhaven, 1984.

21. PUBLISHED PROCEEDINGS OF A CONFERENCE

> Martin, John Steven, and Christine Mason
>   Sutherland, eds. <u>Proceedings of the
>   Canadian Society for the History of
>   Rhetoric</u>. Calgary, Alberta: Canadian
>   Soc. for the History of Rhetoric,
>   1986.

22. PUBLISHER'S IMPRINT

> Rose, Phyllis. <u>Parallel Lives: Five
>   Victorian Marriages</u>. New York: Vintage-
>   Random, 1984.

23. TITLE WITHIN A TITLE

> Gilbert, Stuart. <u>James Joyce's</u> Ulysses. New
>   York: Vintage-Random, 1955.

▌ Periodicals

The basic entry for a periodical includes the following elements: the author's name, last name first; the article title, in quotation marks; and the publication information, including the periodical title (underlined or, if your instructor permits, italicized), the volume and issue numbers (if any), the date of publication, and the page number(s). Each of the three elements ends with a period (which in the article title goes inside the closing quotation marks).

24. ARTICLE IN A JOURNAL PAGINATED BY VOLUME

Norris, Margot. "Narration under a
    Blindfold: Reading Joyce's 'Clay.'"
    PMLA 102 (1987): 206-15.

25. ARTICLE IN A JOURNAL PAGINATED BY ISSUE

Lofty, John. "The Politics at Modernism's
    Funeral." Canadian Journal of Political
    and Social Theory 6.3 (1987): 89-96.

26. ARTICLE IN A MONTHLY MAGAZINE

Weiss, Philip. "The Book Thief: A True Tale
    of Bibliomania." Harper's Jan. 1994:
    37-56.

27. ARTICLE IN A WEEKLY MAGAZINE

Van Biema, David. "Parodies Regained." Time
    21 Mar. 1994: 46.

28. ARTICLE IN A NEWSPAPER

Markoff, John. "Cyberspace's Most Wanted:
    Hacker Eludes F.B.I. Pursuit." New York
    Times 4 July 1994, late ed.: A1+.

29. EDITORIAL OR LETTER TO THE EDITOR

Magee, Doug. "Soldier's Home." Editorial.
    Nation 26 Mar. 1988: 400-01.

30. UNSIGNED ARTICLE

"The Odds of March." Time 15 Apr. 1985:
    20+.

31. REVIEW

Rafferty, Terrence. "Lover in Chief." Rev.
    of The American President, dir. Rob
    Reiner. New Yorker 20 Nov. 1995:
    116-18.

World Wide Web sources

Setting guidelines for regulating and using the information available through the **Internet** is an ongoing
process. Whereas the preceding guidelines are derived
from the *MLA Handbook for Writers of Research Papers,* the
following formats are from the MLA's Web site,
<http://www.mla.org>. The site advises that entries for

sources accessed from the World Wide Web should include all items from the following list that are "relevant and available." Each item except the date of access should be followed by a period.

- *Author.* The name of the author, editor, compiler, or translator, with last name first, and followed by an abbreviation such as *ed.* if appropriate.
- *Title.* The title of the document or subject line of the posting, in quotation marks. If the document is a book, give the book title, underlined, instead of the document title; if it is part of a book, give both titles.
- *Editor, compiler, or translator.* If not cited earlier, preceded by the appropriate abbreviation.
- *Publication information for any print version of the source.*
- *Title of the scholarly project, database, periodical, or Web site,* underlined. For a site with no title, include a description such as *Home page.*
- *Editor of the scholarly project or database*, in normal order, preceded by *Ed.*
- *Identifying number of the source.* The version number (if not part of the title) or, for a journal, the volume, issue, or other identifying number.
- *Date of electronic publication or posting.* Use the date of the most recent update, if known.
- *Discussion list information.* The description *Online posting* and the name of the discussion list.
- *Page, paragraph, or section numbers.*
- *Sponsorship or affiliation.* The name of any institution or organization sponsoring or associated with the site.
- *Date of access.*
- *Address.* The URL, in angle brackets.

32. SCHOLARLY PROJECT

The Orlando Project: An Integrated History of Women's Writing in the British Isles. 1997. U of Alberta. 9 Oct. 1997 <http://www.ualberta.ca/ORLANDO/>.

33. PROFESSIONAL SITE

Digital Future Coalition. Washington, D.C. 8 Oct. 1997 <http://www.dfc.org/dfc/>.

34. PERSONAL SITE

Evanitsky, Olya. Home page. 9 Oct. 1997
   <http://www.cohums.ohio-state.edu
   /english/people/evanitsky.1/>.

35. BOOK

Brewer, F. Cobham. <u>The Dictionary of Phrase
   and Fable</u>. London, 1894. Hypertext
   edition. <u>Bibliomania: Data Text
   Publishing Ltd</u>. 1996. 9 Oct. 1997
   <http://www.bibliomania.com/Reference
   /PhraseAndFable/>.

36. POEM

Dickinson, Emily. "The Grass." <u>Poems/Emily
   Dickinson</u>. Boston, 1891. <u>Humanities
   Text Initiative American Verse
   Collection</u>. Ed. Nancy Kushigian. 1995.
   U of Michigan. 9 Oct. 1997 <http://www
   .planet.net/pkrisxle/emily/poemsOnline
   .html>.

37. ARTICLE IN A REFERENCE DATABASE

"Jonestown." <u>Collier's Encyclopedia</u>. 1996.
   p. 625 (2). Cogito Student Research.
   10 Oct. 1997 <http://www.cogito.com
   /cgi-bin/cgi_app1.cgi/5/8/17585
   /10?xrn_1>.

38. ARTICLE IN A JOURNAL

Browning, Tonya. "Embedded Visuals: Student
   Design in Web Spaces." <u>Kairos: A
   Journal for Teachers of Writing</u> 2.1
   (1997): hypertext. 9 Oct. 1997
   <http://english.ttu.edu/kairos/current
   /toc.html>.

39. ARTICLE IN A MAGAZINE

Gawande, Atul. "Drowsy Docs." <u>Slate</u> 9 Oct.
   1997. 10 Oct. 1997 <http://www.slate
   .com/MedicalExaminer/97-10-09
   /MedicalExaminer.asp>.

40. POSTING TO A DISCUSSION LIST (LISTSERV OR NEWSGROUP)

```
Stegall, Nancy. "Web Publishing and
     Censorship." Online posting. 2 Feb.
     1997. ACW: The Alliance for Com-
     puters and Writing Discussion List.
     10 Oct. 1997 <http://english.ttu
     .edu/acw-l/archive.htm>.
```

41. FTP (FILE TRANSFER PROTOCOL), TELNET, OR GOPHER SITE

These sites are cited the same way as sites accessed directly except that *ftp, telnet,* or *gopher* is substituted for http at the beginning of the URL.

```
Korn, Peter. "How Much Does Breast Cancer
     Really Cost?" Self Oct. 1994. 5 May
     1997 <gopher://nysernet.org:70/00/BCIC
     /Sources/SELF/94/how-much>.
```

▓ Other Internet sources

Formats for the following four kinds of sources, for which the MLA does not yet offer guidelines, are from *Online! A Reference Guide to Using Internet Sources,* by Andrew Harnack and Eugene Kleppinger. The basic entry for all four should include the following elements in the order listed:

- *Author.* The author's name and **email address** (in **angle brackets**), if given, with last name first. End with a period.
- *Title.* The title of the document or subject line of the message or posting, in quotation marks. End with a period inside the closing quotation marks.
- *Publication date.* End with a period.
- *Date of access.*
- *Address.* The URL, in angle brackets, or the path followed to locate the site or file. End with a period.

42. UNARCHIVED LISTSERV MESSAGE. The date of access is followed by the address of the listserv, in angle brackets.

```
Lackey, Noel. <eeinly@ath.ericsson.se>
     "From Clare to Here." 30 Jan. 1995.
     1 May 1997 <nanci@world.std.com>.
```

43. UNARCHIVED NEWSGROUP MESSAGE. If the author is unknown, cite the email address first. After the date of
access, give the name of the newsgroup in angle brackets.

```
Sand, Paul. <psand@unh.edu> "Java Disabled
     by Default in Linux Netscape." 20 Apr.
     1996. 10 May 1996 <keokuk.unh.edu>.
```

44. EMAIL. Include the kind of communication (*Personal
email, Distribution list*), after the publication date.

```
Talbot, Casey J. <ctalbot@pop.interport.net>
     "Do This." 26 Jan. 1996. Personal
     email. 10 May 1996.
```

45. SYNCHRONOUS COMMUNICATION. To cite MOOs, MUDs,
and IRCs, provide the speaker's name and site name;
the title of the event, if appropriate, in quotation marks;
and its date. List the type of communication (*Group discussion, Personal interview*) if necessary and either the
URL or command line directions.

```
LambdaMOO. "Seminar Discussion on Neti-
     quette." 28 May 1996. 28 May 1996
     <telnet://lambda.parc.xerox.edu:8888>.
```

Other kinds of sources

46. CD-ROM, PERIODICALLY REVISED. Include the author's
name, if given, and publication information for print
source, if any: title; volume and issue, if appropriate;
date; and page numbers. (If the material is not available
in print, list only the title and, if given, the date.)
Include the title of the electronic database medium (*CD-
ROM*), name of the company producing it, and electronic publication date: month and year, if possible.

```
Natchez, Gladys. "Frida Kahlo and Diego
     Rivera: The Transformation of
     Catastrophe to Creativity."
     Psychotherapy-Patient 4.1 (1987): 153-
     74. PsycLIT. CD-ROM. SilverPlatter.
     Nov. 1994.
```

47. CD-ROM, DISKETTE, OR MAGNETIC TAPE, SINGLE ISSUE

```
"Poem." The Oxford English Dictionary. 2nd
     ed. CD-ROM. Oxford: Oxford UP, 1992.
```

48. COMMERCIAL ONLINE DATABASE SERVICE. Include the publication information: title; volume and issue, if appropriate; date; and page numbers. (If the material is not available in print, list only the title of the material and, if given, the date.) Include the title of the database, medium *(Online)*, name of the computer service, and date of access: day, month, and year.

> Johnson, Lawrence B. "Television Grows a
>   Brain." New York Times 16 May 1996,
>   late ed.: C1+. New York Times Online.
>   Online. America Online. 30 Aug. 1996.

49. UNPUBLISHED DISSERTATION

> LeCourt, Donna. "The Self in Motion: The
>   Status of the (Student) Subject in
>   Composition Studies." Diss. Ohio State
>   U, 1993.

50. PUBLISHED DISSERTATION

> Botts, Roderic C. Influences in the Teaching
>   of English, 1917-1935: An Illusion of
>   Progress. Diss. Northeastern U, 1970.
>   Ann Arbor: UMI, 1971. 71-1799.

51. INTERVIEW

> Schorr, Daniel. Interview. Weekend Edition.
>   Natl. Public Radio. WEVO, Concord. 26
>   Mar. 1988.
> Merget, Astrid. Telephone Interview. 16 Mar.
>   1994.

52. LETTER

> Frost, Robert. "Letter to Editor of the
>   Independent." 28 Mar. 1894. Selected
>   Letters of Robert Frost. Ed. Lawrance
>   Thompson. New York: Holt, 1964. 19.
> Moller, Willie. Letter to the author. 10
>   Sept. 1994.

53. FILM OR VIDEOTAPE

> The Night of the Hunter. Dir. Charles
>   Laughton. Perf. Robert Mitchum, Shelley
>   Winters, and Lillian Gish. United
>   Artists, 1955.

54. TELEVISION OR RADIO PROGRAM

<u>Hill Street Blues</u>. Writ. Michael Kozoll and
        Stephen Bochco. Perf. Daniel J.
        Travanti, Joe Spano, and Charles Haid.
        NBC. WNBC, New York. 15 Jan. 1981.

55. RECORDING

Grieg, Edvard. Concerto in A-minor, op. 16.
        Cond. Eugene Ormandy. Philadelphia
        Orch. RCA, 1989.

56. WORK OF ART

Kahlo, Frida. <u>Self-Portrait with Cropped
        Hair</u>. Museum of Modern Art, New York.

57. LECTURE OR SPEECH

Stern, Virginia. "Sir Stephen Powle as
        Adventurer in the Virginia Company."
        Seminar on the Renaissance. Columbia
        University. New York, 15 Oct. 1985.

58. PERFORMANCE

<u>Frankie and Johnny in the Clair de Lune</u>. By
        Terrence McNally. Dir. Paul Benedict.
        Westside Arts Theater, New York. 18
        Jan. 1988.

59. MAP OR CHART

Pennsylvania. Map. Chicago: Rand. 1985.

60. CARTOON

Trudeau, Garry. "Doonesbury." Cartoon.
        <u>Philadelphia Inquirer</u> 9 Mar. 1988: 37.

61. ADVERTISEMENT

NordicTrack. Advertisement. <u>Cooking Light</u>
        Jan.-Feb. 1995: 9.

32d Manuscript format

The MLA recommends the following format for the
manuscript of a research paper. Your instructor may
have different preferences, however, so always check
before preparing your final draft.

Heading and title. The MLA does not require a title page, but your instructor may require one. If so, follow the format shown on page 154. Center the title about one-third of the way down the page. Center your name, preceded by the word *by*, two double spaces below the title. Two double spaces below your name, center the course name and number, the instructor's name, and the date, double-spacing between each item.

If you are not using a title page, type each of the following items on a separate line on the first page, beginning one inch from the top and flush with the left margin: your name, the instructor's name, the course name and number, and the date. Double-space between each item; then double-space again and center the title, double-spacing between lines if necessary. Double-space once more between the title and the beginning of the text. An example is shown on page 155.

Margins, spacing, and pagination. Leave one-inch margins at the top and bottom and on both sides of each page. Double-space the entire text, including set-off quotations, notes, and the list of works cited. Indent the first line of a paragraph one-half inch, or five spaces if you are using a typewriter. Indent set-off quotations one inch, or ten spaces, from the left margin. Type your last name and the page number on each page, one-half inch below the top and flush with the right margin.

The "Works Cited" list. Start the list of works cited on a new page at the end of the paper and after any notes. Number each page, continuing the page numbers of the text. Center the heading an inch from the top of the page; do not underline or italicize it or enclose it in quotation marks. Double-space between the heading and the first entry, and double-space the entire list. Start each entry flush with the left margin; indent any subsequent lines one-half inch, or five typewriter spaces. An example of this format is shown on page 156.

Alphabetize the list by the authors' (or editors') last names. If a work has no author or editor, alphabetize it by the first word of the title, disregarding *A*, *An*, or *The*. If a list has two or more works by the same author, use the author's name only in the first entry; in subsequent entries, instead of the name use three hyphens followed by a period. Alphabetize the works by title.

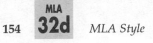

SAMPLE MLA TITLE PAGE

Frida Kahlo: More Than a Life

by Daniel Taffe

English 231
Professor Connors
15 May 1996

SAMPLE MLA FIRST PAGE

Daniel Taffe

Professor Connors

English 231

15 May 1997

Frida Kahlo: More Than a Life

Who is Frida Kahlo?
Ten or fifteen years ago,
few people would have known.
Today, however, Kahlo is
being recognized as a major
figure in twentieth-century
art. Her paintings, primarily self-portraits, con-
tinue to gain popularity
in the United States and

Fig. 1. "Self
Portrait," Frida
Kahlo, from <u>The
Original Frida
Kahlo Home Page</u>

in her native Mexico. <u>My Birth</u>, for example, was recently purchased by Madonna, and
<u>Self-Portrait with Loose Hair</u> sold in 1991
for $1.65 million, a record price for any
Latin American artist (Plagens et al. 54).

Much of the scholarship on Kahlo and
her art has been produced by Hayden
Herrera, author of <u>Frida: A Biography of
Frida Kahlo</u> and numerous periodical articles
about the artist. Indeed, it is nearly
impossible to read anything about Kahlo
without encountering a reference to
Herrera's research. Although her biography
was published almost thirty years after
Kahlo's death, her information comes, as
Angela Carter notes in her review, from

SAMPLE MLA LIST OF WORKS CITED

Works Cited

Carter, Angela. "A Ribbon around a Bomb."
    Rev. of <u>Frida: A Biography of Frida
    Kahlo</u>, by Hayden Herrera. <u>New Statesman
    & Society</u> 12 May 1989: 32-33.

Delavoy, Robert L. <u>Bosch</u>. Trans. Stuart
    Gilbert. Cleveland: World, 1984.

Gardner, Helen. <u>Art through the Ages</u>. 7th
    ed. Vol. 2. New York: Harcourt, 1980.
    3 vols.

Hartt, Frederick. <u>History of Italian
    Renaissance Art</u>. Englewood Cliffs:
    Prentice, 1981.

Herrera, Hayden. <u>Frida: A Biography of
    Frida Kahlo</u>. New York: Harper, 1983.

Honeywell, Richard. Telephone interview.
    15 Apr. 1991.

Janson, H. W. <u>Key Monuments in the History
    of Art</u>. New York: Abrams, 1959.

Jenkins, Nicholas. "Calla Lilies and Kahlos:
    The Frida Kahlo Museum, Mexico City."
    <u>ARTnews</u> Mar. 1989: 104-05.

<u>The Life of Frida Kahlo</u>. 13 Oct. 1997
    <http://www.eccs.uic.edu/~ngalindo
    /frida1@html>.

Natchez, Gladys. "Frida Kahlo and Diego
    Rivera: The Transformation of
    Catastrophe to Creativity."
    <u>Psychotherapy-Patient</u> 4.1 (1987): 153-
    74. PsycINFO. Online. Dialog. 12 July
    1994.

33

APA Style

This chapter discusses the basic formats prescribed by the American Psychological Association (APA), guidelines that are widely used in the social sciences. For further reference, consult the *Publication Manual of the American Psychological Association*, fourth edition, 1994.

33a In-text citations

APA style requires parenthetical citations in the text to document quotations, paraphrases, summaries, and other material from a source. These in-text citations correspond to full bibliographic entries in a list of references at the end of the text.

Directory to APA style for in-text citations

1. AUTHOR NAMED IN A SIGNAL PHRASE. Generally, use the author's name in a signal phrase to introduce the cited material, and place the date, in parentheses, immediately after the author's name. For a quotation, the page number, preceded by *p.*, appears in parentheses after the quotation. For electronic texts or other works without page numbers, paragraph numbers may be used instead. For a long, set-off quotation, position the page reference in parentheses two spaces after the final punctuation.

```
Key (1983) has argued that the placement of
women in print advertisements is subliminal-
ly important.
```

```
As Briggs (1970) observed, parents play an
important role in building their children's
self-esteem because "children value them-
selves to the degree that they have been
valued" (p. 14).
```

2. AUTHOR NAMED IN PARENTHESES. When you do not mention the author in a signal phrase, give the name and the date, separated by a comma, in parentheses at the end of the cited material.

```
One study has found that only 68% of let-
ters received by editors were actually pub-
lished (Renfro, 1979).
```

3. TWO AUTHORS. Use both names in all citations. Use *and* in a signal phrase, but use an ampersand (&) in parentheses.

```
Murphy and Orkow (1985) reached somewhat
different conclusions by designing a study
that was less dependent on subjective judg-
ment than were previous studies.
```

```
A recent study that was less dependent on
subjective judgment resulted in conclusions
somewhat different from those of previous
studies (Murphy & Orkow, 1985).
```

4. THREE TO FIVE AUTHORS. List all the authors' names for the first reference. In subsequent references, use just the first author's name plus *et al.*

```
Belenky, Clinchy, Goldberger, and Tarule
(1986) have suggested that many women rely
on observing and listening to others as
ways of learning about themselves.
```

```
From this experience, observed Belenky et
al. (1986), women learn to listen to them-
selves think, a step toward self-expression.
```

5. SIX OR MORE AUTHORS. Use only the first author's name and *et al.* in *every* citation.

```
As Mueller el al. (1980) demonstrated,
television holds the potential for distort-
ing and manipulating consumers as free-
willed decision makers.
```

6. ORGANIZATION AS AUTHOR. If the name of an organization or a corporation is long, spell it out the first time, followed by an abbreviation in brackets. In later citations, use the abbreviation only.

FIRST CITATION   `(Centers for Disease Control`
                        `[CDC], 1990)`
LATER CITATION   `(CDC, 1990)`

7. UNKNOWN AUTHOR. Use the title or its first few words in a signal phrase or in parentheses.

> `The school profiles for the county substan-`
> `tiated this trend (`<u>`Guide to Secondary`</u>
> <u>`Schools,`</u> `1983).`

8. AUTHORS WITH THE SAME LAST NAME. If your list of references includes works by different authors with the same last name, include the authors' initials in each citation.

> `G. Jones (1984) conducted the groundbreaking`
> `study of retroviruses.`

9. TWO OR MORE SOURCES IN THE SAME CITATION. List sources by different authors in alphabetical order by author's last name, separated by semicolons: (Chodorow, 1978; Gilligan, 1982). List works by the same author in chronological order, separated by commas: (Gilligan, 1977, 1982).

10. SPECIFIC PARTS OF A SOURCE. Use abbreviations (*chap.*, *p.*, and so on) in a parenthetical citation to name the part of a work you are citing.

> `Montgomery (1988, chap. 9) argued that his`
> `research yielded the opposite results.`

11. PERSONAL COMMUNICATION. Cite any personal letters, email, electronic bulletin-board correspondence, telephone conversations, or interviews by giving the person's initial(s) and last name, the identification *personal communication,* and the date.

> `J. L. Morin (personal communication, October`
> `14, 1990) supported with new evidence the`
> `claims made in her article.`

33b Content notes

APA style allows you to use content notes to expand or supplement your text. Indicate such notes in your text by superscript numerals. Type the notes themselves on a separate page after the last page of the text, under the heading *Footnotes*, centered at the top of the page. Double-space all entries. Indent the first line of each note five to seven spaces, but begin subsequent lines at the left margin.

SUPERSCRIPT NUMERAL IN TEXT

> The age of the children involved was an important factor in the selection of items for the questionnaire.[1]

FOOTNOTE

> [1]Marjorie Youngston Forman and William Cole of the Child Study Team provided great assistance.

33c List of references

The alphabetical list of the sources cited in your document is called *References*. (If your instructor asks that you list everything you have read as background—not just the sources you cite—call the list *Bibliography*.) Following are some guidelines for preparing entries for such a list.

For print sources, APA style specifies the treatment and placement of four basic elements—author, publication date, title, and publication information.

- *Author.* List all authors last name first, and use only initials for first and middle names. Separate the names of multiple authors with commas, and use an ampersand before the last author's name.

- *Publication date.* Enclose the date in parentheses. Use only the year for books and journals; use the year, a comma, and the month or month and day for magazines. Do not abbreviate.

- *Title.* Underline or italicize titles and subtitles of books and periodicals. Do not enclose titles of articles in

quotation marks. For books and articles, capitalize only the first word of the title and subtitle and any proper nouns or proper adjectives. Capitalize all major words in a periodical title.

- *Publication information.* For a book, list the city of publication (and the country or postal abbreviation for the state if the city is unfamiliar), a colon, and the publisher's name, dropping *Inc., Co.,* or *Publishers.* For a periodical, follow the periodical title with a comma, the volume number (underlined or italicized), the issue number (if provided) in parentheses and followed by a comma, and the inclusive page numbers of the article. For newspaper articles and for articles or chapters in books, include the abbreviation *p.* ("page") or *pp.* ("pages").

The following APA-style examples appear in the "hanging indent" format, in which the first line aligns on the left and the subsequent lines indent one-half inch or five spaces. Unless your instructor suggests otherwise, it is the format we recommend. Note, however, that for manuscripts submitted to journals, APA requires the reverse (first lines indented, subsequent lines flush left), assuming that the citations will be converted by a typesetting system to a hanging indent.

Directory to APA style for a list of references

Books

1. ONE AUTHOR

Lightman, A. (1993). <u>Einstein's dreams.</u> New
    York: Warner Books.

2. TWO OR MORE AUTHORS

Newcombe, F., & Ratcliffe, G. (1978).
    <u>Defining females: The nature of women
    in society.</u> New York: Wiley.

3. ORGANIZATION AS AUTHOR

Institute of Financial Education. (1983).
    <u>Income property lending.</u> Homewood, IL:
    Dow Jones-Irwin.

Use the word *Author* as the publisher when the organization is both the author and the publisher.

American Chemical Society. (1978). <u>Handbook for authors of papers in American Chemical Society publications.</u> Washington, DC: Author.

4. UNKNOWN AUTHOR

<u>National Geographic atlas of the world.</u> (1988). Washington, DC: National Geographic Society.

5. EDITOR

Solomon, A. P. (Ed.). (1980). <u>The prospective city.</u> Cambridge, MA: MIT Press.

6. SELECTION IN A BOOK WITH AN EDITOR

West, C. (1992). The postmodern crisis of the black intellectuals. In L. Grossberg, C. Nelson, & P. Treichler (Eds.), <u>Cultural studies</u> (pp. 689-705). New York: Routledge.

7. TRANSLATION

Durkheim, E. (1957). <u>Suicide</u> (J. A. Spaulding & G. Simpson, Trans.). Glencoe, IL: Free Press of Glencoe.

8. EDITION OTHER THAN THE FIRST

Kohn, M. L. (1977). <u>Class and conformity: A study in values</u> (2nd ed.). Chicago: University of Chicago Press.

9. ONE VOLUME OF A MULTIVOLUME WORK

Baltes, P., & Brim, O. G. (Eds.). (1980). <u>Life-span development and behavior</u> (Vol. 3). New York: Basic Books.

10. ARTICLE IN A REFERENCE WORK

Ochs, E. (1989). Language acquisition. In <u>International encyclopedia of communications</u> (Vol. 2, pp. 390-393). New York: Oxford University Press.

If no author is listed, begin with the title.

11. **REPUBLICATION**

Piaget, J. (1952). <u>The language and thought
of the child.</u> London: Routledge &
Kegan Paul. (Original work published
1932.)

12. **GOVERNMENT DOCUMENT**

U.S. Bureau of the Census. (1975).
<u>Historical statistics of the United
States, colonial times to 1870.</u>
Washington, DC: U.S. Government
Printing Office.

13. **TWO OR MORE WORKS BY THE SAME AUTHOR.** List the works
in chronological order. Repeat the author's name in
each entry.

Macrorie, K. (1968). <u>Writing to be read.</u>
New York: Hayden.
Macrorie, K. (1970). <u>Uptaught.</u> New York:
Hayden.

Periodicals

14. **ARTICLE IN A JOURNAL PAGINATED BY VOLUME**

Shuy, R. (1981). A holistic view of language. <u>Research in the Teaching of
English, 15,</u> 101-111.

15. **ARTICLE IN A JOURNAL PAGINATED BY ISSUE**

Maienza, J. G. (1986). The superintendency:
Characteristics of access for men and
women. <u>Educational Administration
Quarterly, 22</u> (4), 59-79.

16. **ARTICLE IN A MAGAZINE**

Gralla, P. (1994, April). How to enter
cyberspace. <u>PC Computing,</u> 60-62.

17. **ARTICLE IN A NEWSPAPER**

Browne, M. W. (1988, April 26). Lasers for
the battlefield raise concern for eye-
sight. <u>New York Times,</u> pp. C1, C8.

18. EDITORIAL OR LETTER TO THE EDITOR

> Russell, J. S. (1994, March 27). The language instinct [Letter to the editor]. <u>New York Times Book Review</u>, 27.

19. UNSIGNED ARTICLE

> What sort of person reads <u>Creative Computing</u>? (1985, August). <u>Creative Computing</u>, 8, 10.

20. REVIEW

> Larmore, C. E. (1989). [Review of the book <u>Patterns of moral complexity</u>]. <u>Ethics</u>, 99, 423-426.

21. PUBLISHED INTERVIEW

> McCarthy, E. (1968, December 24). [Interview with <u>Boston Globe</u> Washington staff]. <u>Boston Globe</u>, p. B27.

22. TWO OR MORE WORKS BY THE SAME AUTHOR IN THE SAME YEAR. List works alphabetically by title, and place lowercase letters (*a, b,* etc.) after the dates.

> Murray, F. B. (1983a). Equilibration as cognitive conflict. <u>Developmental Review</u>, 3, 54-61.
> Murray, F. B. (1983b). Learning and development through social interaction. In L. Liben (Ed.), <u>Piaget and the foundations of knowledge</u> (pp. 176-201). Hillsdale, NJ: Erlbaum.

Electronic sources

In the 1994 edition of its *Publication Manual*, the APA acknowledges that set standards for referencing online information have yet to emerge. However, the APA offers general guidelines for referencing electronic sources (for example, CD-ROMs) and recommends that writers follow standard APA format for listing the author, date, and title of electronic sources. The date should consist of the year of publication or of the most recent update, if available. If the publication year is not available, use the exact date of the search that turned up the item. Following the title, in brackets, put the kind of electronic source (*CD-ROM*).

23. CD-ROM ABSTRACT

> Natchez, G. (1987). Frida Kahlo and Diego
>   Rivera: The transformation of catastro-
>   phe to creativity [CD-ROM].
>   <u>Psychotherapy-Patient, 8,</u> 153-174.
>   Abstract from: SilverPlatter File:
>   PsycLIT Item: 76-11344

24. MATERIAL FROM AN INFORMATION SERVICE OR DATABASE

> Belenky, M. F. (1984). The role of deafness
>   in the moral development of hearing
>   impaired children. In A. Areson & J.
>   De Caro (Eds.), <u>Teaching, learning and
>   development.</u> Rochester, NY: National
>   Institute for the Deaf. (ERIC Document
>   Reproduction Service NO. ED 248 646)

25. SOFTWARE OR COMPUTER PROGRAM

> SuperCalc3 Release 2.1 [Computer program].
>   (1985). San Jose, CA: Computer
>   Associates, Micro Products Division.

Internet sources

With the exception of guidelines for citing some kinds of electronic sources, such as an **online** journal article available via **email** or **FTP**, the APA's *Publication Manual* does not have guidelines for citing **World Wide Web** sites and other **Internet** sources. The following formats—adapted from APA style to include Internet sources—are from *Online! A Reference Guide for Using Internet Sources*, by Andrew Harnack and Eugene Kleppinger.

The basic entry for most sources you access via the Internet should include the following elements:

- *Author.* The author's name, if available, last name first.
- *Date of publication.* The year of Internet publication or the year of the most recent update, if available, in parentheses followed by a period.
- *Title.* The title of the document or **subject line** of the message, in quotation marks. End with a period inside the quotation marks.
- *Address.* The **URL**, in **angle brackets**, or other retrieval information.
- *Date of access.* In parentheses, followed by a period.

26. WORLD WIDE WEB SITE. After the document title, include the title of the complete work, if applicable, underlined.

```
Mullins, B. (1995). Introduction to Robert
     Hass. Readings in Contemporary Poetry
     at Dia Center for the Arts.
     <http://www.diacenter.org/prg/poetry/95
     -96/interhass.html> (1997, April 24).
Shade, L. R. (1993). Gender issues in com-
     puter networking. <http://www.mit.edu
     :8001/people/sorokin/women/lrs.html>
     (1996, May 28).
```

27. LINKAGE DATA. To cite a file or document accessed through a link with a source document, provide information on both the cited document and the source. After the title of the document, include the abbreviation *Lkd.* and the title of the source document, underlined. Then give additional linkage details, if applicable, indicated by *at,* and the source's URL.

```
Williams, T. T. The politics of place. Lkd.
     Insight & Outlook: A Program of Ideas,
     at "Transcripts." <http://www.west.net
     /~insight/> (1997, May 1).
```

28. FTP (FILE TRANSFER PROTOCOL) SITE. After the title of the document, use the abbreviation *ftp* followed by the address of the FTP site, with no closing punctuation, and the full path to follow to find the document, with no closing punctuation.

```
Altar, T. W. (1993). Vitamin B12 and veg-
     ans. ftp wiretap.spies.com Library
     /Article/Food/b12.txt (1996, May 28).
```

29. TELNET SITE. After the title of the document, include the title of the full work, if applicable, underlined and followed by a period. Then include the word *telnet,* followed by the complete telnet address, with no closing punctuation, and directions to access the document.

```
Aquatic Conservation Network. (n.d.). About
     the Aquatic Conservation Network.
     National Capital Freenet. telnet
     freenet.carleton.ca login as guest, go
     acn, press 1 (1996, May 28).
```

30. GOPHER SITE. Include any print publication information, underlined where appropriate. Then give the URL,
or list the word *gopher,* the site name, and the path followed to access information, with slashes to indicate
menu selections.

> Korn, P. How much does breast cancer really
>   cost? <u>Self</u>, October 1994. <gopher
>   ://nysernet.org:70/00/BCIC/Sources/SELF
>   /94/how-much> (1997, May 5).

31. LISTSERV MESSAGE. Include the author's email address,
in angle brackets. The subject line from the posting is followed by the address of the listserv, in angle brackets.

> Lackey, N. <eeinly@ath.ericsson.se> (1995,
>   January 30). From Clare to here.
>   <nanci@world.std.com> (1997, May 1).

To cite a file that can be retrieved from a list's server or
Web address, after the publication date, include the
address of the listserv, in angle brackets, and the
address or URL for the list's archive, indicated by *via*, in
angle brackets.

> Lackey, N. <eeinly@ath.ericsson.se> (1995,
>   January 30). From Clare to here.
>   <nanci@world.std.com> via <http://www
>   .rahul.net/frankf/Nancy/archives/95130
>   .html> (1997, May 1).

32. NEWSGROUP MESSAGE. Include the author's email
address (if known), enclosed in angle brackets. The subject line from the posting is followed by the name of the
newsgroup, in angle brackets.

> Sand, P. <psand@unh.edu> (1996, April 20).
>   Java disabled by default in Linux
>   Netscape. <keokuk.unh.edu> (1996,
>   May 10).

33. EMAIL MESSAGE. The APA's *Publication Manual* dis-
courages including email in a list of references, and
suggests citing email only in text. It is good practice,
however, to document email messages in the list of references, especially when their content is scholarly. In
citing email correspondence, include the author's email
address, in angle brackets, after the author's name.

After the subject line from the posting, include the kind of communication (*Personal email, Office communication*) in square brackets.

```
Talbot, C. J. <ctalbot@pop.interport.net>
    (1996, January 26). Do this [Personal
    email]. (1996, May 10).
```

34. SYNCHRONOUS COMMUNICATION. To cite postings in MOOs, MUDs, and IRCs, provide the speaker's name, if known, or the name of the site; the date of the event, in parentheses; its title, if appropriate; and the kind of communication (*Group discussion, Personal interview*), if necessary, in square brackets. Include the URL or command-line directions and date of access, in parentheses.

```
LambdaMOO. (1996, May 28). Seminar discus-
    sion on netiquette. <telnet://lambda
    .parc.xerox.edu:8888> (1996, May 28).
```

Other sources

35. TECHNICAL OR RESEARCH REPORTS AND WORKING PAPERS

```
Wilson, K. S. (1986). Palenque: An interac-
    tive multimedia optical disc prototype
    for children (Working Paper No. 2).
    New York: Center for Children and
    Technology, Bank Street College of
    Education.
```

36. PAPER PRESENTED AT A MEETING OR SYMPOSIUM, UNPUBLISHED. Cite the month of the meeting, if it is available.

```
Engelbart, D. C. (1970, April). Intellectual
    implications of multi-access computing.
    Paper presented at the meeting of the
    Interdisciplinary Conference on Multi-
    Access Computer Networks, Washington,
    DC.
```

37. DISSERTATION, UNPUBLISHED

```
Leverenz, C. A. (1994). Collaboration and
    difference in the composition class-
    room. Unpublished doctoral disserta-
    tion, Ohio State University, Columbus.
```

38. POSTER SESSION

> Ulman, H. L., & Walborn, E. (1993, March).
>   <u>Hypertext in the composition classroom.</u>
>   Poster session presented at the Annual
>   Conference on College Composition and
>   Communication, San Diego.

39. FILM OR VIDEOTAPE

> Hitchcock, A. (Producer & Director). (1954).
>   <u>Rear window</u> [Film]. Los Angeles: MGM.

40. TELEVISION PROGRAM, SINGLE EPISODE. Begin with the names of the script writers, and give the name of the director, in parentheses, after the episode title.

> Kuttner, P. K., Moran, C., & Scholl, E.
>   (1994, July 19). Passin' it on
>   (W. Chamberlain, Executive Director).
>   In D. Zaccardi (Executive Producer),
>   <u>P.O.V.</u> New York: Public Broadcasting
>   Service.

41. RECORDING. For recordings by an artist other than the writer, begin with the writer's name, followed by the date of copyright. Give the recording date if it is different from the copyright date.

> Colvin, S. (1991). I don't know why.
>   [Recorded by A. Krauss and Union
>   Station]. On <u>Every time you say
>   goodbye</u> [Cassette]. Cambridge, MA:
>   Rounder Records. (1992)

33d Manuscript format

The following guidelines for the format of college papers using APA style are adapted from the APA's recommendations for preparing manuscripts for publication in APA journals. Your instructor may have different preferences, so always check before preparing your final draft.

Title page. Center the title about halfway down the title page. Below it, center your name, the instructor's name, the course name and number, and the date. Double-space between each item. In the top right-hand

corner, begin the page numbering of the paper by typing a short version (two or three words) of the title, skipping five spaces, and typing the number *1*. The title and page number should be about one-half inch from the top of the page and at least one inch from the right side. A sample title page is shown on page 172.

On the first page of the text of the paper, type the full title again, centered one inch below the top. Double-space, and then begin typing the text. A sample first text page is shown on page 173.

■ **Margins, spacing, and pagination.** Leave margins of at least one inch at the top and bottom and on both sides of each page. Do not justify the right margin. Double-space the entire text, including headings, set-off quotations, content notes, and the list of references. Indent five to seven spaces from the left margin for the first line of a paragraph and all lines of a quotation of forty words or longer. Type the short title and the page number in the upper right-hand corner of each page, in the same position as on the title page.

■ **Headings.** Headings are used within the text of many papers in APA style. In college papers and others with only one or two levels of headings, center the main headings; underline or italicize the subheadings and position them flush with the left margin. Capitalize all major words—articles, short prepositions, and coordinating conjunctions are not capitalized unless they are the first word or follow a colon.

■ **List of references.** Start the list of references on a new page at the end of the paper. Identify each page with the short title and page number, continuing the numbering of the text. Center the title *References* one inch from the top, and double-space between the title and the first entry. Unless your instructor specifies otherwise, type the first line of each entry flush with the left margin, and indent any subsequent lines five to seven spaces. An example of this format is shown on page 174.

Alphabetize the list by the authors' (or editors') last names. If a work has no author or editor, alphabetize it by the first word of the title, disregarding *A, An,* or *The.* If the list includes two or more works by the same author, see the examples on pages 164 and 165.

SAMPLE APA TITLE PAGE

Early Detection   1

Early Detection of Child Abuse

Laura Brannon

Professor Phelan

Psychology 101

May 20, 1995

SAMPLE APA FIRST TEXT PAGE

Early Detection of Child Abuse

There is no simple one-word answer to the question of what causes child abuse. The abuse of children results from a complex interaction among parent, child, and environmental factors. This complexity does not necessarily mean, however, that potential victims and abusers cannot be identified before serious damage is done. Some researchers have examined methods of detecting potential or actual child abuse.

Prediction of Child Abuse: Interviews

In a study by Altemeier, O'Connor, Vietze, Sandler, and Sherrod (1984), 1,400 women between 9 and 40 weeks pregnant were interviewed to test their abusive tendencies. Four researchers were present (with an interrater agreement of 90% or better). The Maternal History Interview included questions about the mother's own childhood, self-image, support from others, parenting philosophy, attitudes towards pregnancy, and health-related problems (including substance abuse). Maternal and paternal stresses during the preceding year were measured with a modified Life Stress Inventory. Any information not included in the standard interview but felt by the researchers to make the mother at high risk for abuse of her child

SAMPLE APA LIST OF REFERENCES

References

Altemeier, W. A., O'Connor, S., Vietze, P.,
    Sandler, H., & Sherrod, K. (1984).
    Prediction of child abuse: A prospec-
    tive study of feasibility. <u>Child Abuse
    and Neglect: The International Journal,
    8,</u> 393-400.

Johnson, C. F., & Showers, J. (1985).
    Injury variables in child abuse. <u>Child
    Abuse and Neglect: The International
    Journal, 9,</u> 207-215.

Murphy, S., Orkow, B., & Nicola, R. (1985).
    Prenatal prediction of child abuse and
    neglect: A prospective study. <u>Child
    Abuse and Neglect: The International
    Journal, 9,</u> 225-235.

34

Chicago Style

The fourteenth edition of the style guide of the University of Chicago Press, published in 1993 and called *The Chicago Manual of Style*, covers two systems of documentation at great length. One of them, discussed below as "Chicago style," has long been used in history as well as other areas of the arts and humanities. For further reference, consult *The Chicago Manual* or the following much shorter volume intended for student writers:

> Turabian, Kate L. *A Manual for Writers of Term Papers, Theses, and Dissertations.* 6th ed. Rev. John Grossman and Alice Bennett. Chicago: U of Chicago P, 1996.

34a In-text citations and notes

Chicago style uses superscript numbers (¹) to mark citations in the text. Citations are numbered sequentially throughout the text and correspond to notes that contain either publication information about the sources cited or explanatory or supplemental material that the writer chooses not to include in the main text. The sources are often also listed in a bibliography at the end of the text.

In the text, the superscript number for each note is placed near the cited material—at the end of the relevant quotation, sentence, clause, or phrase. The number is typed after any punctuation mark except the dash, and no space is left between the superscript and the preceding letter or punctuation mark.

IN THE TEXT

    As Luftig notes, true friendship between
    the sexes may simply not be possible.[1]

IN THE NOTE

        1. Victor Luftig, <u>Seeing Together:
    Friendship between the Sexes in English
    Writing</u> (Palo Alto, Calif.: Stanford
    University Press, 1993), 1.

The first note for any source gives full information about the source, whereas subsequent notes are shortened. Here are some guidelines for the format of notes in Chicago style.

Directory to Chicago style for notes

SUBSEQUENT NOTES FOR PREVIOUSLY CITED SOURCES

Books

A note for a book typically includes four elements, separated by commas: the author's name, in normal order; the title and subtitle, underlined or italicized; the publication, including the city of publication, a shortened form of the publisher's name, and the date, all enclosed in parentheses; and the page number(s) to which the note refers, followed by a period.

1. ONE AUTHOR

    1. Hayden Herrera, <u>Frida: A Biography of Frida Kahlo</u> (New York: Harper and Row, 1983), 356.

2. MORE THAN ONE AUTHOR

    2. John T. McNeill and Helena M. Gamer, <u>Medieval Handbooks of Penance</u> (New York: Octagon Books, 1965), 139.

3. UNKNOWN AUTHOR

    3. <u>The New York Times Atlas of the World</u> (New York: New York Times Books, 1980), 67.

4. EDITOR

    4. C. Vann Woodward, ed., <u>Mary Chesnut's Civil War</u> (New Haven, Conn.: Yale University Press, 1981), 214.

5. SELECTION IN AN ANTHOLOGY, OR CHAPTER IN A BOOK, WITH AN EDITOR

    5. Mary Gordon, "The Parable of the Cave," in <u>The Writer on Her Work</u>, ed. Janet Sternburg (New York: W. W. Norton, 1980), 30.

6. EDITION OTHER THAN THE FIRST

    6. Alfred H. Kelly, Winfred A. Harbison, and Herman Belz, <u>The American Constitution: Its Origins and Development,</u> 6th ed. (New York: W. W. Norton, 1983), 187.

7. MULTIVOLUME WORK

    7. Philip S. Foner and Ronald L. Lewis, eds., <u>The Black Worker</u> (Philadelphia: W. P. Lippincott, 1980), 3:134.

Periodicals

A note for a periodical typically includes the following elements, separated by commas: the author's name, in normal order; the article title, in quotation marks; and the periodical title, underlined or italicized. The format

for the rest of the publication information, including the volume and issue numbers (if any), the date of publication, and the page number(s) to which the note refers, varies according to the type of periodical.

8. ARTICLE IN A JOURNAL PAGINATED BY VOLUME

> 8. Margot Norris, "Narration under a Blindfold: Reading Joyce's 'Clay,'" <u>PMLA</u> 102 (1987): 206.

9. ARTICLE IN A JOURNAL PAGINATED BY ISSUE

> 9. John Lofty, "The Politics at Modernism's Funeral," <u>Canadian Journal</u> of <u>Political and Social Theory</u> 6, no. 3 (1987): 89.

10. ARTICLE IN A MAGAZINE

> 10. Sarah Ferguson, "The Comfort of Being Sad: Kurt Cobain and the Politics of Suicide," <u>Utne Reader</u>, July-August 1994, 60.

11. ARTICLE IN A NEWSPAPER

> 11. Dennis Kelly, "A Financial Report Card for Colleges," <u>USA Today</u>, 5 July 1994, sec. D, p. 1.

Internet sources

The Chicago Manual does not include guidelines for citing Internet sources. The following formats, adapted from Chicago style, are from *Online! A Reference Guide for Using Internet Sources*, by Andrew Harnack and Eugene Kleppinger.

The basic entry for most sources you access through the Internet should include the following elements:

- *Author.* The author's name, if available, in normal order, followed by a comma.
- *Title.* The title of the document or subject line of the message, enclosed in quotation marks and followed by a comma.
- *Date of publication.* The date of Internet publication or the most recent update, if available, followed by a comma. (If no date is available, use *n.d.*)
- *Address.* The URL, in angle brackets, or other retrieval information.

- *Date of access.* In parentheses, followed by a comma or by a period if it is the last item in the entry.
- *Text division.* The page number or other internal division of the source, if applicable, followed by a period.

12. WORLD WIDE WEB SITE. After the document title, include the title of the complete work, if applicable, italicized or underlined.

> 12. Stephanie Brail, "Newsflash!"
> <u>Spider Woman: An Online Community &</u>
> <u>Resource for Women Web Designers,</u> n.d.,
> <http://www.amazoncity.com/spiderwoman/web
> .html> (22 May 1997).

13. EMAIL MESSAGE. Include the author's email address, in angle brackets, after the author's name, and the type of communication (*Personal email, Distribution list*) after the subject line.

> 13. Danielle Mitchell, <mitcheld@ucs
> .orst.edu> "PhD Decisions," 28 May 1997,
> Personal email (28 May 1997).

14. HYPERNEWS POSTING. Include the author's email address, in angle brackets, after the author's name, and the type of message (if appropriate), followed by a comma, after the publication date.

> 14. Cyrus, "Students as Creative Users
> of Multimedia," <yku@moe.ac.sg> 21 October
> 1996, reply to "Multimedia--Students as
> Users or Creators?" by Mark Christie,
> <http://www.smedia.com.sg/HyperNews/get.cgi
> /TeachTalk/30/1.html> (28 May 1997).

15. LISTSERV MESSAGE. Include the author's email address, in angle brackets, after the author's name, and the address of the listserv, in angle brackets, after the publication date.

> 15. Ann Welpton Fisher-Wirth,
> <afwirth@sunset.backbone.olemiss.edu>
> "Deserts," 27 May 1997 <asle@unr.edu>
> (28 May 1997).

16. NEWSGROUP MESSAGE. Include the author's email address, in angle brackets, after (or instead of) the

author's name, and the name of the newsgroup, in angle brackets, after the publication date.

> 16. <kunk@astro.phys.unm.edu> "What Did the Vandals Learn?" 30 May 1997, <soc.history.ancient> (2 June 1997).

17. SYNCHRONOUS COMMUNICATION. Cite the name of the speaker(s), if known, or the name of the site, followed by a comma; the title of the event, if appropriate, enclosed in quotation marks and followed by a comma; the date of the event, followed by a comma; the type of communication (*Group discussion, Personal interview*), if not indicated elsewhere in the entry, followed by a comma; and the address, using either a URL or command-line directions; and the date of access, in parentheses, followed by a period.

> 17. MediaMoo, "Netoric's Tuesday Cafe on Megabyte University: A Look Back; a Look Ahead," 13 May 1997, <telnet://purple-crayon.media.mit.edu:8888> (5 June 1997).
>
> 18. Marcy Bauman, "Collaborative Software Environments: What's on Your Wish List?" Group discussion, 15 April 1997, <telnet purple-crayon.media.mit.edu/port=8888> (5 June 1997).

18. TELNET SITE. After the document title, include the full title of the work, if applicable, italicized or underlined and followed by a comma. After the publication date, include the word *telnet* and the complete telnet address, with no closing punctuation, and directions for accessing the document, with no closing punctuation.

> 19. Virginia's Public Education Network, "Legislation Tracking Report," <u>Virginia Department of Education Legislative Tracking Analysis,</u> n.d., telnet pen1.pen.k12.va.us login as guest, press 3, press 4, press 2 (29 May 1997).

19. FTP (FILE TRANSFER PROTOCOL) SITE. After the publication date, include the abbreviation *ftp* followed by the address of the FTP site, with no closing punctuation, and either the URL or the command, address, and path elements used to find the document, with no closing punctuation.

        20. Zheng Wang, "EIP: The Extended
Internet Protocol: A Long-Term Solution to
Internet Address Exhaustion," June 1992,
<ftp://munnari.OZ.AU/big-internet/eip.txt>
(5 June 1997).

20. GOPHER SITE. After the document title, include any print publication information, italicized or underlined where appropriate. Then give either the URL or the word *gopher*, the site name, and the path followed to access the document, with slashes to indicate menu selections.

        21. Steve Martinots, "Spectors of
Sartre: Nancy's Romance with Ontological
Freedom," September 1995, gopher Journals
and Newsletters/OSU Libraries' Electronic
Serials/Postmodern Culture/pmcv6n1/review 4
(29 May 1997).

21. LINKAGE DATA. After the document title, give the abbreviation *lkd.*; the title of the document to which the file is linked, italicized or underlined; and additional linkage information, if applicable, preceded by *at* and followed by a comma. After the publication date, give the URL for the source document.

        22. Meredith Goldstein-LeVande,
"Elizabeth Cady Stanton," lkd. Introduction,
at "To learn about Elizabeth Cady Stanton,
click here," n.d., <http://www.history
.rochester.edu/class/suffrage/home.htm>
(2 June 1997).

Subsequent notes for previously cited sources

After providing a full citation the first time you refer to a work, for any additional reference to that work you need list only the author's name followed by a comma, a shortened version of the title, a comma, and the page number. If the reference is to the same source cited in the previous note, you can use the Latin abbreviation *Ibid.* instead of the name and title.

        23. Herrera, Frida, 32.
        24. Ibid., 33.
        25. Foner and Lewis, Black Worker,
138-39.

26. Ferguson, "Comfort of Being Sad," 63.

27. Martinots, "Spectors of Sartre."

34b Bibliographic entries

The bibliographic entry for a source includes the same information as the first note for that source, except for the specific page reference. However, the author's name is given last name first; the main elements of the entry are separated by periods rather than commas; and the publication information is not enclosed in parentheses. The following examples demonstrate how to arrange the elements of bibliographic entries according to Chicago style.

Directory to Chicago style for bibliographic entries

Books

1. ONE AUTHOR

Herrera, Hayden. <u>Frida: A Biography of Frida Kahlo</u>. New York: Harper and Row, 1983.

2. MORE THAN ONE AUTHOR

McNeill, John T., and Helena M. Gamer. <u>Medieval Handbooks of Penance</u>. New York: Octagon Books, 1965.

3. UNKNOWN AUTHOR

<u>The New York Times Atlas of the World</u>. New York: New York Times Books, 1980.

4. EDITOR

Woodward, C. Vann, ed., <u>Mary Chesnut's Civil War</u>. New Haven, Conn.: Yale University Press, 1981.

5. SELECTION IN AN ANTHOLOGY, OR CHAPTER IN A BOOK, WITH AN EDITOR

Gordon, Mary. "The Parable of the Cave." In <u>The Writer on Her Work</u>, edited by Janet Sternburg, 30-45. New York: W. W. Norton, 1980.

6. EDITION OTHER THAN THE FIRST

Kelly, Alfred H., Winfred A. Harbison, and Herman Belz. <u>The American Constitution: Its Origins and Development.</u> 6th ed. New York: W. W. Norton, 1983.

7. MULTIVOLUME WORK

Foner, Philip S., and Ronald L. Lewis, eds. <u>The Black Worker</u>. Vol. 3. Philadelphia: W. P. Lippincott, 1980.

Periodicals

8. ARTICLE IN A JOURNAL PAGINATED BY VOLUME

Norris, Margot. "Narration under a Blindfold: Reading Joyce's 'Clay.'" <u>PMLA</u> 102 (1987): 206-15.

9. ARTICLE IN A JOURNAL PAGINATED BY ISSUE

> Loffy, John. "The Politics at Modernism's
>   Funeral." <u>Canadian Journal of Political
>   and Social Theory</u> 6, no. 3 (1987):
>   89-96.

10. ARTICLE IN A MAGAZINE

> Ferguson, Sarah. "The Comfort of Being Sad:
>   Kurt Cobain and the Politics of
>   Suicide." <u>Utne Reader</u>, July-August
>   1994, 60-62.

11. ARTICLE IN A NEWSPAPER

> Kelly, Dennis. "A Financial Report Card for
>   Colleges." <u>USA Today</u>, 5 July 1994,
>   sec. D, p. 1.

Internet sources

12. WORLD WIDE WEB SITE

> Brail, Stephanie. "Newsflash!" <u>Spider Woman:
>   An Online Community & Resource for
>   Women Web Designers.</u> n.d. <http://www
>   .amazoncity.com/spiderwoman/web.html>
>   (22 May 1997).

13. EMAIL MESSAGE

> Mitchell, Danielle. <mitcheld@ucs.orst.edu>
>   "PhD Decisions." 28 May 1997, Personal
>   email (28 May 1997).

14. HYPERNEWS POSTING

> Cyrus. "Students as Creative Users of
>   Multimedia." <yku@moe.ac.sg> 21 October
>   1996. Reply to "Multimedia--Students as
>   Users or Creators?" by Mark Christie.
>   <http://www.smedia.com.sg/HyperNews/get
>   .cgi/TeachTalk/30/1.html> (28 May
>   1997).

15. LISTSERV MESSAGE

> Fisher-Wirth, Ann Welpton.
>   <afwirth@sunset.backbone.olemiss.edu>
>   "Deserts." 27 May 1997. <asle@unr.edu>
>   (28 May 1997).

16. NEWSGROUP MESSAGE

<kunk@astro.phys.unm.edu> "What Did the
     Vandals Learn?" 30 May 1997. <soc
     .history.ancient> (2 June 1997).

17. SYNCHRONOUS COMMUNICATION

MediaMoo. "Netoric's Tuesday Cafe on
     Megabyte University: A Look Back; a
     Look Ahead." 13 May 1997.
     <telnet://purple-crayon.media.mit
     .edu:8888> (5 June 1997).
Bauman, Marcy. "Collaborative Software
     Environments: What's on Your Wish
     List?" Group discussion. 15 April 1997.
     <telnet purple-crayon.media.mit.edu
     /port=8888> (5 June 1997).

18. TELNET SITE

Virginia's Public Education Network.
     "Legislation Tracking Report." <u>Virginia
     Department of Education Legislative
     Tracking Analysis.</u> n.d. telnet
     pen1.pen.k12.va.us login as guest,
     press 3, press 4, press 2
     (29 May 1997).

19. FTP (FILE TRANSFER PROTOCOL) SITE

Wang, Zheng. "EIP: The Extended Internet
     Protocol: A Long-Term Solution to
     Internet Address Exhaustion." June
     1992. <ftp://munnari.OZ.AU/big-internet
     /eip.txt> (5 June 1997).

20. GOPHER SITE

Martinots, Steve. "Spectors of Sartre:
     Nancy's Romance with Ontological
     Freedom." September 1995. gopher
     Journals and Newsletters/OSU
     Libraries' Electronic Serials
     /Postmodern Culture/pmcv6n1/review 4
     (29 May 1997).

21. LINKAGE DATA

```
Goldstein-LeVande, Meredith. "Elizabeth Cady
    Stanton." Lkd. Introduction, at "To
    learn about Elizabeth Cady Stanton,
    click here." n.d. <http://www.history
    .rochester.edu/class/suffrage/home.htm>
    (2 June 1997).
```

34c Manuscript format

Notes. Notes can be footnotes (each typed at the bottom of the page on which the citation for it appears in the text) or endnotes (all typed on a separate page at the end of the text under the heading "Notes"). Be sure to check your instructor's preference. The first line of each note is indented like a paragraph and begins with a number followed by a period and one space before the first word of the entry. All remaining lines of the entry are typed flush with the left margin. Type footnotes single-spaced with a double space between each note. Type all endnotes double-spaced. See page 187 for an example of endnotes.

Bibliography. An alphabetical list of sources in Chicago style is usually titled "Bibliography." If "Sources Consulted," "Works Cited," or "Selected Bibliography" better describes your list, however, any of these titles is acceptable. Begin the list on a separate page at the end, following the main text and any endnotes. Continue the consecutive numbering of pages. Type the title (without underlining or quotation marks), and center it two inches below the top of the page. Double-space, and begin each entry at the left margin. Indent the second and subsequent lines of each entry five spaces. Double-space the entire list.

List sources alphabetically by authors' last names (or by the first major word in the title if the author is unknown). See page 188 for an example of a bibliography in Chicago style.

SAMPLE CHICAGO-STYLE ENDNOTES

Notes

1. John A. Garraty, <u>Quarrels That Have Shaped the Constitution</u> (New York: Harper and Row, 1987), 7-14.

2. Garraty, <u>Quarrels</u>, 19.

3. William C. Louthan, <u>The United States Supreme Court: Lawmaking in the Third Branch of Government</u> (Englewood Cliffs, N.J.: Prentice-Hall, 1991), 51.

4. Thomas J. Higgins, <u>Judicial Review Unmasked</u> (West Hanover, Mass.: Christopher Publishing House, 1981), 40-41.

5. <u>Marbury v. Madison</u>, 1 Cranch, 137 (1803).

6. Louthan, <u>Supreme Court</u>, 51.

7. Ibid., 51.

8. Ibid., 50-51.

9. Higgins, <u>Judicial Review</u>, 40-41.

10. Ibid., 32.

11. Ibid., 34.

SAMPLE CHICAGO-STYLE BIBLIOGRAPHY

Bibliography

Garraty, John A. <u>Quarrels That Have Shaped the Constitution</u>. New York: Harper and Row, 1987.

Higgins, Thomas J. <u>Judicial Review Unmasked</u>. West Hanover, Mass.: Christopher Publishing House, 1981.

Louthan, William C. <u>The United States Supreme Court: Lawmaking in the Third Branch of Government</u>. Englewood Cliffs, N.J.: Prentice-Hall, 1991.

<u>Marbury v. Madison</u>, 1 Cranch, 137 (1803).

35

CBE Style

Writers in the natural sciences, the physical sciences, and mathematics can find recommendations for documentation type in the manual of the Council of Biology Editors (CBE): *Scientific Style and Format: The CBE Manual for Authors, Editors, and Publishers,* sixth edition, 1994.

35a In-text citations

In CBE style, citations within an essay follow one of two formats.

- The citation-sequence format calls for a superscript number ([1]) or a number in parentheses after any mention of a source.
- The name-year format calls for the last name of the author and the year of publication in parentheses after any mention of a source. If the last name appears in a signal phrase, the name-year format allows for giving only the year of publication in parentheses.

Dr. Edward Huth, chairperson of the CBE Style Manual Committee, recommends either the name-year or the superscript system rather than the number-in-parentheses system—and suggests that student writers check a current journal in the field or ask an instructor about the preferred style in a particular course or discipline.

1. IN-TEXT CITATION USING CITATION-SEQUENCE SUPERSCRIPT FORMAT

    In his lengthy text, Gilman[1] provides the
    most complete discussion of this phenomenon.

For the citation-sequence system, you would also use a superscript *1* ([1]) for each subsequent citation of this work by Gilman.

2. IN-TEXT CITATION USING NAME-YEAR FORMAT

    In his lengthy text, Gilman provides the
    most complete discussion of this phenomenon
    (Gilman, 1994).

Maxwell's two earlier studies of juvenile
obesity (1988, 1991) examined only children
with diabetes.

The classic examples of such investigations
(Morrow 1968; Bridger and others 1971;
Franklin and Wayson 1972) still shape the
assumptions of current studies.

35b List of references

The citations in the text of an essay correspond to items
on a list called *References*. If you use the citation-
sequence superscript format, number and list the references in the sequence in which the references are *first*
cited in the text. If you use the name-year format, list
the references, unnumbered, in alphabetical order.

The following examples show both the citation-
sequence format and the name-year format for various
types of sources. You will see that the citation-sequence
format calls for listing the date after the publisher's
name in references for books and after the periodical
name in references for articles. The name-year format
calls for listing the date immediately after the author's
name in any kind of reference. See page 198 for an
example of references in name-year format.

■ Directory to CBE style for a list of references

BOOKS

PERIODICALS

ELECTRONIC SOURCES

INTERNET SOURCES

Books

For a book, the basic entry includes the following items: the author, with the last name first, no comma, and initials without periods for the first and middle names; the title, with only the first word and proper nouns and adjectives capitalized; the place and year of publication; the publisher; and the number of pages in the book.

1. ONE AUTHOR

[1]Freidson E. Profession of medicine. New
    York: Dodd-Mead; 1972. 802 p.
Freidson E. 1972. Profession of medicine.
    New York: Dodd-Mead. 802 p.

2. TWO OR MORE AUTHORS

[2]Stalberg E, Trontelj JV. Single fiber elec-
    tromyography: studies in healthy and
    diseased muscle. New York: Raven; 1994.
    291 p.
Stalberg E, Trontelj JV. 1994. Single fiber
    electromyography: studies in healthy
    and diseased muscle. New York: Raven.
    291 p.

3. ORGANIZATION AS AUTHOR. Any organization abbreviation is placed at the beginning of the name-year entry and is used in the corresponding in-text citation.

[3]World Health Organization. World health
    statistics annual: 1993. Geneva: World
    Health Organization; 1994.

[WHO] World Health Organization. 1994. World
    health statistics annual: 1993. Geneva:
    WHO.

4. BOOK PREPARED BY EDITOR(S)

[4]Berge ZL, Collins MP, editors. Computer
    mediated communication and the online
    classroom. Cresskill, NJ: Hampton Pr;
    1995. 230 p.
Berge ZL, Collins MP, editors. 1995.
    Computer mediated communication and the
    online classroom. Cresskill, NJ:
    Hampton Pr. 230 p.

5. SECTION OF A BOOK WITH AN EDITOR

[5]Adler M. Stroke. In: Dulbecco R, editor.
    Encyclopedia of human biology. San
    Diego: Academic; 1991. p 299-308.
Adler M. 1991. Stroke. In: Dulbecco R, edi-
    tor. Encyclopedia of human biology. San
    Diego: Academic. p 299-308.

6. CHAPTER OF A BOOK

[6]Castro J. The American way of health: how
    medicine is changing and what it means
    to you. Boston: Little, Brown; 1994.
    Chapter 9, Why doctors, hospitals, and
    drugs cost so much; p 131-53.
Castro J. 1994. The American way of health:
    how medicine is changing and what it
    means to you. Boston: Little, Brown.
    Chapter 9, Why doctors, hospitals, and
    drugs cost so much; p 131-53.

7. PUBLISHED PROCEEDINGS OF A CONFERENCE

[7][Anonymous]. International Conference on
    the Bus '86; 1986 Sep 9-10; London.
    [London]: Institution of Mechanical
    Engineers; 1986. 115 p.

The place of publication was not stated but inferred and
placed in brackets.

[Anonymous]. 1986. International Conference
    on the Bus '86; 1986 Sep 9-10; London.
    [London]: Institution of Mechanical
    Engineers. 115 p.

■ Periodicals

For a journal article, the basic entry includes: the author, with the last name first, no comma, and initials without periods for the first and middle names; the article title, with only the first word and proper nouns and adjectives capitalized; the journal title, abbreviated; the date of the issue; the volume number; the issue number, if any; and the inclusive page numbers. For newspaper and magazine articles, the entry includes the section designation and column number, if any. For rules on abbreviating journal titles, consult *The CBE Manual,* or ask an instructor or librarian to refer you to other examples. Following are examples using both superscript and name-year systems.

8. ARTICLE IN A JOURNAL PAGINATED BY VOLUME

[8]Finkel MJ. Drugs of limited commercial
        value. New Engl J Med 1980;302:
        643-4.
Finkel MJ. 1980. Drugs of limited commer-
        cial value. New Engl J Med 302:643-4.

9. ARTICLE IN A JOURNAL PAGINATED BY ISSUE

[9]Fagan R. Characteristics of college student
        volunteering. J Vol Admin 1992;11(1):
        5-18.
Fagan R. 1992. Characteristics of college
        student volunteering. J Vol Admin
        11(1):5-18.

10. ARTICLE IN A WEEKLY JOURNAL

[10]Kerr RA. How many more after Northridge?
        Science 1994 Jan 28;263(5146):460-1.
Kerr RA. 1994 Jan 28. How many more after
        Northridge? Science 263(5146):460-1.

11. ARTICLE IN A MAGAZINE

[11]Jackson R. Arachnomania. Natural History
        1995 Mar:28-31.
Jackson R. 1995 Mar. Arachnomania. Natural
        History:28-31.

12. ARTICLE IN A NEWSPAPER

[12]Christopher T. Grafting: playing Dr.
        Frankenstein in the garden. New York
        Times 1995 Feb 19;Sect Y:21(col 1).

```
Christopher T. 1995 Feb 19. Grafting: play-
    ing Dr. Frankenstein in the garden.
    New York Times; Sect Y:21(col 1).
```

Electronic sources

13. ELECTRONIC JOURNAL ARTICLES

```
¹³Harrison CL, Schmidt PQ, Jones JD. Aspirin
    compared with acetaminophen for relief
    of headache. Online J Therap [serial
    online] 1992 Jan 2;Doc nr 1:[4320
    words; 10 paragraphs]. 5 figures; 10
    tables. (Accessed 1992 Dec 26).
```

The abbreviation *nr* stands for "number."

```
Harrison CL, Schmidt PQ, Jones JD. 1992 Jan
    2. Aspirin compared with acetaminophen
    for relief of headache. Online J
    Therap [serial online];Doc nr 1:
    [4320 words; 10 paragraphs]. 5 figures;
    10 tables. (Accessed 1992 Dec 26).
```

14. ELECTRONIC BOOKS (MONOGRAPHS)

```
¹⁴Martindale online [monograph online].
    London: Pharmaceutical Society of Great
    Britain; 1989 [updated 1989 Dec].
    Available from: Dialog. Dialog.
    Accessed 1990 Jan 10.
[PSCB] Pharmaceutical Society of Great
    Britain. 1989. Martindale online [mono-
    graph online]. London: PSGB; [updated
    1989 Dec]. Available from: Dialog.
    Accessed 1990 Jan 10.
```

Internet sources

With the exception of guidelines for citing electronic journal articles and books, some of which are available on the World Wide Web and by FTP and gopher, *The CBE Manual* does not have guidelines for citing Internet sources. The following formats, adapted from CBE style, are from *Online! A Reference Guide for Using Internet Sources*, by Andrew Harnack and Eugene Kleppinger. These examples use the citation-sequence system; to adapt them to the name-year system, simply delete the superscripts and alphabetize the entries.

The basic entry for most sources you access through the Internet should include the following elements:

- *Author.* The author's name, if available, last name first, followed by the initial(s) and a period.
- *Date of publication.* The year of Internet publication or most recent update, if available, followed by a period. If no date is available, use *n.d.*
- *Title.* The title of the document or subject line of the message, followed by a period.
- *Address.* The URL, in angle brackets, or other retrieval information.
- *Date of access.* Preceded by *Accessed* and followed by a period.

15. WORLD WIDE WEB SITE. Include the title of the complete work, if applicable, after the document title.

> [15]Brail S. n.d. Newsflash! Spider woman: an online community & resource for women web designers. <http://www.amazoncity .com/spiderwoman/web.html> Accessed 1997 May 22.

16. EMAIL MESSAGE. Include the author's email address, in angle brackets, after the author's name, and the type of communication (*Personal email, Office communication*), in square brackets, after the subject line.

> [16]Mitchell D. <mitcheld@ucs.orst.edu> 1997 May 28. PhD decisions [Personal email]. Accessed 1997 May 28.

17. HYPERNEWS POSTING. Include the author's email address, in angle brackets, after the author's name, and the type of message (if appropriate), in square brackets, after the subject line or title.

> [17]Cyrus. <yku@moe.ac.sg> 1996 October 21. Students as creative users of multimedia [reply to Multimedia--students as users or creators? by Mark Christie]. <http://www.smedia.com.sg/HyperNews/get .cgi/TeachTalk/30/1.html> Accessed 1997 May 28.

18. LISTSERV MESSAGE. Include the author's email address, in angle brackets, after the author's name, and the

address of the listserv, in angle brackets, after the subject line.

[18]Fisher-Wirth A. <afworth@sunset.backbone
.olemiss.edu> 1997 May 27. Deserts. <asle
@unr.edu> Accessed 1997 May 28.

19. NEWSGROUP MESSAGE. Include the author's email address, in angle brackets, after (or instead of) the author's name, and the name of the newsgroup, in angle brackets, after the subject line.

[19]<kunk@astro.phys.unm.edu> 1997 May 30.
What did the vandals learn? <soc.history
.ancient> Accessed 1997 June 2.

20. SYNCHRONOUS COMMUNICATION. Cite the name(s) of the speaker(s), if known, or the name of the site; the date of the event; its title, if appropriate; the kind of communication (*Group discussion, Personal interview*), if not indicated elsewhere in the entry, in square brackets; and the address, using either a URL or command-line directions.

[20]MediaMoo. 1997 May 13. Netoric's Tuesday
        cafe on Megabyte University: a look
        back; a look ahead. <telnet://purple
        -crayon.media.mit.edu:8888> Accessed
        1997 June 5.
[21]Bauman M. 1997 Apr 15. Collaborative soft-
        ware environments: what's on your wish
        list? [Group discussion]. telnet
        purple-crayon.media.mit.edu/port=8888
        Accessed 1997 June 5.

21. TELNET SITE. After the document title, include the title of the full work, if applicable, followed by a period. Then include the word *telnet* and the complete telnet address, with no closing punctuation, and directions for accessing the document, with no closing punctuation.

[22]Virginia's Public Education Network. n.d.
        Legislation tracking report. Virginia
        Department of Education legislative
        tracking analysis. telnet pen 1.pen.k12
        .va.us login as guest, press 3, press
        4, press 2 Accessed 1997 May 29.

22. FTP (FILE TRANSFER PROTOCOL) SITE. If the date of publication is unknown, use *n.d.* After the document title, include the abbreviation *ftp* followed by the address of the FTP site, with no closing punctuation. Then give either the URL or the command, address, and path elements used to find the document, with no closing punctuation.

> [23]Wang Z. 1992 June. EIP: the extended
> Internet protocol: a long-term solution
> to Internet address exhaustion. <ftp://
> munnari.OZ.AU/big-internet/eip.txt>
> 1997 June 5.

23. GOPHER SITE. After the document title, include any print publication information. Then give either the URL or the word *gopher,* the site name, and the path followed to access the document, with slashes to indicate menu selections.

> [24]Martinots S. 1995. Spectors of Sartre:
> Nancy's romance with ontological free-
> dom. gopher Journals and Newsletters
> /OSU Libraries' Electronic Serials
> /Postmodern Culture/pmcv6n1/review 4
> Accessed 1997 May 29.

24. LINKAGE DATA. After the title of the document, give the abbreviation *Lkd.,* the title of the document to which the file is linked, followed by a comma; and additional linkage details (if applicable), indicated with *at.* Then give the source's URL.

> [25]Meier C. 1997 March 25. How to implement
> Kassebaum-Kennedy. Lkd. The Heartland
> Institute, at Hot Documents. <http://
> www.heartland.org/index.html> Accessed
> 1997 June 2.

SAMPLE CBE LIST OF REFERENCES

References

Gardner EJ. 1960. Principles of genetics. New York: Wiley. 386 p.

Hayward HE. 1938. Structure of economic plants. New York: Macmillan. 674 p.

Knowles RV, Sprienc F, Phillips RL. 1990. Endoreduplication of nuclear DNA in the developing maize endosperm. Dev Genet 11:125-32.

Walden DB. 1978. Maize breeding and genetics. New York: Wiley. 794 p.

Can you use underlining to indicate italics in online writing just as you would in traditional printed text?

Because underlining on the World Wide Web signals an active **HYPERTEXT LINK**, you should not use underlining for italics in Web documents. If you need to signal italics, type an underscore mark (_) before and after the word you want to italicize (_Ebony_).

Do you need permission to use online texts, graphics, or images in your own work?

The concept of "fair use" in copyright allows you to use brief excerpts of copyrighted material (generally 300 words from a book, 150 words from a magazine, or 4 lines from a poem—or even more if your work is for a class and not intended to be "published"), as long as you provide a full citation. To cite personal communication such as **EMAIL** or for **LISTSERV POSTINGS**, however, you should ask permission of the writer before you include any of his or her material in your own text. To use someone else's graphics or images in your text, it is safest to request permission from the creator or owner. Here are two sample email permission requests.

    MAIL TO: litman@mindspring.com
    CC TO: lunsford.2@osu.edu
    SUBJECT: Request for permission

Dear Professor Litman:

I am writing to request permission to quote from your essay, "Copyright, Owners' Rights and Users' Privileges on the Internet: Implied Licenses, Caching, Linking, Fair Use, and Sign-on Licenses." I want to quote some of your work in a hypertext essay I am writing for students in my composition class in order to explain the complex debates over ownership on the Internet and to argue that students in my class should be participating in these debates. My essay, like all the others in my class, will be linked to our class Web page. I will give full credit to you and will cite the URL where I first found your work: <http://www.msen.com/~litman/dayton/htm>.

Please let me know if you are willing to grant me permission to quote from your essay. Thank you very much for considering my request.

Raul Sanchez <sanchez.32@osu.edu>

MAIL TO: fridanet@aol.com
CC TO: lunsford.2@osu.edu
SUBJECT: Request for permission

Dear Kimberley Masters:

I am a student at Ohio State University and am writing to request your permission to download and use your photograph of Frida Kahlo in a three-piece suit <fridanet/suit.htm#top>. This illustration would be used in a project I and two other students are working on for members of our composition class about the later work of Frida Kahlo. In the report on our project, which we will post on our class's Web page, we will cite <http://members.aol.com/fridanet/kahlo.htm> as the URL, unless you want us to use a different source.

Thank you very much for considering our request.

Jennifer Fox <fox.360@osu.edu>

In all cases, remember the difference between the fair use of a document for an assignment that you will submit to a teacher and classmates and one that you will post or publish on the Internet or in print. For your class, you might include the text of an entire song in an essay, but you cannot put such an essay—with the copyrighted song—on the Internet without infringing on the rights of the copyright owner.

What if page numbers aren't included in an online source you want to cite?

You can signal the fact that the document you are citing has no pages by including *n pag* (for "no pagination") in your citation. To be as accurate and helpful as possible, you can count paragraphs and cite the paragraph number in your citation (Selfe, par. 8) or cite a part of the document (Selfe, abstract) if the text indicates various parts—but be careful not to list divisions that come from your browsing software. An online source with divisions can be referenced in one of two ways. You can refer to the part of the source you are citing, and its author, in your own text:

In his abstract to "Rhetorics of the Web: Implications for Teachers of Literacy," Doug Brent asks, "But is rhetorical interchange possible in a form that works against the linear-sequential argumentative structures that have traditionally underpinned rhetoric?"

You can also name the author and the part of the source in a parenthetical citation:

"But is rhetorical interchange possible in a form that works against the linear-sequential argumentative

structures that have traditionally underpinned rhetoric?" (Brent, Abstract).

Here is the works cited entry, following MLA style:

```
Brent, Doug. "Rhetorics of the Web:
     Implications for Teachers of
     Literacy." Kairos: A Journal for
     Teachers of Writing in Webbed
     Environments 2.1 (Spring 1997).
     1 June 1997 <http://english.ttu.edu
     /kairos/current/index_f.html>.
```

How do you cite texts that may exist in different versions or that are subject to change?

If possible, include the *original date of production*—when the document was first produced; the *publication date on the Web*—sometimes a version number or revision date; and the *date you accessed the document*. This information lets readers know that any material you used was part of the document on the date you accessed it—and it allows them to look to other versions to see whether changes have occurred:

```
Cross, Janet, and Kristian Fuglevik.
     "Reflections Onna MOO." Kairos: A
     Journal for Teachers of Writing in
     Webbed Environments 1.3 (Autumn
     1996). 2 July 1997 <http://english
     .ttu.edu/kairos/1.3/index.html>.
```

Online Resources

The *APA Web Site* contains a link to student FAQs that can help you cite information from the Web using APA style:

<http://www.apa.org/journals/webref.html>

The electronic version of Andrew Harnack and Eugene Kleppinger's *Online!* provides guidelines for documenting online sources using four different styles—MLA, APA, Chicago, and CBE:

<http://www.smpcollege.com/online-4styles~help/toc.html>

Janice Walker also provides *Citations of Electronic Sources:*

<http://www.cas.usf.edu/english/walker.mla.html>

For Eric Crump's list of *Citation Guides for Electronic Documents,* see

<http://www.nlc-bnc.ca/ifla/I/training/citation/citing.htm>

EVERYDAY SOURCES FOR 15 SUBJECTS

The yellow pages that follow contain information about useful resources in fifteen disciplinary fields, including annotated lists of URLs and journals. For access to these and other useful resources, visit the EasyWriter Web site at <www.smpcollege.com /easywriter>.

Art

Web sites

WWW VIRTUAL LIBRARY—ART
<http://www.w3.org/pub/Datasources/bySubject/Literature/Overview.html>
An excellent collection of links to both art and literature sites. Includes links to other virtual libraries.

HISTORY OF ART VIRTUAL LIBRARY
<http://www.hart.bbk.ac.uk/VirtualLibrary.html>
Includes links to art history sites, museums, galleries, art history organizations, and university art departments.

NATIONAL GALLERY OF ART
<http://www.nga.gov/>
Images from the collection and news about current displays and educational opportunities.

WORLD ART TREASURES
<http://sgwww.epfl.ch/BERGER/Index.html>
In-depth links to selected artists' works and areas of art, with good links to other sites.

VIRTUAL LIBRARY MUSEUMS PAGE
<http://www.comlab.ox.ac.uk/archive/other/museums.html>
A large number of links to recent and current exhibitions at many major museums, by country.

ART HISTORY RESOURCES ON THE WEB
<http://witcombe.bcpw.sbc.edu/ARTHLinks.html>
An extraordinarily detailed set of chronologically organized links to art history sources, from prehistoric through modern.

H-GIG ART HISTORY
<http://www.ucr.edu/h-gig/hist-art/arthi.html>
Easy links to some of the best art history sources and directories, based in the large HORUS system at the University of California at Riverside. Smaller and more manageable than some of the full-service sites.

Journals

American Artist. Since 1937. Monthly. *Especially relevant to practicing artists, with articles on commercial opportunities, collections, techniques, and profiles of individual artists.*

Art History. Since 1978. Quarterly. *A scholarly magazine that carries book reviews and articles, including those concerning the social history of art.*

Art Journal. Since 1941. Quarterly. *Each issue features a theme that connects all of the articles.*

Artforum. Since 1962. Monthly. *Focuses on modern art with an international emphasis, giving excellent coverage of the contemporary art scene.*

37

Biology and Biosciences

Web sites

BIOSCIENCES INDEX
<http://golgi.harvard.edu/htbin/biopages>
Allows searching by keyword and provides an alphabetical list of links for specialties within the biosciences.

PASTEUR INSTITUTE
<http://web.pasteur.fr/search/>
Allows keyword searches of the Pasteur Institute's server and many other English-language-based bioscience servers.

WWW VIRTUAL LIBRARY—BIOSCIENCES
<http://golgi.harvard.edu/biopages.html>
Categorizes information by provider and subject. A good place to begin research, this site includes many links to journals, FTP sites, and subdisciplines.

HUMAN GENOME PROJECT
<http://www.nhgri.nih.gov/index.html>
The homepage for this important research project; situated at the National Institutes of Health.

NATIONAL SCIENCE FOUNDATION: BIOLOGY
<http://www.nsf.gov/home/bio/start.htm>
The site of the primary government agency funding scientific research. Allows a search of its Biology Directorate's sources and includes links to online documents, grants, and specific fields within biology.

BIOSCIENCES GOPHER RESOURCES
<gopher://genome-gopher.stanford.edu/11/topic>
An alphabetical list of gopher links that relate to biosciences, nearly all in the form of textfiles.

INTERNET RESOURCES OF INTEREST
<http://lib2.med.cornell.edu/Library/HTML/IntRes.html>
From Cornell Medical School; provides constantly updated links to many medical and bioscience resources.

CENTERS FOR DISEASE CONTROL
<http://ftp.cdc.gov/>
The homepage of the famous virus hunters, with links to what they do, to search facilities, to other sites, and to a wide range of useful government data.

NATIONAL INSTITUTES OF HEALTH
<http://www.nih.gov/>
The central government organization dealing with health issues; site includes news, health information, grant descriptions, and links to scientific resources and to NIH suborganizations.

Journals

Journal of Biological Chemistry. Since 1905. Weekly. *Covers a broad range of topics in biochemistry. Each issue includes full-length research papers, information on new developments in the field, and professional announcements.*

Journal of Cell Biology. Since 1955. Twice monthly. *Formerly the Journal of Biophysical and Biochemical Cytology. Focuses on new findings in the field of cell biology. Articles cover a wide range of topics in developmental biology, immunology, neurobiology, and virology.*

Journal of Bacteriology. Since 1916. Twice monthly. *Includes papers and mini-reviews regarding new research on bacteria and microorganisms. Genetics and molecular biology is one of the more prominent areas covered.*

Nature. Since 1869. Weekly. *An international science journal. Latest findings are often reported here.*

Analytical Biochemistry. Since 1960. 16/yr. *Issues include full-length papers and shorter pieces on techniques and methodologies of biochemistry and related fields.*

Biotechnology and Bioengineering. Since 1958. 22/yr. *A primary journal in the field of biomedical engineering. Scholarly papers cover all aspects of biotechnology.*

Quarterly Review of Biology. Since 1923. Quarterly. *Critical reviews, commentaries, and theoretical articles, all designed to appeal to general biologists as well as specialists. Reviews of books and biological software are also included.*

JAMA: Journal of the American Medical Association.
Since 1845. Weekly. *Covers a wide range of medical issues as well as reports from the Centers for Disease Control. Special monthly section for medical students.*

38

Business and Economics

Web sites

GALAXY BUSINESS GENERAL RESOURCES
<http://www.einet.net/galaxy/Business-and-Commerce/Business-General-Resources.html>
Links to a variety of resources for business; includes prices, statistics, trends, and general reading sources.

BUSINESS RESOURCE CENTER
<http://www.morebusiness.com/>
Specific links to advice about marketing, management, and financing. Also includes a search service.

SEC EDGAR DATABASE
<http://www.sec.gov:80/edgarhp.htm>
The Electronic Data Gathering, Analysis, and Retrieval system is the Securities and Exchange Commission's archive of business filings. Includes various search capabilities and a wide range of information.

INTERNATIONAL BUSINESS RESOURCES ON THE WWW
<http://ciber.bus.msu.edu>
Specializes in links to international business sites. Also offers keyword searches, browsing, and a variety of other links.

A BUSINESS RESEARCHER'S INTERESTS
<http://www.brint.com/interest.html>
Provides links to articles, papers, magazines, tools, and many other resources for "contemporary business, management, and information technology issues."

THE MANAGEMENT ARCHIVE
<http://ursus.jun.alaska.edu/>
Information on managing business and public organizations, with links to an archive of working papers, other management sites, and a search facility.

BUSINESS WEEK ONLINE
<http://www.businessweek.com/>
Offers online versions of some BW stories, quick news updates, stock and mutual-fund tracking data, and advertisements—some of which may, in fact, be useful.

BUSINESS AND ECONOMICS—SPECIAL FIELDS
<http://bib10.sub.su.se/sam/sbspec.htm>
*An alphabetical list of links to many different resources, with
an emphasis on economics and investment issues.*

ECONOMICS WORKING PAPER ARCHIVE
<http://econwpa.wustl.edu:80/Welcome.html>
*Working papers in economics, organized by subject areas, with
many links to other sites and sources.*

WEBEC
<http://www.helsinki.fi/WebEc/>
*An award-winning site that attempts to categorize all the free
information on economics available on the Web. Organized by
area of economics, it is easily searchable and contains the valuable List of Economics Journals.*

Journals

Fortune. Since 1930. Twice weekly. *Focuses on general issues
related to industry and the economy.*

Journal of Business. Since 1928. Quarterly. *Theoretical articles reflect a wide range of research in finance and economics.*

Business Week. Since 1929. Weekly. *U.S. business news and
analysis, including company and individual profiles, new technology, financial statistics, and social/political trends.*

Economist. Since 1843. Weekly. *International business news
and in-depth analysis, as well as articles on world politics, current affairs, and charts of economic indicators.*

Harvard Business Review. Since 1922. Bimonthly. *Scholarly
journal with an emphasis on business and economic history.
Many articles by leaders in industry and academe.*

Business Horizons. Since 1957. Bimonthly. *Articles on business and economic conditions. Each issue includes topics such as
marketing, small business, health care, and more.*

39

Chemistry

Web sites

BEGINNER'S GUIDE TO CHEMICAL ABSTRACTS
<http://library.uwaterloo.ca/howto/howto12.html>
*Introduces users to the standard guide to chemical literature
and shows how to do simple searches. A commercial site.*

WWW VIRTUAL LIBRARY—CHEMISTRY
<http://www.chem.ucla.edu/chempointers.html>
Links to universities and organizations as well as to chemistry resources and other VLs. Especially useful are the links to gopher and FTP servers in chemistry.

CHEMCENTER
<http://www.ChemCenter.org/>
From the American Chemical Society; includes links to education, industry, publications, and searchable databases.

CIS-IU
<http://www.indiana.edu/~cheminfo/cisindex.html>
Chemical Information Sources from Indiana University is a guide to Internet and Web resources in chemistry; offers both alphabetical and keyword searches in a useful format.

MOLECULAR VISUALIZATION TOOLS AND SITES
<http://www.indiana.edu/~cheminfo/mvts.html>
Links to all the major Chime and RasMol sites as well as to various other free and commercial visualization sites.

THE ANALYTICAL CHEMISTRY SPRINGBOARD
<http://www.anachem.umu.se/jumpstation.htm>
Presents links to all the analytical chemistry resources on the Net, arranged by analytical techniques. Also includes lists of other Net and Web resources.

MANUAL AND COMPUTER-AIDED LITERATURE SEARCHING
<http://httpl.brunel.ac.uk:8080/depts/chem/ch361a/lect.htm>
A long, detailed explanation of how to use the standard sources in chemical literature, by Dr. J. J. Gosper. Includes a section on Beilstein and full explication of CA and BIDS. Worth downloading.

ACSWEB
<http://www.acs.org/>
Provides searches of American Chemical Society resources as well as information on news, events, and publications.

BIOCHEMNET
<http://schmidel.com/bionet.htm>
Contains a directory and links to a variety of biology and chemistry sources, most of them oriented toward high school and college chemistry and education.

Journals

Accounts of Chemical Research. Since 1968. Monthly. *Links current projects with previous and future trends; includes reviews and critical assessments by experts.*

Angewandte Chemie. International edition. Since 1962. Twice monthly. *The English-language edition; published by the German Chemical Society. Includes review articles, book reviews, new research, and correspondence for all areas of chemistry.*

Chemical Reviews. Since 1924. 8/yr. *Reviews cover all areas of chemistry and assess current work in the field. Every other issue focuses on a specific theme. With its comprehensive bibliographies, this is a good scholarly resource.*

American Chemical Society Journal. Since 1879. Biweekly. *Includes research articles and important preliminary studies in all fields of chemistry.*

Chemical Communications: Journal of the Chemical Society. Since 1965. Twice monthly. *A key source for new research; features short, preliminary surveys of recent research in all areas of chemistry.*

Chemical Abstracts. Since 1907. Weekly. *The most comprehensive coverage for chemistry and one of the largest abstracting services in the world; covers titles, patents issues, conference and symposia proceedings, dissertations, government reports, and books. Abstracts include bibliographic information and summaries of key points.*

40

Communication

Web sites

ACA HOMEPAGE
<http://www.uark.edu/depts/comminfo/www/ACA.html>
The American Communication Association sponsors this full-coverage page, with links to the different subfields that make up communications, organized by field and by interest.

LINKS TO FRIENDLY COMMUNICATIONS HOMEPAGES
<http://www.csufresno.edu/speechcomm/wscalink.htm>
From the Western States Speech Association; provides easy access to many organizational homepages in communications.

APDA
<http://www.mit.edu:8001/activities/debate/apdawww/pgone.html>
The American Parliamentary Debate Association maintains this site for college and university debating, with links to members, officers, a newsletter, and other debating sites.

NATIONAL COMMUNICATION ASSOCIATION
<http://www.scassn.org/>
Formerly the Speech Communication Association. The NCA site offers information on publications and conferences, links to sources, and related communication news and links.

CMU RHETORIC AND COMPOSITION
<http://english-www.hss.cmu.edu/rhetoric/>
A well-organized list of links to classical rhetoric, e-journals, writing centers, rhetoricians, and miscellaneous resources on the Net. An especially good collection of classical texts.

INVESTIGATIVE REPORTERS & EDITORS
<http://www.ire.org>
An organization dedicated to teaching the skills and issues of investigative journalism; the site's resource center includes a database of more than 11,000 abstracts of investigative articles.

LAUNCH PAD FOR JOURNALISTS
<http://www.ccrc.wustl.edu/spj/resources.html>
The Society of Professional Journalists produces this site.

COMMUNICATION STUDIES
<http://www.lib.uiowa.edu/gw/comm/>
From the University of Iowa; offers a wide range of links to list-servs, journals, Web research, and electronic style guides, as well as to a broad range of fields from advertising through rhetoric.

Journals

Communication Education. Since 1952. Quarterly. Formerly Speech Teacher. *A publication of the Speech Communication Association. Includes articles on the study, teaching, and practice of oral communication.*

Quarterly Journal of Speech. Since 1915. Quarterly. *The journal of the Speech Communication Association. Contains essays on many areas of speech communication, including oratory, rhetoric, debate and public speaking, mass communication, and media studies.*

Journalism & Mass Communication Quarterly. Since 1924. Quarterly. *Published by the Association for Education in Journalism and Mass Communication. Includes articles on theory and research as well as book reviews.*

Communication Monographs. Since 1934. Quarterly. Formerly Speech Monographs. *A scholarly journal dedicated to human communication processes. Articles and research reports highlight scientific investigations.*

41

Engineering

Web sites

IEEE SPECTRUM
<http://www.spectrum.ieee.org/>
Provides access to all major publications and resources of the Institute of Electrical and Electronics Engineers.

WWW VIRTUAL LIBRARY—ENGINEERING
<http://arioch.gsfc.nasa.gov/wwwvl/engineering.html>
Lists links to many relevant sources across engineering fields, including all the engineering VLs, from acoustic engineering to welding engineering. Includes information on standards, products, and institutions.

ICE—INTERNET CONNECTIONS FOR ENGINEERING
<http://www.englib.cornell.edu/ice/ice-index.html>
Links for all engineering disciplines; good for finding additional sources and bibliographic information.

WWW VIRTUAL LIBRARY—CHEMICAL ENGINEERING
<http://www.che.ufl.edu/www-che/>
Offers links to meetings, conferences, organizations, and information resources. Good specific subtopic list.

WWW VIRTUAL LIBRARY CIVIL ENGINEERING
<http://www.ce.gatech.edu/WWW-CE/home.html>
Lists servers containing information on civil engineering, most of them from university programs.

ASCE'S CIVIL ENGINEERING DATABASE
<http://www.ascepub.infor.com:8601/chrhome2.html>
Provides access to over 80,000 bibliographic and abstracted records in civil engineering since 1975.

WWW VIRTUAL LIBRARY—ELECTRICAL ENGINEERING
<http://arioch.gsfc.nasa.gov/wwwvl/ee.html>
A good place to start.

ELECTRONIC ENGINEERS' TOOLBOX
<http://www.eetoolbox.com/ebox.htm>
A search utility for specialized issues within electronics engineering. Provides links to both commercial and noncommercial resources.

INSTITUTE OF ELECTRICAL AND ELECTRONICS ENGINEERS
<http://www.ieee.org/>
Links to member services, related technical societies, search engines, databases, publications, and activities.

WWW VIRTUAL LIBRARY—MECHANICAL ENGINEERING
<http://CDR.stanford.edu/html/WWW-ME/home.html>
Provides good links to online services as well as the usual links to universities and societies.

Journals

Civil Engineering ASCE. Since 1930. Monthly. *Includes notices of upcoming ASCE conferences, new publications, news briefs, and new products and applications. Full-length, semi-technical articles on timely topics also included.*

Chemical & Engineering News. Since 1923. Weekly. *Devoted to providing current information on the chemical industry. Valuable for job searching.*

Space Technology. Since 1981. 6/yr. *Aids in the transfer of information on space technology from developers, system designers, and policymakers to the users, suppliers, and specialists of space technology. Covers telecommunications, environmental considerations, manufacturing, and energy research and development.*

Automotive Engineering. Since 1917. Monthly. *Designed to keep engineers abreast of the latest technological developments in the automotive industry.*

Industrial Engineering. Since 1969. Monthly. *Features articles on improving industrial production. Departments include industry news and classified and job ads.*

JOM: The Journal of the Minerals, Metals, and Materials Society. Since 1949. Monthly. *Covers the full range of materials science and engineering. Includes commentary, research summaries, and overviews of materials research.*

42

History

Web sites

HISTORICAL JOURNALS ONLINE
<http://www.tntech.edu/www/acad/hist/journals.html>
Links to many journals, book chapters, and reviews that can be accessed from the WWW. Not all journals are available online, but they can be sampled.

HISTORY SITES BY TIME PERIOD
<http://www.tntech.edu/www/acad/hist/period.html>
Provides access to many sites covering issues from ancient through contemporary history and links to other general sites.

HISTORY SITES BY SUBJECT
<http://www.tntech.edu/www/acad/hist/subject.html>
Offers links to subjects ranging from areas to methodologies.

HORUS'S WEB LINKS TO HISTORY RESOURCES
<http://www.ucr.edu/h-gig/toc.html>
Provides a search engine for browsing databases.

THE HISTORY NET
<http://www.theHistoryNet.com/>
A project of the National Historical Society. Provides a historical magazine as well as a search service.

WWW VIRTUAL LIBRARY—HISTORY
<http://history.cc.ukans.edu/history/WWW_specialized
.html>
Provides links to history servers by subject—General, Americas, Asia, Europe, Topics, and Organizations.

MODERN HISTORY
<http://www.tntech.edu/www/acad/hist/modern.html>
Texts, links, and documents on the period 1775–1945.

GATEWAY TO WORLD HISTORY
<http://library.ccsu.ctstateu.edu/~history/world
_history/>
Supports searches for teachers and students of world history and allows links to more specific areas.

WORLD HISTORY ARCHIVES
<http://library.ccsu.ctstateu.edu/~history/world_history
/archives/index.html>
Offers access to actual versions of important texts in world history and many links to contemporary writings.

GOPHER JEWELS HISTORY MENU
<gopher://cwis.usc.edu:70/11/other_gophers_and
_information_resources/gophers_by_subject/gopher
_jewels/academic/history>
Allows downloading of original archival documents from a variety of U.S. and world history sources.

EURODOCS
<http://library.byu.edu/~rdh/eurodocs/homepage.html>
Offers primary historical documents from western Europe; organized by country.

HISTORICAL TEXT ARCHIVE
<http://www.msstate.edu/Archives/History/>
Provides access to many world history texts; organized by both area and topic.

BEDFORD BOOKS HOME PAGE
<http://www.bedfordbooks.com>
Provides an annotated list of links to history sites.

Journals

American Historical Review. Since 1895. 5/yr. *The official journal of the American Historical Association. Many articles involve history outside of the United States. A good source of book reviews.*

Journal of Women's History. Since 1989. Quarterly. *Features research articles about women in all time periods and includes a section on current issues and trends for women around the world.*

History and Theory: Studies in the Philosophy of History. Since 1960. Quarterly. *Offers interdisciplinary connections to other fields, including philosophy, critical theory, methodology, and more. Issues include articles and book reviews. The fourth issue of each volume is a monograph or bibliography.*

Journal of American History. Since 1914. Quarterly. *Formerly the* Mississippi Valley Historical Review. *Includes scholarly articles, book reviews, film reviews, lists of recent dissertations, and published bibliographies on American history.*

Journal of Social History. Since 1967. Quarterly. *Features articles and book reviews on a broad range of topics in social history. A good source for interdisciplinary studies.*

Journal of Modern History. Since 1929. Quarterly. *Offers a global and comparative focus; typically includes articles and review articles. Occasional issues focus on a single theme.*

Journal of World History. Since 1990. Twice annually. *The official journal of the World History Association. Reflects the need for historical analysis at the global level. Scholarly articles cover a wide range of topics and approaches.*

43

Literature

Web sites

IN OTHER WORDS: A LEXICON OF THE HUMANITIES
<http://www.sil.org/humanities/>
Provides an interesting hyperlinked lexicon and glossary of major terms in literary criticism, rhetoric, and linguistics.

RESOURCES IN ENGLISH LANGUAGE AND LITERATURE
<http://www.lib.cmich.edu/bibliographers/billmiles/english.htm>
Offers many links to American studies, British literary studies, children's literature, and English literary studies in general. A useful place to begin research.

LITERARY RESOURCES ON THE NET
<http://www.english.upenn.edu/~jlynch/Lit/>
Allows you to search for literary materials on the Net, and provides a list of periodicals and genre-based categories to explore.

LITERARY RESOURCES—FEMINISM AND WOMEN'S LITERATURE
<http://www.english.upenn.edu/~jlynch/Lit/women.html>
Devoted entirely to women writers and feminist criticism.

PROJECT GUTENBERG MASTER INDEX
<http://free.systemy.it/gut_berg.htm>
The best current index to PG texts, most of which are now in the public domain.

INTERNATIONAL GAY AND LESBIAN REVIEW
<http://www.usc.edu/Library/oneigla/onepress/index.html>
Provides abstracts and reviews of many books related to lesbian, gay, bisexual, and transgender studies.

AMERICAN STUDIES WEB
<http://www.georgetown.edu/crossroads/asw/lit.html>
Provides links to many elements of American studies, with an emphasis on literary texts, authors, approaches, genres, and associations.

ROMANCE LANGUAGES RESOURCE PAGE
<http://humanities.uchicago.edu/romance/>
Offers links to travel and study, research, university departments, and classroom help for those studying Romance languages.

FRENCH RESOURCES
<http://blair.library.rhodes.edu/ForLanghtmls/french.html>
Guide to French language, literature, and culture.

RESOURCES FOR RUSSIAN AND SLAVIC LANGUAGES AND LITERATURE
<http://www.library.vanderbilt.edu/central/russian.html#russian>
Links to Web sites, dictionaries, literary sites, e-journals, e-texts, departments, and professional organizations.

GERMAN RESOURCES
<http://blair.library.rhodes.edu/ForLanghtmls/german.html>
Links to sites, dictionaries, and texts in German.

Journals

Journal of Modern Literature. Since 1970. Quarterly. *Devoted to the history and analysis of the literature of the twentieth century.*

American Literature. Since 1929. Quarterly. *Includes scholarly, critical, and bibliographical articles.*

Comparative Literature. Since 1949. Quarterly. *Publishes scholarly and critical articles on literature in all languages.*

ELH. Since 1934. Quarterly. *Publishes scholarly and critical articles on English literature and literary history.*

New York Review of Books. Since 1963. Biweekly. *Reviews and review essays about recently published books.*

PMLA. Since 1844. Bimonthly. *The Journal of the Modern Language Association; features scholarly articles on all areas of modern languages and literature.*

Melus: The Journal of the Society for the Study of the Multi-ethnic Literature of the United States. Since 1974. Quarterly. *Focuses on the analysis of multi-ethnic literature. Individual issues focus on a single topic or theme.*

African American Review. Since 1967. Quarterly. *Formerly* Negro American Literature Forum, Black American Literature Forum. *Although one of its strengths is Black literature, this journal is interdisciplinary and includes perspectives from the arts, humanities, and social sciences.*

Women's Review of Books. Since 1983. Monthly. *Provides reviews of books by and about women; issues sometimes feature a special theme.*

44

Mathematics

Web sites

MATH ARCHIVES UNDERGRADS' PAGE
<http://archives.math.utk.edu/undergraduates.html>
Devoted to math issues of special interest to undergraduates. Includes societies, projects, research, competitions, and career issues.

MATH ARCHIVES BIBLIOGRAPHIES
<http://archives.math.utk.edu/cgi-bin/bibliography.html>
A list of bibliographies and subject links; supplements the Math Archives homepage.

THE MOST COMMON ERRORS IN UNDERGRADUATE MATHEMATICS
<http://math.vanderbilt.edu/~schectex/commerrs/>
From Eric Schecter at Vanderbilt University.

AMS MATHEMATICS ON THE WEB
<http://www.ams.org/mathweb/>
Offers literature guides and links both on- and off-line, references, topical guides, and links to individuals.

MATERIALS ORGANIZED BY MATHEMATICAL TOPICS
<http://www.ams.org/mathweb/mi-mathbytopic.html>
Links to specific issues in current mathematical work.

MATHSEARCH
<http://www.maths.usyd.edu.au:8000/MathSearch.html>
Searches over ninety thousand documents on English-language math and statistics servers, keying by phrase.

ERIC'S TREASURE TROVE OF MATHEMATICS
<http://www.astro.virginia.edu/~eww6n/math/math0.html>
An alphabetical search list of important terms and concepts.

Journals

American Journal of Mathematics. Since 1878. Bimonthly. *Includes contributions from American and international scholars in the field.*

American Mathematical Monthly. Since 1894. 10/yr. *Focuses on problem solving and is designed for both professional mathematicians and students at the college level.*

Mathematical Intelligencer. Since 1978. Quarterly. *Designed for a general audience; features articles relating to all areas of the history and culture of mathematics.*

Mathematics Magazine. Since 1926. Bimonthly. *Covers all aspects of mathematics with examples, applications, illustrations, and historical background. Aimed at undergraduates.*

Chance. Since 1988. Quarterly. *For those who use statistical methods in market research, demographics, social sciences, medicine, and other areas. Includes articles on statistical methods, statistical computing programs, and technical problems.*

Bulletin of the American Mathematical Society. Since 1894. Quarterly. *Includes current research, important developments, and book reviews.*

Mathematical Reviews. Since 1940. Monthly. *A basic indexing and abstracting service for mathematics.*

Quantum: Tomorrow's Magazine of Math and Science Today. Since 1990. Bimonthly. *A magazine by and for math students. In English and Russian. Regular features include an analysis in recreational mathematics, an update on current events for science students, and a selection of problems.*

Journal of Recreational Mathematics. Since 1968. Quarterly. *Devoted to the lighter side of math, with thought-provoking games, puzzles, and articles.*

45

Music

Web sites

SIBELIUS ACADEMY MUSIC RESOURCES
<http://www.siba.fi/Kulttuuripalvelut/music.html>
Provides links to every aspect of music appreciation, production, and education.

UNIVERSITY OF MARYLAND MUSIC RESOURCES
<http://www.lib.umd.edu/UMCP/MUSIC/LINKS.HTM>
Provides electronic access to sources by composers, journals, indexes, libraries, and musicology and theory sites.

ONLINE RESOURCES IN MUSIC
<http://www.ruf.rice.edu/~brownlib/music/music.html#hplibs>
Links to databases, musicians, libraries, and publishers.

MUSIC SOURCES ON THE WEB
<http://www.idbsu.edu/carol/music.htm>
Organized by kinds of music.

WORLDWIDE INTERNET MUSIC RESOURCES
<http://www.music.indiana.edu/music_resources/>
A general list of links to musicians, composers, performance sites, genres, research, industry, and journals.

CLASSICAL MUSIC ON THE WEB
<http://www.unc.edu/~baker/music.html>
An "organized jumpstation" to the best classical music sites on the Web.

Journals

Journal of Music Theory. Since 1957. Twice annually. *Focuses on music theory and composition from all periods. Each issue includes reviews, a listing of new articles and books in the field, and a correspondence column.*

Journal of the American Musicological Society. Since 1948. 3/yr. *Scholarly articles by musicologists cover a wide range of topics. Each issue includes a bibliography of the latest works in the field.*

Journal of Musicology. Since 1982. Quarterly. *A review of music history, criticism, analysis, and performing practice. Occasional issues focus on a single theme.*

Musical Quarterly. Since 1915. Quarterly. *Covers a wide range of topics in music composition and performance, from classical to contemporary.*

Ethnomusicology. Since 1953. 3/yr. *An excellent source for information on world music and vernacular music. Includes a current bibliography, discography, and filmography; dissertations and theses; and reviews of books, recordings, and films.*

Choral Journal. Since 1980. Monthly. *Articles cover numerous topics related to choral conducting, performing, and teaching. Regular features include book and chorale reviews as well as annotated lists of choral music.*

Instrumentalist. Since 1946. Monthly. *Articles are designed for conductors, teachers, and performers. Includes reviews of books, new music, and software, as well as a calendar of competitions and works.*

Current Musicology. Since 1965. Twice annually. *"An international forum for scholars," with articles on all aspects of musicology, reviews, and information on conferences.*

46

Physics

Web sites

PHYSICS NEWS
<http://www.het.brown.edu/news/index.html>
Lists latest work being done in physics, including NASA's Hot Topics and the newsletter the Scientist; science news from wire services; and links to other journals and magazines.

AIP PHYSICS INFORMATION
<http://www.aip.org/>
Links to societies, publications, career services, and databases from the American Institute of Physics.

HEPIC GLOBAL SEARCH
<http://www.hep.net/search/global.html>
Covers all the major electronic databases in physics, using a keyword search.

CONTEMPORARY PHYSICS EDUCATION PROJECT
<http://pdg.lbl.gov/cpep.html>
Provides links to several interactive explanations of fields in physics and lists of other sites.

THE NET ADVANCE OF PHYSICS
<http://www.mit.edu/afs/athena.mit.edu/user/r/e /redingtn/www/netadv/welcome.html>
Includes the Physicist's Encyclopedia, *a collection of review articles in physics arranged by subject.*

TIPTOP
<http://www.tp.umu.se/TIPTOP/>
Allows access to physics societies, databases, projects, news, and events.

AMERICAN PHYSICAL SOCIETY
<http://www.aps.org/>
Allows quick access to professional activities and databases.

WWW VIRTUAL LIBRARY—PHYSICS
<http://www.w3.org/vl/Physics/Overview.html>
Categorizes its links by subject.

US DEPARTMENT OF ENERGY
<http://www.doe.gov/>
Contains data on current research and developments in physics; subsidized by the Department of Energy.

THE NASA HOMEPAGE
<http://www.gsfc.nasa.gov/NASA_homepage.html>
Contains useful links to current NASA projects.

Journals

Annals of Physics. Since 1957. 16/yr. *Publishes works of broad significance, written in a manner understandable to a wide audience. Articles tend to be long—over fifty pages.*

Physical Review. The most prestigious journal of physics published today. Divided into five sections, each devoted to a specific topic. **Part A** (since 1970; monthly) *includes current research on atomic, molecular, and optical physics in original research articles and brief commentaries.* **Part B** (since 1970; 48/yr.) *devoted to the field of condensed matter and the solid state.* **Part C** (since 1970; monthly) *concentrates on nuclear physics, including nuclear structure, nuclear reactions, particle reactions, relativistic collisions, hadrons, and sub-nucleon aspects of nuclei.* **Part D** (since 1970; bimonthly) *covers particles, fields, gravitation, and cosmology.* **Part E** (since 1993; monthly) *covers the fields of statistical physics, kinetics, plasmas, fluid structures and fluid dynamics, as well as classical, biological, and computational physics.*

Physics Letters. Part A. General, Atomic, and Solid. Since 1962. Weekly. *Original research important to the field that cannot have been published elsewhere.*

Physics Letters. Part B. Nuclear, Elementary Particle, and High-Energy Physics. Since 1962. Weekly. *Often used to establish scientific precedence, and competition for discovery is fierce.*

47

Political Science

Web sites

POLITICAL SCIENCE VIRTUAL LIBRARY
<http://spirit.lib.uconn.edu/PoliSci/polisci.htm>
Links to departments, libraries, journals, government agencies, newsgroups and listservs, and related fields.

THOMAS: LEGISLATIVE INFORMATION ON THE INTERNET
<http://thomas.loc.gov/>
The homepage of the U.S. Congress, with links to current legislation, Congressional Record *archives, historical documents, and other government resources.*

THE WHITE HOUSE
<http://www.whitehouse.gov>
The presidential site, with links to the president and vice-president, commonly requested federal services, news, a virtual library, and other executive branch links.

FEDWORLD
<http://www.fedworld.gov/>
Links to government services and databases. Good search facilities and explanations, with information on how to order materials.

LEGAL INFORMATION INSTITUTE
<http://www.law.cornell.edu/>
A service of Cornell Law School. Access to recent and historic Supreme Court decisions and a hypertext version of all major federal laws. Good links to other central legal sites.

DEMOCRATIC PARTY ONLINE
<http://www.democrats.org/>
The homepage of the Democratic National Committee. Useful links to Democratic news, issues, and initiatives.

REPUBLICAN MAIN STREET
<http://www.rnc.org/>
The homepage of the Republican National Committee. Has many useful links, not all to party issues.

THE GALLUP ORGANIZATION
<http://www.gallup.com/>
The homepage of the organization, with short descriptions of some of its latest polls. No archive or search ability.

DTIC
<http://www.dtic.dla.mil>
The Defense Technical Information Center is the U.S. military's own information service, with very detailed coverage of the Defense Technical Information Web and links to specific databases.

UNITED NATIONS
<http://www.un.org/>
A good general site, with links to many UN offices, policies, and activities. Also available in French and Spanish.

FOREIGN GOVERNMENT RESOURCES ON THE WEB
<http://www.lib.umich.edu/libhome/Documents.center /foreign.html>
Offers easy-to-find information about other countries and governments; organized by area or by governmental issue.

ST. MARTIN'S POLITICAL SCIENCE HOMEPAGE
<http://www.smpcollege.com/smp_govt>
Over 1,000 links to sites of interest to political science students.

Journals

Political Science Quarterly. Since 1886. Quarterly. *Provides scholarly analysis of political events.*

Foreign Affairs. Since 1922. Quarterly. *Publishes articles on international relations and world politics.*

Congressional Quarterly. Since 1945. Quarterly. *Offers serious articles about national politics.*

48
Psychology

Web sites

THE VIRTUAL PSYCHOLOGY LIBRARY
<http://www-mugc.cc.monash.edu.au/psy/ol/psylinks .html>
Good general links to major North American psychology sites.

AMERICAN PSYCHOLOGICAL ASSOCIATION
<http://www.apa.org/>
The APA homepage, with access to their PsychNet document site and information for students in psychology.

AMERICAN PSYCHOLOGICAL SOCIETY
<http://psych.hanover.edu/APS/>
Links to journals, departments, Net resources and discussion groups, and research information.

COGNITIVE AND PSYCHOLOGICAL SCIENCES ON THE NET
<http://www-psych.stanford.edu/cogsci>
Indexes resources on the Net that deal with research in cognition and psychology. Note that this site does not cover clinical psychology or mental health issues.

GALAXY PSYCHOLOGY PAGE
<http://galaxy.einet.net/galaxy/Social-Sciences
/Psychology.html>
A large site divided into Clinical, Developmental, Educational, and Experimental lists. Also offers a search facility with links to academic organizations, collections, directories, and discussion groups.

FREUDNET: THE BRILL LIBRARY
<http://plaza.interport.net/nypsan/>
Psychoanalytic news, services, and links to electronic research.

NEUROPSYCHOLOGY CENTRAL
<http://www.premier.net/~cogito/neuropsy.html>
Links to almost any aspect of neuropsychology.

BEHAVIOR ANALYSIS RESOURCES
<http://www.coedu.usf.edu/behavior/bares.htm>
Links to resources in behavioral psychology.

INTERNET MENTAL HEALTH
<http://www.mentalhealth.com/main.html>
Links to the most common mental disorders and medications, news, diagnosis, and help.

Journals

American Journal of Psychology. Since 1887. Quarterly. *Addresses issues in the basic science of the mind. Includes research reports, theoretical and experimental analysis, historical commentaries, discussions, and reviews.*

American Psychologist. Since 1946. Monthly. *Publishes articles with a theoretical or empirical emphasis.*

Clinical Psychology Review. Since 1981. 8/yr. *Provides substantive reviews covering issues in clinical psychology.*

Psychological Review. Since 1894. Quarterly. *Emphasizes work that advances psychological theory.*

Journal of Personality and Social Psychology. Since 1965. Monthly. *Empirical reports on "Attitudes and Social Cognition," "Interpersonal Relations and Group Processes," and "Personality and Individual Differences."*

Counseling Psychologist. Since 1973. Quarterly. *Focuses on the theory, research, and practice of counseling psychology.*

49

Sociology

Web sites

SOCIAL SCIENCE SITES
<http://www.tntech.edu/www/acad/hist/data.html>
A historically weighted list of social sciences for general information.

SOCIAL WORK AND SOCIAL SERVICES WEB SITES
<http://www.gwbssw.wustl.edu/%7Egwbhome/websites.html>
Information on abuse and violence, addiction, alternative medicine, emotional support, gender issues, and welfare.

SOCIOLOGICAL ABSTRACTS
<http://www.socabs.org/>
Provides links to other free sites in sociology.

WWW VIRTUAL LIBRARY—SOCIOLOGY
<http://www.w3.org/pub/DataSources/bySubject/Sociology/Overview.html>
Links to sites covering research centers, discussion groups, e-journals, organizations, and university departments.

ANNUAL REVIEWS SOCIOLOGY ON-LINE
<http://www.annurev.org/soc/home.htm>
Allows searches of twelve years' worth of databases for downloadable abstracts. Full articles can be ordered.

INTERNET/WEB RESOURCES FOR SOCIOLOGY
<http://don.skidmore.edu/academics/sociology/soclinks.html>
Offers links to sociology resources and areas of interest, including journals and listservs.

A SOCIOLOGICAL TOUR THROUGH CYBERSPACE
<http://www.trinity.edu/~mkearl/index.html>
Provides links within sociology, including theory, data, methods, paper-writing guides, and inquiry help.

THE SOCIOWEB
<http://www.socioweb.com/~markbl/socioweb/>
A general site of links and resources, including searches by topic.

Journals

Journal of Social Issues. Since 1944. Quarterly. *Provides broad coverage of research on the psychological aspects of major social issues.*

American Sociological Review. Since 1936. Twice monthly. *Provides broad coverage of all topics in the field, including new theoretical developments, results of research, and methodological innovations.*

Journal of Sociology and Social Welfare. Since 1973. Quarterly. *Articles focus on the connection between social science theory and social work practice.*

SMR: Sociological Methods and Research. Since 1972. Quarterly. *Articles focus on methods of quantitative research, including all fields of the social sciences.*

absolute phrase   See *phrase.*

abstract noun   See *noun.*

acronym   a word, usually a noun, formed from the first letter(s) of several words, such as FAQ for *frequently asked questions.*

active voice   See *voice.*

adjective   a word that modifies, quantifies, identifies, or describes a noun or a word or words acting as a noun. Most adjectives precede the noun or other word(s) they modify (*a good book*), but a **predicate adjective** follows the noun or pronoun it modifies (*the book is good*).

adjective clause   See *clause.*

adjective forms   changes in an adjective from the positive degree (*tall, good*) to the comparative (comparing two—*taller, better*) or the superlative (comparing more than two—*tallest, best*). Short regular adjectives (*tall*) add -er and -est, but most adjectives of two syllables or more form the comparative by adding *more* (*more beautiful*) and the superlative by adding *most* (*most beautiful*). A few adjectives have irregular forms (*good, better, best*), and some adjectives (*only, forty*) do not change form.

adverb   a word that qualifies, modifies, limits, or defines a verb, an adjective, another adverb, or a clause, frequently answering the questions *where? when? how? why? to what extent?* or *under what conditions?* Adverbs derived from adjectives and nouns commonly end in the suffix -ly. *She will soon travel south and will probably visit her very favorite sister.* See also *conjunction.*

adverb clause   See *clause.*

adverb forms   changes in an adverb from the positive degree (*eagerly*) to the comparative (comparing two—*more eagerly*) or the superlative (comparing more than two—*most eagerly*). Most adverbs add *more* to form the comparative and *most* to form the superlative, but a few add -er and -est or have irregular forms (*fast, faster, fastest; little, less, least*).

agreement   the correspondence of a pronoun with its antecedent in person, number, and gender or of a verb with its subject in person and number. See also *antecedent, gender, number, person.*

< > angle brackets   an Internet convention (sometimes called "right and left arrows") meaning that all characters within the brackets must be treated as a single unit, with no spaces between

parts. Example: <http://www.mapquest.com>. Angle brackets are used to enclose email addresses or Web site locations.

antecedent   the specific noun that a pronoun replaces and to which it refers. A pronoun and its antecedent must agree in person, number, and gender. *Ginger Rogers moved her feet as no one else has.*

appositive   a noun or noun phrase that identifies or adds identifying information to a preceding noun phrase. *Michael Jordan, the best player in the NBA, scored thirty-one points. My sister Janet has twin boys.*

Archie   an early Internet tool for discovering and retrieving files from linked computers.

archive   a collection of electronic files stored on a computer.

article   *a, an,* or *the,* the most common adjectives. *A* and *an* are **indefinite**; they do not specifically identify the nouns they modify. *I bought an apple and a peach. The* is **definite** or specific. *The peach was not ripe.*

ASCII   American Standard Code Information Interchange, the most basic format allowing for transfer of text files between different computers and programs.

asynchronous ("asynch") communication   online communication, such as email, involving a delay between the time a message is posted and the time it is received.

@ (the "at" sign)   the part of every email address that occurs between the username and the domain name, indicating that someone is "at" a particular electronic address. For example, <jrobinson@osu.edu> indicates that Jane Robinson gets email at OSU, an educational institution.

auxiliary verb   a verb that combines with the base form or with the present or past participle of a main verb to form a verb phrase. The primary auxiliaries are forms of *do, have,* and *be. Did he arrive? We have eaten. She is writing.* **Modal** auxiliaries such as *can, may, shall, will, could, might, should, would,* and *ought [to]* have only one form and show possibility, necessity, obligation, and so on.

\ (the backslash)   the backward slash mark used mainly in DOS directory paths. An example would be: <C:\windows \desktop\pcfile\survey>.

bandwidth   a measure of the speed at which a given amount of electronic data can be transmitted. Fiber-optic data lines on computer networks allow for much greater bandwidth than do telephone lines.

base form   the form of a verb that is listed in dictionaries, such as *go* or *listen.* For all verbs except *be,* it is the same as the first-person singular form in the present tense.

BBS (bulletin board service or **bulletin board system)** a local computer system that functions as an information clearinghouse for users, allowing people with common interests to post and receive messages.

bookmark a Web site listed in a bookmark list.

bookmark list a pulldown menu in Netscape or Explorer browsers that allows a user to save the addresses of favorite Web sites so they can easily be revisited.

Boolean term a word like *and* or *or* that allows for computer database searches using multiple words. Example: *Kahlo, Frida <u>and</u> American Literature.*

browser a World Wide Web program for negotiating the Internet. Browsers display Web sites and homepages and allow users to click on hyperlinks to move among sites. Netscape Navigator and Microsoft Explorer are the two most commonly used. Some browsers display text but not graphics; Lynx is the most popular of these.

bulletin board service See *BBS.*

bulletin board system See *BBS.*

case the form of a noun or pronoun that reflects its grammatical role in a sentence. Nouns and indefinite pronouns can be **subjective, possessive,** or **objective,** but they change form only in the possessive case. *The <u>dog</u>* (subjective) *barked. The <u>dog's</u>* (possessive) *tail wagged. The mail carrier called the <u>dog</u>* (objective). The personal pronouns *I, he, she, we,* and *they,* as well as the relative or interrogative pronoun *who,* have different forms for all three cases. *<u>We</u>* (subjective) *took the train to Chicago. <u>Our</u>* (possessive) *trip lasted a week. Maria met <u>us</u>* (objective) *at the station.* See also *person, pronoun.*

chat rooms See *IRC.*

clause a group of words containing a subject and a predicate. An **independent clause** can stand alone as a sentence. *The car hit the tree.* A dependent clause, as the name suggests, is grammatically subordinate to an independent clause, linked to it by a subordinating conjunction or a relative pronoun. A dependent clause can function as an adjective, an adverb, or a noun. *The car hit the tree <u>that stood at the edge of the road</u>* (**adjective clause**). *The car hit the tree <u>when it went out of control</u>* (**adverb clause**). *The car hit <u>what grew at the side of the road</u>* (**noun clause**). See also *nonrestrictive element, restrictive element.*

collective noun See *noun.*

comma splice an error resulting from joining two independent clauses with only a comma.

common noun See *noun.*

comparative degree See *adjective forms, adverb forms.*

complement   a word or group of words completing the predicate in a sentence. A **subject complement** follows a linking verb and renames or describes the subject. It can be a **predicate noun** (*Anorexia is an illness*) or a **predicate adjective** (*Karen Carpenter was anorexic*). An **object complement** renames or describes a direct object (*We considered her a prodigy and her behavior extraordinary*).

complete predicate   See *predicate.*

complete subject   See *subject.*

complex sentence   See *sentence.*

compound adjective   a combination of words that functions as a single adjective (*blue-green sea, ten-story building, get-tough policy, high school outing, north-by-northwest journey*). Most, but not all, compound adjectives need hyphens to separate their individual elements.

compound noun   a combination of words that functions as a single noun (*go-getter, in-law, Johnny-on-the-spot, oil well, southeast*).

compound sentence   See *sentence.*

compound subject   See *subject.*

concrete noun   See *noun.*

conjunction   a word or words that join words, phrases, clauses, or sentences. **Coordinating conjunctions** (such as *and, but, or,* or *yet*) join grammatically equivalent elements (*Marx and Engels* [two nouns]; *Marx wrote one essay, but Engels wrote the other* [two independent clauses]). **Correlative conjunctions** (such as *both, and; either, or;* or *not only, but also*) are used in pairs to connect grammatically equivalent elements (*neither Marx nor Engels; Marx not only studied the world but also changed it*). A **subordinating conjunction** (such as *although, because, if, that,* or *when*) introduces a dependent clause and connects it to an independent clause. *Marx moved to London, where he did most of his work. Marx argued that religion was an "opiate."* A **conjunctive adverb** (such as *consequently, moreover,* or *nevertheless*) modifies an independent clause following another independent clause. A conjunctive adverb generally follows a semicolon and is followed by a comma. *Thoreau lived simply at Walden; however, he regularly joined his aunt for tea in Concord.*

coordinating conjunction   See *conjunction.*

correlative conjunction   See *conjunction.*

count noun   See *noun.*

cyber-   a prefix overused to mean anything created or existing electronically or online, as in *cybernovel, cyberkitchen, cybergeek.*

cyberspace   originally a term describing a complex melding of mind and computer in William Gibson's science-fiction

novel *Neuromancer*; now generalized to mean simply the Internet or the World Wide Web.

dangling modifier a word, phrase, or clause that does not logically modify any element in the sentence to which it is attached. *Studying Freud, the meaning of my dreams became clear* is incorrect because *the meaning* could not have been studying Freud. *Studying Freud, I began to understand the meaning of my dreams* is correct because now *I* was doing the studying.

degree See *adjective forms, adverb forms*.

dependent clause See *clause*.

descriptor a keyword used in a Web or Net search.

digital From its specific original meaning of "composed of binary on-off pulses," this term has come to mean simply "electronic" or "wired."

direct address construction that uses a noun or pronoun to name the person or thing being spoken to. *Hey, Jack. You, get moving.*

direct discourse a quotation that reproduces a speaker's exact words, marked with quotation marks.

direct object a noun or pronoun receiving the action of a transitive verb. *McKellan recited Shakespearean soliloquies*. See also *indirect object*.

directory a list or group of computer files that are somehow related; also called a folder. A directory can contain other directories, which are then called subdirectories.

directory path a listing of the order of directories and subdirectories a user must open to find a particular computer file in DOS and Windows applications. Directory paths are delineated by backslashes. For example, <c:\wp52\memos\walter.1> indicates that the file <walter.1> is in the directory <wp52>, subdirectory <memos>, on the hard disk drive designated <c:>.

domain name the characters and symbols identifying elements within a computer server on the Internet. Usually designating Web sites or email addresses, domain names have at least two parts, separated by dots. The first part designates the organization or server, and the final part identifies the type of organization operating the server, such as *.com* (commercial), *.edu* (educational), *.gov* (government), *.mil* (military), *.net* (network management), and *.org* (noncommercial/nonprofit). Domains outside the United States often identify the country in which a server is located, such as *.uk* for Great Britain and *.fi* for Finland.

. (the dot) the period symbol called "dot" when used to separate parts of email addresses, URLs, and newsgroup names, as in <bgm2@umnvm1.umn.edu>.

download to move data electronically, usually from a server or mainframe to a microcomputer or PC.

email address the string of characters identifying a location for sending or receiving email. An email address contains a username, the @ symbol, and the domain name, as in <gbowe @hopper.unh.edu>.

email (electronic mail) sending or receiving electronic messages by means of various programs that allow asynchronous communication over a network.

emoticons combinations of ASCII characters used in email to indicate moods or facial expressions. (Look at them sideways.) Common emoticons include :-) (smile), :-((frown), ;-/ (skeptical), and :-o (surprised).

expletive a construction that introduces a sentence with *there* or *it*, usually followed by a form of *be*. *There are four candidates for this job. It was a dark and stormy night.*

FAQ (frequently asked questions) a file containing common questions about an online program or service (such as a listserv or newsgroup) and their answers.

file name the last part of a URL, indicating the specific computer file for which the URL is the address.

first person See *person*.

flaming personal attacks in email or other electronic communication. Considered bad manners.

FTP (file transfer protocol) the electronic commands used to transfer files between computers on the Internet.

fused sentence a sentence in which two independent clauses are run together without a conjunction or punctuation between them. Also known as a *run-on sentence*.

future tense See *tense*.

gender the classification of a noun or pronoun as masculine (*god, he*), feminine (*goddess, she*), or neuter (*godliness, it*).

gerund a verbal form ending in *-ing* and functioning as a noun. *Sleeping is a bore.*

gopher a set of programs for accessing information on the Internet through a series of hierarchically arranged menus. Gopher underlies the search capabilities of Web browsers, but it is usually used to seek out text-based files.

hard copy a version of an electronic document or file that is printed out onto paper.

header the subject line of a listserv or newsgroup posting. By looking at the index of headers, users can determine the different threads of a discussion.

helping verb See *auxiliary verb*.

hit   an electronic connection on the World Wide Web. A hit can be either a match with a keyword a user is searching for with a search engine (as in: *HOTBOT's search for* firewalking *turned up thirty* <u>hits</u>) or the accessing of a Web homepage by a remote browser (as in *The Beanie Babies page received two thousand* <u>hits</u> *today*).

homepage   the introductory page users see when they access a Web site, which controls access to other links the site offers.

hotlink   See *hyperlink*.

HTML (Hypertext Markup Language)   an electronic coding system for creating World Wide Web pages, which indicates how browsers should display text and graphic images onscreen.

hyperlink   a connection between two points on the World Wide Web, which may be in the same or different sites. Hyperlinks are indicated in Web text by the use of different-colored letters and/or underlining.

hypertext   a document coded in HTML that contains hyperlinks, or a collection of such documents.

imperative mood   the form of a verb used to express a command or a request. An imperative uses the base form of the verb and may or may not have a stated subject. <u>Leave</u>. *You* <u>be</u> *quiet.* <u>Let</u>'s go. See also *mood*.

indefinite pronoun   See *pronoun*.

independent clause   See *clause*.

indicative mood   the form of a verb used to state a fact or opinion or to ask a question. *Washington* <u>crossed</u> *the Delaware.* <u>Did</u> *he* <u>defeat</u> *the Hessians?* See also *mood*.

indirect discourse   a paraphrased quotation that does not repeat another's exact words and hence is not enclosed in quotation marks. *Coolidge said that if nominated he would not run.*

indirect object   a noun or pronoun identifying to whom or to what or for whom or for what a transitive verb's action is performed. The indirect object almost always precedes the direct object. *I handed the* <u>dean</u> *my application and told* <u>her</u> *that I needed financial aid.* See also *direct object*.

indirect question   a sentence pattern in which a question is the basis of a subordinate clause. An indirect question should end with a period, not a question mark. *Everyone wonders* <u>why young people continue to take up smoking</u>. (The question, phrased directly, is "Why do young people continue to take up smoking?")

infinitive   the base form of a verb preceded by *to* (*to go, to run, to hit*). An infinitive can serve as a noun, an adverb, or an adjective. <u>To go</u> *would be unthinkable* (noun). *We stopped* <u>to rest</u> (adverb). *The company needs space* <u>to grow</u> (adjective). An infini-

tive can be in either the active (*to hit*) or passive (*to be hit*) voice and in either the present (*to [be] hit*) or perfect (*to have [been] hit*) tense. An **infinitive phrase** consists of an infinitive together with its modifiers, objects, or complements. See *phrase*.

intensifier   a modifier that increases the emphasis of the word or words it modifies. *I would very much like to go. I'm so happy.* Despite their name, intensifiers are stylistically weak; they are best avoided in academic and professional writing.

interjection   a grammatically independent word or group of words that is usually an exclamation of surprise, shock, dismay, or the like. *Ouch! For heaven's sake, what do you think you're doing?*

Internet   originally a network of academic and military mainframe computers; now a worldwide "network of networks," linking computers of all sizes and types and providing access to the World Wide Web, among other services.

Internet service provider (ISP)   an individual or group that provides access to the Internet, such as America Online and CompuServe.

intransitive verb   a verb that does not need a direct object to complete its meaning. *The children laughed.*

IRC (Internet relay chat)   an Internet service that allows synchronous online communication (like telephone conference calls) with others; sometimes called "chat rooms."

irregular verb   a verb whose past tense and past participle are not formed by adding *-ed* or *-d* to the base form, such as *see, saw, seen.*

keyword   a word or phrase used to search a computer database. In a World Wide Web or Internet search, it is typed into the search engine's dialog box.

linkage data   information about a hypertext document's links to other documents.

linking verb   a verb that joins a subject with a subject complement or complements. Common linking verbs are *appear, be, become, feel,* and *seem. The argument appeared sound. It was actually a trick.* See also *verb*.

listserv   the central server that controls an ongoing email discussion group about a particular topic. Participants subscribe to a listserv by sending a "subscribe" command to the server.

main clause   an independent clause. See *clause*.

main verb   the verb that carries the central meaning in a verb phrase, such as *given* in the phrase *could be given.*

misplaced modifier   a word, phrase, or clause positioned so that it appears to modify a word other than the one the writer intended. *With a credit card, the traveler paid for the motel room*

and opened the door. Unless the writer intended to indicate that the traveler used the credit card to open the door, *with a credit card* should follow *paid* or *room*.

modal   See *auxiliary verb.*

modem   an electronic device connecting a computer to a telephone line or another line that allows it to communicate with other computers.

modifier   a word, phrase, or clause that acts as an adjective or an adverb and qualifies the meaning of another word, phrase, or clause. See also *adjective, adverb, clause, phrase.*

MOO (multi-user domain, object-oriented)   an online service that enables many people to communicate synchronously at prearranged times, usually to discuss a particular topic.

mood   the form of a verb that indicates the writer's or speaker's attitude toward the idea expressed by the verb. Different moods are used to state a fact or opinion or to ask a question (indicative); to give a command or request (imperative); and to express a wish, a suggestion, a request or requirement, or a condition that does not exist (subjunctive). *The sea is turbulent* (indicative). *Stay out of the water* (imperative). *I wish the water were calm enough for swimming* (subjunctive). See also *imperative mood, indicative mood, subjunctive mood.*

mouse   a handheld device, with two buttons and a cord at one end, used to enter commands into a computer.

MUD (multi-user domain)   an online service for synchronous communication, usually in the form of role-playing games.

netiquette   a set of standards for behavior on a computer network or the Internet.

newsgroup   an arrangement by a group of people with a particular interest to maintain a space for postings about the topic on the Usenet network.

noncount noun   See *noun.*

nonrestrictive element   a word, phrase, or clause that modifies but does not change the essential meaning of a sentence element. A nonrestrictive element is set off from the rest of the sentence with commas, dashes, or parentheses. *Quantum physics, a difficult subject, is fascinating.* See also *restrictive element.*

noun   a word that names a person, place, object, concept, action, or the like. Nouns serve as subjects, objects, complements, and appositives. Most nouns form the plural with the addition of *-s* or *-es* and the possessive with the addition of *'s* (see *number, case*). **Common nouns** (*president, state, month*) name classes or general groups. **Proper nouns** (*Hillary Clinton, Florida, July*) name particular persons or things and are capitalized. **Collective nouns** (*family, committee, jury*) refer to a group

of related elements. **Count nouns** (*women, trees*) refer to things that can be directly counted. **Noncount nouns** (*sand, rain, violence*) refer to collections of things or to ideas that cannot be directly counted.

noun clause See *clause.*

noun phrase See *phrase.*

number the form of a noun or pronoun that indicates whether it is singular (*book, I, he, her, it*) or plural (*books, we, they, them, their*).

object a word or words, usually a noun or pronoun, influenced by a transitive verb, a verbal, or a preposition. See also *direct object, indirect object, object of a preposition.*

object complement See *complement.*

objective case See *case.*

object of a preposition a noun or pronoun connected to a sentence by a preposition. The preposition, the object, and any modifiers make up a **prepositional phrase**. *I went to the party without her.*

online connected to a network; on the Internet or the World Wide Web.

participial phrase See *phrase.*

participle a verbal with properties of both an adjective and a verb. Like an adjective, a participle can modify a noun or pronoun; like a verb, it has present and past forms and can take an object. The **present participle** of a verb always ends in *-ing* (*going, being*). The **past participle** usually ends in *-ed* (*ruined, injured*), but many verbs have irregular forms (*gone, been, brought*). Present participles are used with the auxiliary verb *be* to form the **progressive tenses** (*I am making, I will be making, I have been making*). Past participles are used with the auxiliary verb *have* to form the **perfect tenses** (*I have made, I had made, I will have made*) and with *be* to form the passive voice (*I am seen, I was seen*). These combinations of auxiliary verbs and participles are known as **verb phrases**. See also *adjective, phrase, tense, verbal, voice.*

parts of speech the eight grammatical categories into which words can be grouped depending on how they function in a sentence. Many words act as different parts of speech in different sentences. The parts of speech are *adjectives, adverbs, conjunctions, interjections, nouns, prepositions, pronouns, and verbs.*

passive voice See *voice.*

password a personal code used to access a computer account.

past participle See *participle.*

past perfect tense See *tense.*

past tense   See *tense*.

perfect tenses   See *participle, tense, verb*.

person   the relation between a subject and its verb, indicating whether the subject is speaking about itself (**first person**—*I* or *we*), being spoken to (**second person**—*you*), or being spoken about (**third person**—*he, she, it,* or *they*). *Be* has several forms depending on the person (*am, is,* and *are* in the present tense and *was* and *were* in the past tense). Other verbs change form only in the present tense with a third-person singular subject (*I fall, you fall, she falls, we fall, they fall*).

personal pronoun   See *pronoun*.

phrase   a group of words that functions as a single unit but lacks a subject, verb, or both. An **absolute phrase** modifies an entire sentence. It usually includes a noun or pronoun followed by a participle (sometimes implied) or participial phrase. *The party being over, everyone left*. A **gerund phrase** includes a gerund and its objects, complements, and modifiers. It functions as a noun, acting as a subject, a complement, or an object. *Exercising regularly and sensibly is a key to good health* (subject). An **infinitive phrase** includes an infinitive and its objects, complements, and modifiers. It functions as an adjective, an adverb, or a noun. *The Pacific Coast is the place to be* (adjective). *She went to pay her taxes* (adverb). *To be young again is all I want* (noun). A **noun phrase** includes a noun and its modifiers. *A long, rough road crossed the barren desert*. A **participial phrase** includes a present or past participle and its objects, complements, or modifiers. It functions as an adjective. *Absentmindedly climbing the stairs, he stumbled. They bought a house built in 1895*. A **prepositional phrase** is introduced by a preposition and ends with a noun or pronoun, called the object of the preposition. It functions as an adjective, an adverb, or a noun. *The gas in the laboratory was leaking* (adjective). *The firefighters went to the lab to check* (adverb). *The smell came from inside a wall* (noun). A **verb phrase** is composed of a main verb and one or more auxiliaries, acting as a single verb in the sentence predicate. *I should have come to the review session*.

plural   the form of a noun, pronoun, or adjective that refers to more than one person or thing, such as *books, we,* or *those*.

possessive case   See *case*.

post   to send a message, or *posting*, to an electronic correspondent, a listserv, or a newsgroup.

predicate   the verb and related words in a clause or sentence. The predicate expresses what the subject does, experiences, or is. The **simple predicate** is the verb or verb phrase. *For years the YMHA has been a cultural center in New York City*. The **complete predicate** includes the simple predicate and any modifiers, objects, or complements. *John gave Sarah an engagement ring*. A

compound predicate has more than one simple predicate. *The athletes <u>swam</u> in a relay and <u>ran</u> in a marathon.*

predicate adjective See *complement.*

predicate noun See *complement.*

prefix an addition to the beginning of a word to alter its meaning (<u>*anti*</u>*-French,* <u>*un*</u>*dress*).

preposition a word or group of words that indicates the relationship of a noun or pronoun, called the *object of the preposition,* to another part of the sentence. *He was <u>on top of</u> the ladder before the other contestants had climbed <u>to</u> the fourth rung.* See *phrase.*

present participle See *participle.*

present perfect See *participle, tense, verb, verbal.*

present progressive See *participle, tense, verb, verbal.*

present tense See *tense, verb.*

progressive tenses See *participle, tense, verb.*

pronoun a word used in place of a noun, usually called the antecedent of the pronoun. **Indefinite pronouns** do not refer to specific nouns and include *any, each, everybody, some,* and similar words. <u>*Many*</u> *are called, but <u>few</u> are chosen.* **Personal pronouns** (*I, you, he, she, it, we, you,* and *they*) refer to particular people or things. They have different forms (*I, me, my, mine*) depending on their case. (See also *case.*) **Relative pronouns** (*who, whom, whose, which, that, what, whoever, whomever, whichever,* and *whatever*) connect a dependent clause to a sentence. *I wonder <u>who</u> will win the prize.*

proper noun See *noun.*

protocol the agreed command set used by many different kinds of computers to allow data exchange. Examples include FTP, telnet, and gopher.

real-time communication See *synchronous communication.*

regular verb a verb whose past tense and past participle are formed by adding *-d* or *-ed* to the base form (*care, cared, cared; look, looked, looked*). See also *irregular verb.*

relative pronoun See *pronoun.*

restrictive element a word, phrase, or clause that limits the essential meaning of the sentence element it modifies or provides necessary identifying information about it. A restrictive element is not set off from the rest of the sentence with commas, dashes, or parentheses. *The tree <u>that I hit</u> was an oak.* See also *nonrestrictive element.*

run-on sentence See *comma splice, fused sentence.*

search engine one of a variety of programs on the World Wide Web that allows users to search for information by key-

word. When a keyword is typed into a search engine, the program seeks out all Web sites containing that keyword and displays them in a list of "hits." Examples: Alta Vista, Lycos, Yahoo, Excite.

second person See *person*.

sentence a group of words containing a subject and a predicate and expressing a complete thought. In writing, a sentence begins with a capital letter and ends with a period, a question mark, or an exclamation point. A **compound sentence** contains two or more independent clauses linked with a coordinating conjunction, a correlative conjunction, or a semicolon. *I did not wish to go, but she did.* See also *clause*.

sentence fragment a group of words that is not a grammatically complete sentence but is punctuated as one. Usually a fragment lacks a subject, verb, or both or is a dependent clause that is not attached to an independent clause. In academic and professional writing, fragments should be revised to be complete sentences.

server a computer that provides services, such as email or file transfer, in response to requests from other computers; often still called a "mainframe."

.sig file identifying information that many writers attach to the end of their electronic messages, such as their name, title, address, and phone and fax numbers.

simple predicate See *predicate*.

simple subject See *subject*.

singular the form of a noun, pronoun, or adjective that refers to one person or thing, such as *book*, *it*, or *this*.

/ (the slash) the forward slash, called just "slash" when used to separate parts of email addresses, URLs, and newsgroup names, as in <http://quinine.lists/quinine.html>.

snailmail mail delivered in hard copy form through the postal service, so called because it takes so much longer than email.

split infinitive the often awkward intrusion of an adverb between *to* and the base form of the verb in an infinitive (*to better serve* rather than *to serve better*).

squinting modifier a misplaced word, phrase, or clause that could refer equally, but with different meanings, to words either preceding or following it. For example, in *Playing poker often is dangerous*, the position of *often* fails to indicate whether the writer meant that frequent poker playing is dangerous or that poker playing is often dangerous.

subject the noun or pronoun and related words that indicate who or what a sentence is about. The **simple subject** is the

noun or pronoun. The **complete subject** is the simple subject and its modifiers. In *The timid gray mouse fled from the owl*, *mouse* is the simple subject; *The timid gray mouse* is the complete subject. A **compound subject** includes two or more simple subjects. *The mouse and the owl heard the fox.*

subject complement   See *complement*.

subject directory   a hyperlinked list of sites, classified by subject, that results from a World Wide Web search.

subjective case   See *case*.

subjunctive mood   the form of a verb used to express a wish, a suggestion, a request or requirement, or a condition that does not exist. The present subjunctive uses the base form of the verb. *I asked that he be present. Long live the Queen!* The past subjunctive uses the same verb form as the past tense except for the verb *be*, which uses *were* for all subjects. *If I were president, I would change things.* See also *mood*.

subordinate clause   a dependent clause. See *clause*.

subordinating conjunction   See *conjunction*.

suffix   an addition to the end of a word that alters the word's meaning or part of speech, as in *migrate* (verb) and *migration* (noun) or *late* (adjective or adverb) and *lateness* (noun).

superlative degree   See *adjective forms, adverb forms*.

surf   to browse intensively on the Internet. A *surfer* is an Internet enthusiast, whose fun is always also an application of expertise.

synchronous communication   online communication in which messages are sent and received as they are being typed, with no delay, as in IRCs, MOOs, and MUDs; also called **real-time communication**.

syntax   the arrangement of words in a sentence in order to reveal the relation of each to the whole sentence and to one another.

telnet   a program that allows use of one computer from another computer.

tense   the form of a verb that indicates the time at which an action takes place or a condition exists. The times expressed by tense are basically **present**, **past**, and **future**. Each tense has **simple** (*I love*), **perfect** (*I have loved*), **progressive** (*I am loving*), and **perfect progressive** (*I have been loving*) forms.

third person   See *person*.

thread   a series of postings to a listserv or newsgroup about a particular topic.

transitive verb   a verb that takes a direct object, which receives the action expressed by the verb. A transitive verb

may be in the active or passive voice. *The artist drew the sketch. The sketch was drawn by the artist.* See also *verb.*

URL (uniform resource locator) a series of characters identifying the address of a homepage or a whole Web site. The URL for the *EasyWriter* Web site is <www.smpcollege.com /easywriter>.

Usenet a network within the Internet that provides access to newsgroups. Access to Usenet requires a newsreader program on a computer's local server.

username a series of characters that identifies a computer user and, together with a password, provides access to the user's computer account. Email addresses usually begin with a username.

verb a word or group of words, essential to a sentence, that expresses what action a subject takes or receives or what the subject's state of being is. *Edison invented the incandescent bulb. Gas lighting was becoming obsolete.* Verbs change form to show tense, number, voice, and mood. See also *auxiliary verb, intransitive verb, irregular verb, linking verb, mood, person, regular verb, tense, transitive verb, verbal, voice.*

verbal a verb form that functions as a noun, an adjective, or an adverb. The three kinds of verbals are gerunds, infinitives, and participles. See also *gerund, infinitive, participle.*

verbal phrase a phrase using a gerund, a participle, or an infinitive. See *phrase.*

verb phrase See *phrase.*

virtual existing only in electronic form; having no physical reality.

voice the form of a transitive verb that indicates whether the subject is acting or being acted on. When a verb is in the **active voice**, the subject performs the action. *Parker played the saxophone fantastically.* When a verb is in the **passive voice**, the subject receives the action. *The saxophone was played by Parker.* The passive voice is formed with the appropriate tense of the verb *be* and the past participle of the transitive verb. See also *verb.*

WAIS (Wide Area Information Server) a program that searches Internet databases for keywords. Usually found at central sites like libraries, it is often a service that must be purchased.

Web See *World Wide Web.*

Web site any World Wide Web location.

wired electronic; online.

World Wide Web (WWW) a graphically based international service connecting hypertext data on the Internet.

GLOSSARY OF USAGE

Conventions of usage might be called the "good manners" of discourse. And just as our notions of good manners vary from culture to culture and time to time, so do conventions of usage. The word *ain't*, for instance, now considered inappropriate in academic and professional discourse, was once widely used by the most proper British speakers and is still commonly used in some spoken U.S. dialects. In short, matters of usage, like other language choices you must make, depend on what your purpose is and on what is appropriate for a particular audience at a particular time. This glossary provides usage guidelines for some commonly confused or otherwise problematic words and phrases.

a, an Use *a* with a word that begins with a consonant (*a book*), a consonant sound such as "y" or "w" (*a euphoric moment, a one-sided match*), or a sounded *h* (*a hemisphere*). Use *an* with a word that begins with a vowel (*an umbrella*), a vowel sound (*an X-ray*), or a silent *h* (*an honor*).

accept, except The verb *accept* means "receive" or "agree to." *Except* is usually a preposition that means "aside from" or "excluding." *All the plaintiffs except Mr. Kim decided to accept the settlement.*

advice, advise The noun *advice* means "opinion" or "suggestion"; the verb *advise* means "offer advice." *Charlotte's mother advised her to dress warmly, but Charlotte ignored the advice.*

affect, effect As a verb, *affect* means "influence" or "move the emotions of"; as a noun, it means "emotions" or "feelings." *Effect* is a noun meaning "result"; less commonly, it is a verb meaning "bring about." *The storm affected a large area. Its effects included widespread power failures. The drug effected a major change in the patient's affect.*

aggravate The formal meaning is "make worse." *Having another mouth to feed aggravated their poverty.* In academic and professional writing, avoid using *aggravate* to mean "irritate" or "annoy."

all ready, already *All ready* means "fully prepared." *Already* means "previously." *We were all ready for Lucy's party when we learned that she had already left.*

all right, alright Avoid the spelling *alright*.

all together, altogether *All together* means "all in a group" or "gathered in one place." *Altogether* means "completely" or "everything considered." *When the board members were all together, their mutual distrust was altogether obvious.*

allude, elude *Allude* means "refer indirectly." *Elude* means "avoid" or "escape from." *The candidate did not even allude to her opponent. The suspect eluded the police for several days.*

allusion, illusion An *allusion* is an indirect reference. An *illusion* is a false or misleading appearance. *The speaker's allusion to the Bible created an illusion of piety.*

already See *all ready, already.*

alright See *all right, alright.*

altogether See *all together, altogether.*

among, between In referring to two things or people, use *between.* In referring to three or more, use *among. The relationship between the twins is different from that among the other three children.*

amount, number Use *amount* with quantities you cannot count; use *number* for quantities you can count. *A small number of volunteers cleared a large amount of brush.*

an See *a, an.*

and/or Avoid this term except in business or legal writing. Instead of *fat and/or protein,* write *fat, protein, or both.*

any body, anybody, any one, anyone *Anybody* and *anyone* are pronouns meaning "any person." *Anyone* [or *anybody*] *would enjoy this film. Any body* is an adjective modifying a noun. *Any body of water has its own ecology. Any one* is two adjectives or a pronoun modified by an adjective. *Customers could buy only two sale items at any one time. The winner could choose any one of the prizes.*

anyplace In academic and professional discourse, use *anywhere* instead.

anyway, anyways In writing, use *anyway,* not *anyways.*

apt, liable, likely *Likely to* means "probably will," and *apt to* means "inclines or tends to." In many instances they are interchangeable. *Liable* often carries a more negative sense and is also a legal term meaning "obligated" or "responsible."

as Avoid sentences in which it is not clear if *as* means "because" or means "when." For example, does *Carl left town as his father was arriving* mean "at the same time as his father was arriving" or "because his father was arriving"?

as, as if, like In academic and professional writing, use *as* or *as if* instead of *like* to introduce a clause. *The dog howled as if* [not *like*] *it were in pain. She did as* [not *like*] *I suggested.*

assure, ensure, insure *Assure* means "convince" or "promise"; its direct object is usually a person or persons. *She assured voters she would not raise taxes. Ensure* and *insure* both mean "make certain," but *insure* usually refers specifically to protection against financial loss. *When the city rationed water to ensure that the supply*

would last, the Browns could no longer afford to <u>*insure*</u> *their car-wash business.*

as to   Do not use *as to* as a substitute for *about*. *Karen was unsure* <u>*about*</u> [not <u>*as to*</u>] *Bruce's intentions.*

at, where   See *where*.

awful, awfully   *Awful* and *awfully* mean "awe-inspiring" and "in an awe-inspiring way." In academic and professional writing, avoid using *awful* to mean "bad" (*I had an* <u>*awful*</u> *day*) and *awfully* to mean "very" (*It was* <u>*awfully*</u> *cold*).

awhile, a while   Always use *a while* after a preposition such as *for, in,* or *after*. *We drove* <u>*awhile*</u> *and then stopped for* <u>*a while*</u>.

bad, badly   Use *bad* after a linking verb such as *be, feel,* or *seem*. Use *badly* to modify an action verb, an adjective, or another verb. *The hostess felt* <u>*bad*</u> *because the dinner was* <u>*badly*</u> *prepared.*

because of, due to   Use *due to* when the effect, stated as a noun, appears before the verb *be*. *His illness was* <u>*due to*</u> *malnutrition.* (*Illness*, a noun, is the effect.) Use *because of* when the effect is stated as a clause. *He was sick* <u>*because of*</u> *malnutrition.* (*He was sick*, a clause, is the effect.)

being as, being that   In academic or professional writing, use *because* or *since* instead of these expressions. <u>*Because*</u> [not <u>*being as*</u>] *Romeo killed Tybalt, he was banished to Padua.*

beside, besides   *Beside* is a preposition meaning "next to." *Besides* can be a preposition meaning "other than" or an adverb meaning "in addition." *No one* <u>*besides*</u> *Francesca would sit* <u>*beside*</u> *him.*

between   See *among, between*.

breath, breathe   *Breath* is a noun; *breathe*, a verb. "<u>*Breathe*</u>," *said the nurse, so June took a deep* <u>*breath*</u>.

bring, take   Use *bring* when an object is moved from a farther to a nearer place; use *take* when the opposite is true. *Take the box to the post office;* <u>*bring*</u> *back my mail.*

but, yet   Do not use these words together. *He is strong* <u>*but*</u> [not <u>*but yet*</u>] *gentle.*

but that, but what   Avoid using these as substitutes for *that* in expressions of doubt. *Hercule Poirot never doubted* <u>*that*</u> [not <u>*but that*</u>] *he would solve the case.*

can, may   *Can* refers to ability and *may* to possibility or permission. *Since I* <u>*can*</u> *ski the slalom well, I* <u>*may*</u> *win the race.*

can't hardly   *Hardly* has a negative meaning; therefore *can't hardly* is a double negative. This expression is commonly used in some varieties of English but is not used in standard academic English. *Tim* <u>*can*</u> [not <u>*can't*</u>] *hardly wait.*

can't help but This expression is redundant. Use the more formal *I cannot but go* or less formal *I can't help going* rather than *I can't help but go*.

censor, censure *Censor* means "remove that which is considered offensive." *Censure* means "formally reprimand." *The newspaper <u>censored</u> stories that offended advertisers. The legislature <u>censured</u> the official for misconduct.*

complement, compliment *Complement* means "go well with." *Compliment* means "praise." *Guests <u>complimented</u> her on how her earrings <u>complemented</u> her gown.*

comprise, compose *Comprise* means "contain." *Compose* means "make up." *The class <u>comprises</u> twenty students. Twenty students <u>compose</u> the class.*

conscience, conscious *Conscience* means "a sense of right and wrong." *Conscious* means "awake" or "aware." *After lying, Lisa was <u>conscious</u> of a guilty <u>conscience</u>.*

consensus of opinion Use *consensus* instead of this redundant phrase. *The family <u>consensus</u> was to sell the old house.*

consequently, subsequently *Consequently* means "as a result"; *subsequently* means "then." *He quit, and <u>subsequently</u> his wife lost her job; <u>consequently</u>, they had to sell their house.*

continual, continuous *Continual* means "repeated at regular or frequent intervals." *Continuous* means "continuing or connected without a break." *The damage done by <u>continuous</u> erosion was increased by the <u>continual</u> storms.*

could of *Have,* not *of,* should follow *could, would, should,* or *might. We should <u>have</u>* [not *of*] *invited them.*

criteria, criterion *Criterion* means "standard of judgment" or "necessary qualification." *Criteria* is the plural form. *Image is the wrong <u>criterion</u> for choosing a president.*

data *Data* is the plural form of the Latin word *datum,* meaning "fact." Although *data* is used informally as either singular or plural, in academic or professional writing, treat *data* as plural. *These <u>data</u> indicate that fewer people are smoking.*

different from, different than *Different from* is generally preferred in academic and professional writing, although both phrases are used widely. *Her lab results were no <u>different from</u>* [not *than*] *his.*

discreet, discrete *Discreet* means "tactful" or "prudent." *Discrete* means "separate" or "distinct." *The leader's <u>discreet</u> efforts kept all the <u>discrete</u> factions unified.*

disinterested, uninterested *Disinterested* means "unbiased." *Uninterested* means "indifferent." *Finding <u>disinterested</u> jurors was difficult. She was <u>uninterested</u> in the verdict.*

distinct, distinctive *Distinct* means "separate" or "well defined." *Distinctive* means "characteristic." *Germany includes many <u>distinct</u> regions, each with a <u>distinctive</u> accent.*

doesn't, don't *Doesn't* is the contraction for *does not*. Use it with *he, she, it,* and singular nouns. *Don't* stands for *do not;* use it with *I, you, we, they,* and plural nouns.

due to See *because of, due to.*

each other, one another Use *each other* in sentences involving two subjects and *one another* in sentences involving more than two.

effect See *affect, effect.*

elicit, illicit The verb *elicit* means "draw out." The adjective *illicit* means "illegal." *The police <u>elicited</u> from the criminal the names of others involved in <u>illicit</u> activities.*

elude See *allude, elude.*

emigrate from, immigrate to *Emigrate from* means "move away from one's country." *Immigrate to* means "move to another country." *We <u>emigrated</u> from Norway in 1957. We <u>immigrated</u> to the United States.*

ensure See *assure, ensure, insure.*

enthused, enthusiastic Use *enthusiastic* rather than *enthused* in academic and professional writing.

equally as good Replace this redundant phrase with *equally good* or *as good.*

every day, everyday *Everyday* is an adjective meaning "ordinary." *Every day* is an adjective and a noun, meaning "each day." *I wore <u>everyday</u> clothes almost <u>every day</u>.*

every one, everyone *Everyone* is a pronoun. *Every one* is an adjective and a pronoun, referring to each member of a group. *Because he began after <u>everyone</u> else, David could not finish <u>every one</u> of the problems.*

except See *accept, except.*

explicit, implicit *Explicit* means "directly or openly expressed." *Implicit* means "indirectly expressed or implied." *The <u>explicit</u> message of the ad urged consumers to buy the product, while the <u>implicit</u> message promised popularity if they did so.*

farther, further *Farther* refers to physical distance. *How much <u>farther</u> is it to Munich? Further* refers to time or degree. *I want to avoid <u>further</u> delays.*

fewer, less Use *fewer* with nouns that can be counted. Use *less* with general amounts that you cannot count. *The world will be safer with <u>fewer</u> bombs and <u>less</u> hostility.*

finalize *Finalize* is a pretentious way of saying "end" or "make final." *We <u>closed</u> [not <u>finalized</u>] the deal.*

firstly, secondly, etc.   *First, second,* etc., are more common in U.S. English.

flaunt, flout   *Flaunt* means to "show off." *Flout* means to "mock" or "scorn." *The drug dealers <u>flouted</u> authority by <u>flaunting</u> their wealth.*

former, latter   *Former* refers to the first and *latter* to the second of two things previously mentioned. *Kathy and Anna are athletes; the <u>former</u> plays tennis, and the <u>latter</u> runs.*

further   See *farther, further.*

good, well   *Good* is an adjective and should not be used as a substitute for the adverb *well*. *Gabriel is a <u>good</u> host who cooks <u>well</u>.*

good and   *Good and* is colloquial for "very"; avoid it in academic and professional writing.

hanged, hung   *Hanged* refers to executions; *hung* is used for all other meanings.

hardly   See *can't hardly.*

herself, himself, myself, yourself   Do not use these reflexive pronouns as subjects or as objects unless they are necessary. *Jane and I* [not *<u>myself</u>*] *agree. They invited John and me* [not *<u>myself</u>*].

he/she, his/her   Better solutions for avoiding sexist language are to write out *he or she*, to eliminate pronouns entirely, or to make the subject plural. Instead of writing *Everyone should carry <u>his/her</u> driver's license,* try *<u>Drivers</u> should carry <u>their</u> licenses* or *<u>People</u> should carry <u>their</u> driver's licenses.*

himself   See *herself, himself, myself, yourself.*

hisself   Use *himself* instead in academic or professional writing.

hopefully   *Hopefully* is often misused to mean "it is hoped," but its correct meaning is "with hope." *Sam watched the roulette wheel <u>hopefully</u>* [not *<u>Hopefully</u>, Sam will win*].

hung   See *hanged, hung.*

illicit   See *elicit, illicit.*

illusion   See *allusion, illusion.*

immigrate to   See *emigrate from, immigrate to.*

impact   Avoid the colloquial use of *impact* or *impact on* as a verb meaning "affect." *Population control may <u>reduce</u>* [not *<u>impact</u>*] *world hunger.*

implicit   See *explicit, implicit.*

imply, infer   To *imply* is to suggest indirectly. To *infer* is to guess or conclude on the basis of an indirect suggestion. *The note <u>implied</u> they were planning a small wedding; we <u>inferred</u> we would not be invited.*

infer   See *imply, infer.*

inside of, outside of Use *inside* and *outside* instead. *The class regularly met <u>outside</u>* [not <u>outside of</u>] *the building.*

insure See *assure, ensure, insure.*

interact, interface *Interact* is a vague word meaning "do something that somehow involves another person." *Interface* is computer jargon for "discuss" or "communicate." Avoid both words in academic and professional writing.

irregardless, regardless *Irregardless* is a double negative. Use *regardless.*

is when, is where These vague expressions are often incorrectly used in definitions. *Schizophrenia <u>is a psychotic condition in which</u>* [not <u>is when</u> or <u>is where</u>] *a person withdraws from reality.*

its, it's *Its* is the possessive form of *it. It's* is a contraction for *it is* or *it has. <u>It's</u> important to observe the rat before it eats <u>its</u> meal.*

kind, sort, type These singular nouns should be modified with *this* or *that,* not *these* or *those,* and followed by other singular nouns, not plural nouns. *Wear <u>this kind</u> of <u>dress</u>* [not <u>those kind</u> of <u>dresses</u>].

kind of, sort of Avoid these colloquialisms. *Amy was somewhat* [not <u>kind of</u>] *tired.*

later, latter *Later* means "after some time." *Latter* refers to the second of two items named. *Juan and Chad won all their early matches, but the <u>latter</u> was injured <u>later</u> in the season.*

latter See *former, latter* and *later, latter.*

lay, lie *Lay* means "place" or "put." Its main forms are *lay, laid, laid.* It generally has a direct object, specifying what has been placed. *She <u>laid</u> her books on the desk. Lie* means "recline" or "be positioned" and does not take a direct object. Its main forms are *lie, lay, lain. She <u>lay</u> awake until two.*

leave, let *Leave* means "go away." *Let* means "allow." *Leave alone* and *let alone* are interchangeable. *<u>Let</u> me <u>leave</u> now, and <u>leave</u>* [or <u>let</u>] *me <u>alone</u> from now on!*

lend, loan In academic and professional writing, do not use *loan* as a verb; use *lend* instead. *Please <u>lend</u> me your pen so that I may fill out this application for a <u>loan</u>.*

less See *fewer, less.*

let See *leave, let.*

liable See *apt, liable, likely.*

lie See *lay, lie.*

like See *as, as if, like.*

likely See *apt, liable, likely.*

literally *Literally* means "actually" or "exactly as stated." Use it to stress the truth of a statement that might otherwise be

understood as figurative. Do not use *literally* as an intensifier in a figurative statement. *Mirna was <u>literally</u> at the edge of her seat* may be accurate, but *Mirna is so hungry that she could <u>literally</u> eat a horse* is not.

loan See *lend, loan.*

loose, lose *Lose* is a verb meaning "misplace." *Loose* is an adjective that means "not securely attached." *Sew on that <u>loose</u> button before you <u>lose</u> it.*

lots, lots of Avoid these informal expressions meaning "much" or "many" in academic or professional discourse.

man, mankind Replace these terms with *people, humans, humankind, men and women,* or similar wording.

may See *can, may.*

may be, maybe *May be* is a verb phrase. *Maybe* is an adverb that means "perhaps." *He <u>may be</u> the president today, but <u>maybe</u> he will lose the next election.*

media *Media* is the plural form of the noun *medium* and takes a plural verb. *The <u>media are</u>* [not *<u>is</u>*] *obsessed with scandals.*

might of See *could of.*

moral, morale A *moral* is a succinct lesson. *The <u>moral</u> of the story is that generosity is rewarded. Morale* means "spirit" or "mood." *Office <u>morale</u> was low.*

myself See *herself, himself, myself, yourself.*

nor, or Use *either* with *or* and *neither* with *nor.*

number See *amount, number.*

off of Use *off* without *of. The spaghetti slipped <u>off</u>* [not *<u>off of</u>*] *the plate.*

OK, O.K., okay All are acceptable spellings, but avoid the term in academic and professional discourse.

on account of Use this substitute for *because of* sparingly or not at all.

one another See *each other, one another.*

or See *nor, or.*

outside of See *inside of, outside of.*

owing to the fact that Avoid this and other wordy expressions for *because.*

per Use the Latin *per* only in standard technical phrases such as *miles per hour.* Otherwise, find English equivalents. *As mentioned in* [not *<u>As per</u>*] *the latest report, the country's average food consumption each day* [not *<u>per day</u>*] *is only 2,000 calories.*

percent, percentage Use *percent* with a specific number; use *percentage* with an adjective such as *large* or *small. Last year, 80*

percent of the members were female. A large percentage of the members are women.

plenty *Plenty* means "enough" or "a great abundance." *They told us America was a land of plenty.* Colloquially, it is used to mean "very," a usage you should avoid in academic and professional writing. *He was very [not plenty] tired.*

plus *Plus* means "in addition to." *Your salary plus mine will cover our expenses.* Do not use *plus* to mean "besides" or "moreover." *That dress does not fit me. Besides [not Plus], it is the wrong color.*

precede, proceed *Precede* means "come before"; *proceed* means "go forward." *Despite the storm that preceded the ceremony, it proceeded on schedule.*

pretty Avoid using *pretty* as a substitute for "rather," "somewhat," or "quite." *Bill was quite [not pretty] disagreeable.*

principal, principle When used as a noun, *principal* refers to a head official or an amount of money; when used as an adjective, it means "most significant." *Principle* means "fundamental law or belief." *Albert went to the principal and defended himself with the principle of free speech.*

proceed See *precede, proceed.*

quotation, quote *Quote* is a verb, and *quotation* is a noun. *He quoted the president, and the quotation [not quote] was preserved in history books.*

raise, rise *Raise* means "lift" or "move upward." (Referring to children, it means "bring up.") It takes a direct object; someone raises something. *The guests raised their glasses to toast. Rise* means "go upward." It does not take a direct object; something rises by itself. *She saw the steam rise from the pan.*

rarely ever Use *rarely* by itself, or use *hardly ever.* *When we were poor, we rarely went to the movies.*

real, really *Real* is an adjective, and *really* is an adverb. Do not substitute *real* for *really.* In academic and professional writing, do not use *real* or *really* to mean "very." *The old man walked very [not real or really] slowly.*

reason is because Use either *the reason is that* or *because*—not both. *The reason the copier stopped is that [not is because] the paper jammed.*

reason why This expression is redundant. *The reason [not reason why] this book is short is market demand.*

regardless See *irregardless, regardless.*

respectfully, respectively *Respectfully* means "with respect." *Respectively* means "in the order given." *Karen and David are, respectively, a juggler and an acrobat. The children treated their grandparents respectfully.*

rise See *raise, rise.*

set, sit *Set* usually means "put" or "place" and takes a direct object. *Sit* refers to taking a seat and does not take an object. *Set your cup on the table, and sit down.*

should of See *could of.*

since Be careful not to use *since* ambiguously. In *Since I broke my leg, I've stayed home, since* might be understood to mean either "because" or "ever since."

sit See *set, sit.*

so In academic and professional writing, avoid using *so* alone to mean "very." Instead, follow *so* with *that* to show how the intensified condition leads to a result. *Aaron was so tired that he fell asleep at the wheel.*

someplace Use *somewhere* instead in academic and professional writing.

some time, sometime, sometimes *Some time* refers to a length of time. *Please leave me some time to dress. Sometime* means "at some indefinite later time." *Sometime I will take you to London. Sometimes* means "occasionally." *Sometimes I eat sushi.*

sort See *kind, sort, type.*

sort of See *kind of, sort of.*

stationary, stationery *Stationary* means "standing still"; *stationery* means "writing paper." *When the bus was stationary, Pat took out stationery and wrote a note.*

subsequently See *consequently, subsequently.*

supposed to, used to Be careful to include the final -*d* in these expressions. *He is supposed to attend.*

sure, surely Avoid using *sure* as an intensifier. Instead use *surely* (or *certainly* or *without a doubt*). *I was surely glad to see you.*

take See *bring, take.*

than, then Use *than* in comparative statements. *The cat was bigger than the dog.* Use *then* when referring to a sequence of events. *I won, and then I cried.*

that, which A clause beginning with *that* singles out the item being described. *The book that is on the table is a good one* specifies the book on the table as opposed to some other book. A clause beginning with *which* may or may not single out the item, although some writers use *which* clauses only to add more information about an item being described. *The book, which is on the table, is a good one* contains a *which* clause between the commas. The clause simply adds extra, nonessential information about the book; it does not specify which book.

theirselves Use *themselves* instead in academic and professional writing.

then See *than, then.*

to, too, two *To* generally shows direction. *Too* means "also." *Two* is the number. *We, too, are going to the meeting in two hours.* Avoid using *to* after *where. Where are you flying* [not *flying to*]?

two See *to, too, two.*

type See *kind, sort, type.*

uninterested See *disinterested, uninterested.*

unique *Unique* means "the one and only." Do not use it with adverbs that suggest degree, such as *very* or *most. Adora's paintings are unique* [not *very unique*].

used to See *supposed to, used to.*

very Avoid using *very* to intensify a weak adjective or adverb; instead, replace the adjective or adverb with a stronger, more precise, or more colorful word. Instead of *very nice,* for example, use *kind, warm, sensitive, endearing,* or *friendly.*

way, ways When referring to distance, use *way. Graduation was a long way* [not *ways*] *off.*

well See *good, well.*

where Use *where* alone, not with words such as *at* and *to. Where are you going?* [not *Where are you going to?*]

which See *that, which.*

who's, whose *Who's* is the contraction of *who* and *is* or *has. Who's on the patio? Whose* is a possessive form. *Whose sculpture is in the garden? Whose is on the patio?*

would of See *could of.*

yet See *but, yet.*

your, you're *Your* shows possession. *Bring your sleeping bag along. You're* is the contraction of *you* and *are. You're in the wrong sleeping bag.*

yourself See *herself, himself, myself, yourself.*

REVISION SYMBOLS

abb	abbreviation 26a	**//**	faulty parallelism 11
ad	adjective / adverb 4	**para**	paraphrase 31b
agr	agreement 3, 6b	**pass**	inappropriate passive 12e, 10d
awk	awkward	**ref**	unclear pronoun reference 6c
cap	capitalization 25	**run-on**	run-on sentence 7
case	case 6a	**sexist**	sexist language 6b, 14b
cliché	cliché 13e	**shift**	shift 12
com	incomplete comparison 4b	**slang**	slang 13a
concl	weak conclusion	**sp**	spelling
cs	comma splice 7	**sum**	summarize 31b
d	diction 13	**trans**	transition
def	define	**verb**	verb form 2
dm	dangling modifier 5c	**vs**	verb sequence 2d
doc	documentation 32–35	**vt**	verb tense 2c–d
emph	emphasis unclear	**wv**	weak verb 10d
ex	example needed	**wrdy**	wordy 10
frag	sentence fragment 8	**ww**	wrong word 13c
fs	fused sentence 7	**. ? !**	period, question mark, exclamation point 21
hyph	hyphen 28	**,**	comma 19
inc	incomplete construction 9	**;**	semicolon 20
intro	weak introduction 12d	**'**	apostrophe 22
it	italics (or underlining) 27	**"a"**	quotation marks 23
jarg	jargon 13a	**()[ ]—**	parentheses, brackets, dash 24
lc	lower case 25	**: / ...**	colon, slash, ellipses 24
lv	language variety 13a	**∧**	insert
mix	mixed construction 9a, 13e	**~**	transpose
mm	misplaced modifier 5a	**⌒**	close up
ms	manuscript form 32d, 33d, 34c	**X**	obvious error
no ,	no comma 19i	**< >**	angle brackets
num	number 26b		
¶	paragraph		

CONTENTS

FAQs ABOUT ONLINE WRITING

Writing online has made communication faster and, in some ways, simpler than ever. But it has also raised a number of questions. You can find some of these questions — along with easy-to-understand answers — on the pages noted below.

Praise for *EasyWriter:*

"The strongest Internet and online resources I've
seen in a handbook."

— Donelle R. Ruwe, *Fitchburg State College*

"I especially like the materials from across different
disciplines. This makes *EasyWriter* a book my
students will use in all their classes."

— Joseph Tuman, *San Francisco State University*

"The FAQs are exactly the sort of questions my
students ask — and the answers given are excep-
tionally helpful, easy to understand, and technically
correct."

— Andrew Harnack, *Eastern Kentucky University*

"I like the everyday language — many students
feel distanced from academic prose and need
bridges between what they know (which is plenty!)
and academic texts."

— Margaret E. Sokolik,
University of California at Berkeley

"The focus on appropriateness and rhetorical
choices is particularly appealing; it will intrigue
and comfort students."

— Martin M. McKoski, *The University of Akron*

ST. MARTIN'S PRESS

ISBN 0-312-17085-8

90000

9 780312 170851